APPLYING THEORY TO POLICY AND PRACTICE

Applying Theory to Policy and Practice
Issues for Critical Reflection

Edited by

STEVEN R. SMITH
University of Wales, Newport, UK

ASHGATE

Published by
Ashgate Publishing Limited
Gower House
Croft Road
Aldershot
Hampshire GU11 3HR
England

Ashgate Publishing Company
Suite 420
101 Cherry Street
Burlington, VT 05401-4405
USA

Ashgate website: http://www.ashgate.com

British Library Cataloguing in Publication Data
Applying theory to policy and practice : issues for
    critical reflection
    1. Policy sciences 2. Social policy 3. Theory (Philosophy)
    4. Practice (Philosophy) 5. Professional ethics
    I. Smith, Steve, 1961-
    320.6

Library of Congress Cataloging-in-Publication Data
Applying theory to policy and practice: issues for critical reflection / edited by
Steven R. Smith.
        p. cm.
    Includes bibliographical references and index.
    ISBN: 978-0-7546-4599-3
    1. Policy sciences. 2. Social policy. 3. Theory (Philosophy) 4. Practice
(Philosophy) 5. Professional ethics. I. Smith, Steve, 1961-
    H97.A62 2007
    320.6--dc22

2007011097

ISBN 13: 978 0 7546 4599 3

Printed and bound in Great Britain by Antony Rowe Ltd, Chippenham, Wiltshire.

Contents

Notes on Contributors

Gideon Calder is Senior Lecturer in ethics and social theory at the University of Wales, Newport, and has taught ethics on various vocational programmes. He has written two books on the philosophy of Richard Rorty, and articles on issues including sexual consent, the ownership of bodily organs, and the ethics of sporting boycotts. He is co-editor of *Res Publica: A Journal of Legal and Social Philosophy*, director of the Newport Social Ethics Research Group (SERG), and is currently involved in EU-funded comparative research on ethically-grounded exemption from the law.

Alan Carling is Senior Honorary Research Fellow in Sociology at the University of Bradford. He has published extensively in areas of sociological theory, rational choice and political philosophy, including (1991), *Social Division* (Verso) and (2006), *Globalization and Identity* (IB Tauris). He served as Chair of Bradford University's Programme for a Peaceful City from 2002–2004. He has since stood as an Independent candidate in the local elections, and worked as a producer and presenter for Bradford Community Broadcasting (106.6 fm).

Francis Cowe is Associate Dean, Academic Development and Planning, at the University of Wales, Newport School of Health and Social Sciences. He has worked as a practitioner, practice-teacher, and lecturer in criminal and community justice and is also Head of the Newport Centre for Criminal and Community Justice. His current research interests are in approved premises and offender practitioner relationships. He recently contributed to the first National Offender Management Service (NOMS) research forum, co-hosting a workshop on the offender–practitioner relationship.

John Deering is Senior Lecturer in Criminal and Community Justice, at the University of Wales, Newport, and is Programme Leader for the Diploma in Probation Studies. He spent 14 years in the probation service as a practitioner and manager, and conducted research into the effectiveness of 'one-to-one' supervision, publishing evaluative articles in *The Probation Journal*. He is currently conducting research into changes in the probation service, the creation of the National Offender Management Service (NOMS) and the extent to which this has affected face-to-face probation practice.

Nadia Heredia is Professor of Philosophy in the Department of Educative Policy, Faculty of Science of Education and Faculty of Humanities in National University of Comahue (Neuquen, Argentina). She is also a member of CLACSO-CEHEPYC (Center of Historical, Political and Cultural Studies) and works in the Commission of Accessibility, National University of Comahue coordinating disability projects in the university and outside. Her publications are on the topics of disability, and ethical and political philosophy from a Latin American perspective.

David Morgans is Research Fellow in the Philosophy Department in the University of Wales, Lampeter. He has been a social worker, community worker and probation officer and has taught in higher education for the last 15 years. His current research is in the relationship between subject, self-identity and consciousness and the influence (or not) of such theories on practice. He has published in various journals, and is currently working on a research monograph relating to the above subject areas.

Lana Morris is programme director of the BA (Hons) Social Work at the University of Wales, Newport. She has previously worked as a residential social worker, a care manager for people with learning disabilities, and a manager of a peer advocacy project for people who are homeless or disabled. Her current research focuses on the experience of people absent from the workplace due to stress, and its impact upon them and their relatives. She has published in this area, as well as on depression in nurses, homelessness, and peer advocacy.

Steven R. Smith is Reader in Social Policy and Political Philosophy at the University of Wales, Newport, and founding member of the Newport Social Ethics Research Group (SERG). His practice background includes social work, psychiatric nursing and political lobbying, and he has published various studies in social policy, as well as numerous articles in internationally renowned policy and philosophy journals. He is also author of (1998), *The Centre-Left and New Right Divide?* (Ashgate) and (2002), *Defending Justice as Reciprocity* (Edwin Mellen).

Sheila Spong is Senior Lecturer in Counselling at the University of Wales, Newport. She has worked as a counsellor, trainer and supervisor since the 1980s, specialising in addiction counselling and workplace counselling. She adopts a pluralist approach in her client work, drawing particularly on the person-centred and cognitive-behavioural traditions. Her recent research involving the analysis of counsellors' talk around issues of power and influence has been published in the *British Journal of Guidance and Counselling* and *Counselling and Psychotherapy Research*.

James A. Sweeney is Lecturer in Law at the University of Durham. He is an academic human rights lawyer whose work has appeared in, amongst others, the journals *International and Comparative Law Quarterly*, *Legal Issues of Economic Integration* and *Connecticut Journal of International Law*. Recent volunteer work with destitute 'failed' asylum seekers in Newcastle-upon-Tyne encouraged him to question the reasoning upon which asylum determinations are founded, and informed the contribution presented here.

Maurice Vanstone is Reader in Criminal Justice and Criminology at the University of Wales, Swansea. He has experience of practice, training and research on community sentences over a 30-year period, and is author of (2004), *Supervising Offenders in* *the Community* (Ashgate); and (2002), *Understanding Community Penalties* (Open University Press); with Peter Raynor (1996), *Betrayal of Trust* (Free Association Books); with Mathew Colton (1996), *Beyond Offending Behaviour* (Arena), and with Mark Drakeford (1994), *Effective Probation Practice* (Macmillan), as well as publishing numerous articles and reports on community sentences, sex-offenders, and prison after-care, most recently relating to Black and Asian offenders.

Chapter 1

Applying Theory to Policy and Practice: Methodological Problems and Issues[1]

Steven R. Smith

Introduction

This collection is unusual in that it is borne both from the rigours of theoretical and philosophical reflections and from addressing the many difficulties of applying these reflections to the detail of policy and practice. The shared premise of all the contributors is that too often the business of theoretical and philosophical rigour and issues of detailed application are kept apart to the profound detriment of both pursuits. Particular attention is paid to the methodological problems of moving from theoretical generalisation (including normative and ethical arguments) to specific policy and practice-based issues.

We anticipate that interested readers will comprise a number of audiences including, practitioners in the legal profession, probation, counselling, social work, and social and public policy analysts and political campaigners, as well as political and ethical philosophers and theorists concerned with policy and practice-based issues. Although the collection is clearly not targeted to one audience we believe that specific audiences will nevertheless be interested in the whole of the collection for two main reasons. First, we have deliberately focused on issues that overlap between different disciplines and practices in order to draw out general lessons regarding the application of theory to policy and practice. Second, we expect that the collection will provide various interesting case studies concerning the difficulties of moving from theoretical generality to specific policy and practice-based concerns.

Given the above, the contributors have been chosen to reflect a wide range of academic backgrounds including from social policy, political philosophy, political theory, legal theory, social philosophy, and applied ethics, as well as reflecting a diverse range of practice-based backgrounds, in legal practice, probation, counselling, social work, and political campaigning most notably relating to 'race' and disability issues. This combination we believe provides especially fertile ground for exploring the above methodological problems.

With the risk of over-simplification, these problems can be summarised under three broad headings providing a basic organising principle for the collection:

---

1   Parts of this chapter appear in the first chapter of my book (2002), *Defending Justice as Reciprocity*. I would like to thank the publisher Edwin Mellen for permitting these sections to be reproduced here.

1. problems of accessibility for policy analysts and practitioners concerning the theoretical language used and the abstract nature of theoretical argument;
2. problems of relevance and applicability to policy and practice given the structure and purpose of theoretical modelling and the 'environmental constraints'[2] of theory and its application to policy/practice; and
3. problems of how philosophical moves can be made from theoretical generalisation to policy and practice given specific recommendations for implementation are often not axiomatically reflected in generalised abstract principles.

Therefore, the first aim of this collection is to ensure chapters are written in a style that would allow non-philosophers and theorists to follow and engage with the arguments presented. The second aim is to also make clear throughout how theory might be seen as both relevant and applicable to policy and practice, despite the above environmental constraints. The third aim is to directly engage with more abstract philosophical issues concerning the application of theory to policy and practice and the structure of abstract thinking and argument.

We need though, as a preface to the above, to address two more fundamental questions which apply to all areas of policy and practice-based issues. Why is it important to apply theory and ethical argument to policy and practice? And, can this application add anything to our existing knowledge and understanding?

By way of introducing this collection, what therefore follows is an attempt to address these questions in order to affirm, not only the importance, but also the necessity of applying theory and ethical argument to policy and practice. As well as sketching out personal views concerning the way normative generalisations relate to policy and practice, in the process, I give a brief outline of how the other contributors have applied and explored theory in respect to their own areas, given the basic assumption shared by us all. Namely, that engaging in this application will help equip practitioners and policy recommenders and analysts with what might be termed 'critical tools to think with', which then will hopefully better inform the purpose and direction of both policy and practice.

Applying Theory to Policy and Practice

It is the case that academic analysts over the last two or three decades have made significant advances in the application of theory to the study of policy and practice (see Pierson and Castles, 2000, 1–113; Blakemore, 2003, 1–16). At times commentators have regretted these applications, but for most the use of theory has made very positive contributions to understanding both policy and practice.

For example, in the past, academic social policy analysts, skilled in empirical data collection and often motivated by Fabian political perspectives, would only on occasion make explicit applications of theory to social policy studies, usually derived

---

2   These constraints might include financial and resource constraints, but also perceived constraints of the practitioner and policy-maker, that the situation or circumstances confronted do not neatly 'fit' with the theory.

from sociology. Consequently, analysis was frequently based on descriptive accounts of the 'outputs' and 'outcomes' of policy and practice. Roughly, outputs refer to the specific intentions of policy-makers and how effective policy and practice has been in implementing these intentions. Whereas outcomes mainly concern the affect that policy and practice implementation has on particular groups and individuals. However, whilst these accounts have provided very important and useful data, the highly descriptive approach failed to properly address disputes over why and how policy and practice is implemented and justified. It is at this point that theory is able to contribute to the analysis of policy and practice, providing various explanatory frameworks that directly address these disputes (see Pierson and Castles, 2000, 1–10; Blakemore, 2003, 1–16).

It is important at this point to make a distinction between theoretical explanation (which might be morally neutral in that a moral position is not necessarily explicitly promoted); and normative justification of policy (which involves a defence and/or critique of moral and ethical positions in relation to policy). Both assume that empirical data collection is insufficient for analysing policy and practice. To this extent normative or ethical analysis can be seen as a particular branch of theory, given the premise that an interpretation of facts is required when analysing policy and practice. However, this in turn involves theoretical analysis that might (or might not be) philosophical and normative in character.

The central problem to be addressed here though is that, in any event, there is no straightforward delineation between generalised theory and values committed to and specific policy and practice responses. Many complications occur when theoretical and philosophical generality is applied to the detail of policy and practice implementation. Indeed, these complications have themselves become the focus of considerable debate. For example, in relation to the application of political philosophy to the detail of social policy, I have argued elsewhere that political positions usually represented as being very different from each other often provide similar normative justifications for social security policy. Nevertheless, even slight variances of philosophical emphasis can result in large differences regarding policy outcomes, whereas at other times the philosophical differences over value commitment may be large between political positions, with the policy outcome effect being relatively minimal (Smith, 1997, 79–97; Smith, 1998, 246–262; Smith, 2002a, 1–40; Also see Goodin, 1988; Freeden, 1994).

Despite these difficulties, maintaining an engagement in normative political philosophy is an essential part of social policy analysis. Policy-makers need to explain and give normative or ethical reasons why a particular social policy or provision of welfare is being promoted. However, for some 'positivists' within policy analysis moral debates are insubstantial or even nonsensical. Similarly, certain 'post-modern' approaches claim that moral points of view are merely relative to the observer and therefore cannot offer any objective standpoint (despite pretensions to the contrary that such a standpoint can be identified). These issues will be explored in more detail below. Suffice it to say here, various criticisms will be made of these positions but acknowledging the force of some of their arguments.

My main assertion is that without moral analysis, any debates concerning the promotion or justification of welfare and other forms of public provision are likely rendered incoherent. This is because the making of policy and its application in practice is in part legitimated by ethical justifications. For example, politicians appeal to what ought to happen, as well as to what is happening, which then demands moral analysis. Quite how this moral analysis can be applied to policy-making is open to question (and reflects some of the issues outlined above). Despite this, some kind of moral analysis is clearly needed particularly within the field of normative and political philosophy, being centrally concerned with ethical arguments relating to the distribution of economic and political resources.

An additional (perhaps more pragmatic reason) for applying theoretical and ethical questions to social policy analysis is that welfare states (and practitioners) being represented via institutional entities, have become increasingly criticised by commentators from both the left and right, and from within what might be described as 'New Social Movements' (see Pierson, 1990; McIntosh, 2000; Pateman, 2000). The welfare state is now no longer viewed as a benign provider of citizens' needs as was anticipated by its supporters in the aftermath of the Second World War. Policy positions from all sides of the political spectrum exhibit a more complex and ambivalent attitude to state provision.

I will now explore further the general role of normative discussion within policy debate, in an attempt to justify the importance and necessity of applying theoretical and ethical argument to policy and practice.

There are a number of reasons a person could be sceptical about the relevance of applying normative argument to the political realities of policy recommendation and practice implementation. For example, a sceptic might argue that the main motivation of politicians (and policy-makers generally) is often very different from any explicit ethical justifications made in relation to policy proposals. Government and other policy-makers claim that their intentions for implementing X set of policies are to promote a particular value(s) through encouraging Y type of practice. However, their real intentions can be located in less morally bound motivations such as political and/or economic expediency.

Indeed, the above sceptical position can be found within various academic policy-analysis conducted during the 1970s. For example, some policy analysts proposed that the value of equality, relating to the re-distribution of resources from the better-off to the worst-off, had no impact at all on policy-makers and governments (even if the latter were rhetorically highly committed to this value). Wilensky argued that there was no correlation whatsoever between the polemical commitments of particular governments to the value of equality and actual distributive patterns found within their respective countries (Wilensky, 1975; also see Pierson, 1990, 16–18).

However, the lack of correlation between value commitment and the effects of policy implementation does not necessarily mean the value itself is irrelevant to policy and practice debates. First, a particular value may genuinely have a strong resonance within a specific set of proposals for policy-makers and practitioners even though other hidden agendas exist. Motives, in other words, are often mixed. Second, many social, political and economic events are outside the control of the policy-maker and practitioner but will have impacts on policy and practice outcomes whatever the intentions of either, but might then require a moral response. Third, having a commitment to certain values might at least 'put brakes' on the various influences which pull the policy-maker and practitioner in opposite directions. For example, it might be conjectured that countries where there are large degrees of inequality (even if their governments are committed to the value of equality) would be even more unequal without this commitment.

In addition, political philosophers make the point that the importance of normative discussion concerning policy is that the articulation of value can be considered in abstraction from other non-normative intentions and factors. Goodin, for example, distinguishes between conventional intentions (that is the institutional norms which are implied within policy and legislation) and the particular intentions of policy-makers (that is the motivations or intentions of the political actors who create policy) (Goodin, 1988, 13–14). According to Goodin, specifying the normative characteristics of a welfare state should only refer to conventional and not individual intentions, as the latter are likely to be varied and disconnected from policy and practice (for the reasons identified by the sceptic above). Nevertheless, the former normative characteristics still allow for certain philosophical inferences concerning how policy and practice ought to be shaped and formulated.

> Just as we infer the meaning of words from the connotations that speakers conventionally intend by them... so too should we base our classification of policy instruments on the conventional intentions that characteristically lie (or are said to lie) behind them (Goodin, 1988, 14).

Following from the above, a philosophical abstraction process can be engaged in to understand why, on normative grounds, X proposal may be preferred over Y (both understood as 'conventional intentions'). Therefore, the degree to which particular policy proposals are motivated by, say, political expediency is irrelevant, as what matters is the explicit delineation of values in relation to the policy convention itself rather than the policy-maker's intentions. Indeed, it is this Goodin type of distinction that I believe is often behind much of the sceptic's concerns. By seeking to uncover the cynical motivations of governments, the sceptic is not necessarily implying values do not matter, in relation to policy and practice debates. Rather, she could be emphasizing the importance of being explicit about the very mixed motives of a government in order to articulate what *ought* to be its intentions regarding the promotion of particular sets of value, expressed through certain policies and practices understood as conventions (in Goodin's sense above).

Another approach or attitude to the normative analysis of policy and practice might also be dismissive of its worth but not because of the cynical political intentions or motivations of policy-makers. As referred to above, a positivist approach to policy analysis can be taken emphasizing the importance of fact collection over normative evaluation. The term 'positivism' was first used by the nineteenth-century philosopher Auguste Comte in his *Cours de Philosophie Positive* (also see West, 1996, 53–59). It encapsulates what Comte claimed as being a more advanced form of knowledge inherited from the natural sciences, replacing religion and speculative philosophy. Perhaps the most unadulterated form of positivist epistemology is the 'logical positivism' of the early twentieth century that discredited completely ethical discourse arguing that it is literally nonsensical (also see Smith, 1998, 44–59).

An inheritor of the above approach may therefore assert that theories and normative debate are at best only of secondary importance to the positivist job of implementing 'what works' as practice instruments in relation to particular policy goals or aims. Consequently, if theory is to be useful according to the positivist then it is merely to establish testable hypotheses explaining how X policy aim or goal is achieved given certain facts. For example, theoretical models of individual or group behaviour can be constructed, which then are used to predict certain outcomes if and when policy-goal X is aimed for. This type of analysis is prevalent in micro-economic analysis and certain forms of 'games theory' which try to predict behaviour based on the premise that individuals act either to fulfil individual preferences and/or act in their self-interest. Philosophical arguments over the ways values and norms affect the legitimatisation and justification of policy and practice, are as a result often sidelined. Policy and practice analysis instead focuses on technical questions concerning the most efficient method of implementing the goals of Government policy recognising the problem of coordinating and adjudicating between conflicting individual preferences and interests.

Chapter Outline

In defence of theoretical and ethical analysis, the response throughout this collection is two-fold. First, philosophically at least, the above what we will call 'naïve positivist position' has been almost completely discredited. The position (either explicitly or implicitly) states roughly – 'facts speak for themselves and therefore we only need theory when we have a 'gap' in the facts.' Or, put another way – 'theory is used to generate hypotheses that can be tested against the facts but once the right amount of facts are found (via the appropriate research) theory is redundant'. Although this perhaps has overly-caricatured a certain style of policy and practice analysis popular in the first two or three decades after the war (and has since been rejected by most policy academics – see Pierson and, Castles 2000, 1–10; Blakemore, 2003, 1–10) this positivist attitude still informs much contemporary policy-making and practice paradigms to the detriment of those at the receiving end of implementation. For example, in Chapter 2 James Sweeney critically evaluates the relationship between facts and theory in his analysis of decisions made by judges in respect to asylum seekers. Practical problems and issues are derived, he argues, from judges trying to make complex decisions whilst denying their theoretical context. The difficulty being for Sweeney is that judges, as a result, frequently over-rely on their so-called 'common-sense', disguising highly subjective and evaluative assumptions when establishing the factual 'credibility' of asylum seekers personal accounts of their circumstances, but which then lead to judges jettisoning commitments to the rigour of applying consistently legal theory in specific cases. What is required, according to Sweeney, is a more explicit recognition by judges of the socially constructed nature of fact accumulation and how 'facts' are interpreted which will then assist them making consistent and justifiable decisions.

In parallel to this particular criticism of 'naïve positivism', my philosophical objection to the above positivist approach, is based on well-trodden ground and so

I will not dwell on it in too much detail here. Nevertheless, it is important to first emphasise that the demise of logical positivism at least was largely due to a basic incoherence at the heart of its philosophy. It argued for a 'verification principle' functioning as a yardstick for sensible utterances but which was then found to be unverifiable according to its own rules (also see Plant, 1991, 12–21). In addition, even those who were sympathetic to the positivist cause rejected the non (and even anti)-theoretical tendencies of its proponents. Karl Popper, for example, famously argued that a scientific hypothesis can never be verified (at least in the strong verifiable logical positivist sense) as scientists cannot test all possibilities in the universe, but are 'falsifiable' concerning the discovery of new facts (Popper, 1968; Popper, 1972). Scientific hypotheses must therefore be testable but as to whether or not they are demonstrably false, not true. As long as this demonstration has not occurred but it is possible to test for its falsity, then exploring and working with any hypothesis is seen by Popper as a legitimate part of scientific investigation – even if the hypothesis proves to be false at some later date. Clearly this, what I will now term a 'non-naïve positivist position', gives more credence to the importance of theory in factual investigations of the kind explored by Sweeney, than the naïve positivist position explored above, given various and competing theories can be used in these investigations.

Moreover, because of the above developments in debate it is now more or less commonly recognised, amongst academics at least, that facts do not simply 'speak for themselves' as at some point they require a theoretical interpretation (Lewins, 1992, 9–15). One of the main problems addressed in this collection is that the naïve perspective concerning the explanatory force of facts is often implicitly adhered to by practitioners and politicians who assert that establishing 'what works' as related to facts about an 'individual case' is all that is needed in being an effective practitioner. So, the slogan 'What Works' is a central part of the New Labour strategy for developing practice and training within the probation services. However, following from the above, the contention here is that this strategy (while at least acknowledging the potential effectiveness of probation work) tends to oversimplify the relationship between practice and theory, as it requires or expects the practitioner to test their practice against sets of 'facts' gathered (often via government research agencies) concerning how the offender is supposedly responding to intervention.

This expectation of practitioners will be critically evaluated in Chapter 3 by Francis Cowe, John Deering, and Maurice Vanstone. Particular attention will be paid to the reasons why certain types of theoretical approaches historically are dominant over others, and as related to the increasingly perceived need to control and punish offenders. The methodological implications this has for the application of theory to practice across this profession are then explored, with the recommendation that 'evidence-based' practice should be worked-out and tested through what the authors call a 'collaborative relationship' between the academy and the professional agency which is both interdependent and critically reflexive.

The more general point I want to stress here is that because interpretations of facts are bound to generate different and competing theories of human behaviour and organisation, this necessitates putting theoretical speculation at the centre of any gathering of evidence and data analysis (including that which relates to policy and practice). Therefore, theory is not just useful as a fall-back when there are gaps in the facts but it is an integral part of how facts are analysed even when all the facts are demonstrated or at least demonstrable. The non-naïve positivist still insists some theories would need to be adjusted or even abandoned in the light of discovering certain facts. Nevertheless, what has been conceded by the latter-day positivists is that the importance of theory is not simply dependent upon the paucity of facts to be remedied by a more developed science. Rather, it is found in its explanatory input and the many ways the same facts can often be both coherently but variously interpreted. This is particularly the case when social and political relations are a focus for study, which has an important bearing on how policy-making and practice is subsequently analysed. For example, the fact that women are under-represented in UK politics is undisputed. Nevertheless, it is a fact that can be explained and interpreted in different ways depending upon the application of specific theoretical frameworks. According to liberal feminists under-representation is symptomatic of inequalities in individual opportunity and realisable sets of rights afforded to women in politics. Whereas, according to more radical feminists the lack of opportunity and realisable individual rights is symptomatic of a deeper structural bias that tends to serve men's interests (as a group) over women's interests (as a group). In stark contrast with either of the above accounts, traditional conservative and/or socio-biological theories of behaviour will often explain and interpret the fact of under-representation by reference to the natural or biological role of men in leadership roles (also see Goodwin, 1994, 62–64).

The competing character of theory and its relation to practice is examined further in Chapter 4 by Sheila Spong. In short, she argues that the counsellor should hold in tension a belief needed for therapy to be effective, and the scepticism required to maintain openness to alternative interpretations of experience, especially those from the client. It is in this context that Spong argues for what she calls 'theoretical scepticism' – acting as a bulwark against a counsellor's tendency to be authoritarian in her practice, and so helps prevent her impose her 'expert' interpretation of the world onto the client's own narrative or 'personal story'. In the process, the counsellor should also recognise that theories beyond counselling – for example, in social theory – can make valuable contributions to the understanding of her practice and how to more effectively critically reflect on it.

Lana Morris develops some of these themes further in Chapter 5, by exploring some of the methodological considerations in applying theory to the assessment role within care management. The focus is on the unified assessment process, and the identification of tensions between the eclecticism of theories offered to social work students and an assessment process which perpetuates, what she calls, a 'reductionist functionalist' position. For Morris, this position leads to an insufficient consideration of values and the critical evaluation of practice; devalues front-line knowledge to second place within the assessment process, and fails to account for social workers' emotional experience of their relationship with service-users. She also considers how students utilise theory to support their development of creativity and expertise within care management in an attempt to move from this reductionist functionalist position, to one which is more likely to treat service-users holistically, and so take service-users' understanding of their own needs seriously.

Following these themes in Chapters 4 and 5, my second main objection to the naïve positivist in defence of normative and theoretical analysis is again well-trodden but is more direct in that it explicitly highlights how fact-gathering and fact-analysis (as a basis for informing policy and practice) is not only theory-laden but value-laden. It is in this context that Gideon Calder in Chapter 6 examines the training of practitioners and in particular the problems of translating ethical theory into practice, exploring various issues arising from his teaching of ethics on vocational programmes in higher education. He argues that doing justice to both ethics and practice, and ethics in practice, requires providing a critique of what he sees as reductive and instrumentalist models of 'learning outcomes'. For Calder, ethical theories cannot be taught and applied to practice in any straightforward way, but require students and practitioners to creatively engage *in* ethical practice – the latter understood as a personal as well as creative process, and is seen as distinct from learning a set of pre-established rules which then are supposedly applied to practice as ready-made formulas.

In a very different arena, but still exploring similar themes concerning the *process* of putting social and political ethics in practice, Alan Carling in Chapter 7 provides a detailed exegesis of the relationship between different social groups within the city of Bradford in West Yorkshire, during the aftermath of the Bradford riots in 2001. In response to various racial and ethnic tensions and divisions across the district, the Programme for a Peaceful City (PPC) was established, which sought to develop a network of concerned local academics, citizens and practitioners, who would reflect together on the situation, and think about strategies of fruitful intervention which would reduce polarisation across the city. Carling served as Chair of the PPC from July 2002 until June 2004, and this chapter is his accumulated reflections of these and other experiences, and more generally the relationship between theory and social and political practices. Amongst other things, he argues that, through collective deliberation, it is possible to converge on workable and substantive normative principles concerning these practices, but provided 'safe spaces' are allowed across disparate communities for constructive dialogue, interaction and mutual learning. He argues that it is through these types of social and political processes, in the context of assuming that knowledge and understanding is essentially progressive in character, that normative principles and practices can be converged upon, which are egalitarian, tolerant and democratic.

Following from the above, it might be concluded that the facts chosen for analysis in policy and practice-based research are always informed (to some degree at least) by normative judgements concerning how and why individuals and groups behave. Moreover, I would argue that denying the presence of these judgements is dishonest and misleading and (if held to) is a result of the policy-maker's and practitioner's positivist pretence of 'objectivity'. That is, falsely assuming facts can be gathered and analysed from a morally neutral point of view.

However, it is within this latter context that much of 'post-modernism' makes its attacks on all value claims, including many ethical applications of the kind embarked upon in this collection. Consequently, various strands of 'post-modernist' thought has provided radical critiques of positivism *and* theoretical/normative analysis, and has become highly pertinent to debates within policy and practice.

Post-modernism comes in a multitude of guises (see West, 1996, 189–220). However, one theme uniting post-modernist thought is the undermining of the 'Enlightenment Project' through a rejection of all 'totalising' or 'grand' theories, as misplaced attempts at discovering (and imposing) order and unity on the world through unitary explanations and 'objective narratives'. Significantly, these grand theories could include positivism's commitment to scientific explanation, and political theories and philosophies that attempt to access so-called normative 'truths' concerning human relations and behaviour. Given the above critique regarding the objectivity of positivism *and* value-commitment, what is left for the role of theorising and ethical analysis in policy and practice?

First, according to the critique this type of analysis cannot provide an objective account of what ought and ought not to be promoted through policy. This simply recreates the objectivity pretence but this time within the sphere of morality rather than scientific theory and data collection. The first job of normative or ethical analysis might therefore be to lay bare what value judgements are being made, but this should be kept separate from issues concerning what values ought to be promoted. Legitimate 'reflexive questions' can be raised and addressed in relation to, for example, the similarities and differences between the values contained within various policy and practice goals, how competing values are expressed within the same polices and practices, and the complex relationship between normative generality and specific policy instruments.

Indeed, it is within this latter context that Nadia Heredia in Chapter 8 explores the way language and discourse is used around disability, and the implications this might have for the above type of 'reflexive questions' for disabled people (most notably within Latin America). Particular attention is paid to how Eurocentric theory has interrelated with Latin American culture and the impact this has had on disabled people. The main argument being that the presence of dominant medical discourses and dialogue concerning the character of 'The Other' (as 'disabled' and 'in need') allow for oppressive mechanisms of social control of 'the disabled' being exercised through various health and welfare practices. According to Heredia, what is required are new ways of talking about disability that encourages what she calls 'social responsibility' – that is recognising 'The Other' as valuable to society and not a threat.

However, even if the above type of discourse analysis is 'allowed in' so as to provide radically alternative solutions to policy and practice, we are still left with the troubling problem that addressing 'foundational questions' concerning what values ought to be promoted are dismissed by the post-modernist as yet another expression of modernity's aspiration to 'totalise' and devise grand theory. Simply put, foundational questions often assume there is a moral objective standpoint leading to universal imperatives that then can be accessed via rational enquiry or reflection. Kantian universalistic ethical positions typically reflect this assumption and can be expressed in, for example, human rights declarations, as well as in declarations found within policy and practice-based codes of ethics. That is, declarations conceived of as being legitimate or valid over and above the value-judgements made by particular cultures or societies, and including dominant oppressive discourses of the kind described above. However, the post-modern critique often seeks to substitute this commitment to objective and universal rights with 'value-relativism'. So, the moral significance of holding particular values is seen by many as being merely relative to the 'holder' (whether conceived of individually or in respect to a named culture) and is not therefore provided by any objective moral standpoint.[3] In this way, the stress is on differences between peoples and cultures and the subsequent lack of unity and universal value commitments that are held between them.

But one obvious problem with post-modernism is that its critique of moral objectivism as an attempt at grand theorising can be too indiscriminate and used as a *reductio ad absurdum* against those who wield it. A radical critique, it might be argued, must exist outside of the paradigmatic framework being critiqued and therefore is prone to claiming a privileged position or vantage-point for seeing the world. Nevertheless, claiming this objective privileged position is precisely what grand theorising is being critiqued for. The dilemma faced by post-modern value-relativists is that to abandon grand theorising and subsequently the moral objectivity pretence (as its aim) risks abandoning the critique (as its method) (also see Habermas, 1990).

It is in the full glare of these post-modern debates that David Morgans in the final Chapter 9 examines some of the limitations of using *any* theory to explain social life. Using a Wittgensteinian approach to understanding the relation between theory and practice, and seemingly alongside some elements of post-modernism, he argues that the primary task is not that of finding the single, objective standpoint from which to devise a final, true theory. However, he argues that neither is the task to promote 'value-relativism' as a new post-modern theory. Instead, for Morgans we need to create new ways of acting which then can be critically reflected upon through identifying the ways in which 'meaning making' occurs through the social use of language. Therefore, effective critical reflection is done, not through the postulation of theory as representations of reality and words. Neither is it done through an examination of the relationship *between* theory and practice, but rather through reflecting on the minutia of the unique sensed responses of human beings to the world(s) we live in, and our respective 'forms of life'. That is, forms of life that are acted out and 'made sense of' through our social relations.

Normative Generalisation and the Implementation of Social Policy

For my part (and by way of concluding this chapter), I will now briefly outline other methodological issues that need to be recognised when considering more precisely the relationship between normative generalisation and social policy implementation. My main contention is that we need to be attentive not only to the ways in which values conflict, amongst a set of ethical commitments held by particular policy positions, but also to how persons themselves are viewed (in relation to their environment, circumstances and their 'personal identity').

---

3   There is considerable dispute as to whether, or the degree to which, post-modernism is necessarily value-relativist. For example, see West (1996, 197–201) and his exploration of Jean-Francois Lyotard's defence of the post-modern condition as an expression of radical politics. Also, many of these and related issues are explored by Nadia Heredia in Chapter 8.

The Complex Relationship between Normative Generalisation and Specific Policy

Even if the importance of normative analysis and ethical argument to policy debate is recognised in the ways explored above, there is no straightforward relationship between normative generalisation and how policy recommendation is developed. This I believe is for three main reasons, all of which have a bearing on the way policy is subsequently viewed and responded to:

1. The same policy may be susceptible to a range of different moral justifications. For example, political supporters of the New Labour policy in the UK to cut lone parent benefits tried to provide different justifications to those made by the previous Conservative Government regarding the same policy proposals. According to one Labour Member of Parliament (MP) the previous Government recommendations were made in order '...to save money and in response to a moral panic attack in the Conservative Party and some elements of the press about single parents.' (*Hansard*, 10/12/97, c1051, para. 5). For this MP, the Conservative justification is in sharp contrast with the same policy being recommended by New Labour proposals. The latter were instead supposedly intended as part of modernising the welfare state and the wider goal of 'getting people into work... the aim to create more employment opportunities and a fairer society.' (*Hansard*, 01/12/97, c1052, para. 1). Of course, both the interpretation of previous Conservative Government proposals and its claims for an alternative justification from New Labour are open to question. However, whatever the accurateness of this particular interpretation it exposes the complex and varied ways in which the same policies can be justified by reference to different normative principles (also see Smith, 1999, 313–334);

2. Applying philosophical generality to policy-making often involves commitments to various values which may, to lesser or greater degrees, be held in tension by policy-makers. This tension within policies is produced partly because these commitments will come from a variety of different political pressures and influences. For example, I have argued elsewhere that UK Government training policy has often developed out of a response to political pressures – from Trade Unions, business interests, and public opinion (Smith, 1998, 201–213). However, often within one set of identifiable value commitments there exists tensions and conflicts that can be considered, in a more philosophical sense, as difficult or impossible to resolve. Philosophical ethical systems are often justified via pluralistic sets of values that in turn are hard to reconcile internally. This internal conflict of values will also I believe have a bearing on how policy and practice is developed and promoted;

3. Even if value-ends are agreed upon there may still be large conflicts over precisely how these ends are achieved via policy mechanisms. Again, in relation to policy debate over the payment of UK lone parent premiums, a number of defenders and critics of the cuts were in agreement over the value of encouraging paid work as a worthwhile policy aim. The disagreement was over which policy mechanism would be the best or most efficient means for achieving this end.

Quick-fixes and Utilitarianism

A quick 'philosophical solution' to the difficulties presented in 1) and 2) above is possible through a monistic commitment to utilitarianism. This would promote one highest principle allowing for a systematic adjudication between other lower or secondary policy aims (also see Gowans, 1987, 4–31). In relation to social policy, 'maximising human welfare' for utilitarians might be the yardstick for deciding which policy ought to be pursued. Other goals, such as the reduction of inequalities, would only act as a means to the end of serving the utilitarian principle. However, again I have argued elsewhere that whilst utilitarianism might appear superficially attractive providing a 'solution' of sorts to decision-making, it is an inadequate normative response to policy and practice debate for a number of reasons (Smith, 1997, 92–93; Smith, 1998, 214–262; Smith, 2005a, 77–79; Smith, 2005b, 556–559).

First, it may be that overall justifications for distributive policies can be subsumed under generalised higher principles such as 'maximising human welfare is desirable' or 'social assistance is necessary to attain individual and social welfare'. Nevertheless, these principles (although are relatively uncontroversial at least in these generalised forms) are notably unhelpful when articulating and addressing questions that are extremely pertinent in relation to the justification of specific policy and practice. So, fulfilling the principle 'maximising human welfare is desirable' fails to address the moral question of who is responsible for delivering welfare, and more specifically what broad levels of state benefit should be paid, and what type. For example, in relation to the question of 'who should be responsible' for delivering welfare outcomes, an important distinction has been made within ethical debate between 'states of affairs' and 'moral agency' (Parfit, 1987, 430). So bringing about X state of affairs is not the same ethical question as who is responsible for bringing X about, and most ethical positions need to take account of both domains to make proper sense of the moral claims being made. However, the principle that 'maximising human welfare is desirable' risks merely referring to a particular state of affairs without necessarily taking into account issues relating to moral agency – such as who should deliver particular welfare outcomes. For example, in relation to questions concerning what type of benefit ought to be distributed, I (and Mike O'Neill) have explored why disabled people (according to the Disability Rights Movement) often prefer to be paid in 'cash' rather than 'kind' for the provision of social services such as home-helps. Our main argument being that this particular preference over which types of benefit be distributed, is usually implicitly justified by reference to promoting the value of individual autonomy and responsibility. This is then linked to a commitment to resource equality, operating as an independent value-commitment from references to, say, increases in the welfare of disabled people (Smith and O'Neill, 1997, 123–143).

My point here is that the above issues and complexities leave considerable room for non-utilitarian positions that might allow for diminishments in overall welfare. For example, higher levels of benefit (if paid to unemployed people) might well increase overall welfare considerably as the marginal utility gains of the worst-off more than compensate for the welfare losses of relatively rich tax-payers (who could be required to fund such an increase). However, this policy recommendation still does not address the question of whether the relatively rich tax-payer ought to pay for higher rate benefits in any event – that is, whether or not non-payment or payment leads to reductions or increases in overall welfare.

Following from the above, further difficult normative questions arise, not only concerning who should pay and how wealth is initially accumulated, but also relating to the moral objections of the payers themselves. Consider the general question: are the normative objections of relatively rich tax-payers morally justifiable when (and if) their welfare is diminished as a result of paying higher taxes? Now include the fact that this might be implemented to increase the welfare of the least well-off (over and above the diminishment of welfare to the better-off) and yet it is also conceded that the wealth of tax-payers has been gained legitimately. In this scenario answers to the initial question will often be justified through referring to non-monistic value commitments. More specifically, the debate is complicated (and impossible to resolve through utilitarianism) because the value of making gains over others (producing inequalities) may be defended in some, but not necessarily all, forms. What might be termed, 'limited gain-making' then puts a moral brake on any commitment to utilitarian principles as, for example, property rights are respected (or at least taken into account in these moral calculations) despite this leading to an overall diminishment of welfare. This could be conceded even if *some* degree of priority is given to increasing the welfare of the worst-off over the better-off.

Finer Distinctions in Policy and Value-Conflict

I contend that it is at these finer and more difficult points of policy debate that philosophical discussions concerning value conflict can be readily applied. My main argument is that pluralistic value frameworks yield more morally relevant and politically realistic results than the monistic 'solutions' above, but these frameworks ought to be applied differently depending upon how situations and persons within these situations are specifically defined and viewed. For example, when faced with a multiple accident on a motorway, according to most people the principle of need fulfilment (alongside giving priority to the worst-off) provides sufficient justification for how victims of the accident ought to be treated. As raised above, this position still leaves open the question of who should pay for the treatment once it is made. However, in relation to how the treatment is in the first place distributed by any health service (whether this is, say, state or privately funded) need fulfilment, and priority to the worst-off would I believe be the most likely candidates consistent with our moral intuitions. In contrast, it seems radically inconsistent with our moral intuitions that the alternative principle of, say, treating people according to what they 'deserve' can play a normatively legitimate role in these circumstances. A desert principle, for example, could allow the person who is least to blame for the accident to be given priority for treatment. Whereas the person who is most to blame is treated last, even if the former happened to sustain the lesser injuries and the latter the greatest. Of course, it might be that in a road accident no one is to blame but in this particular instance what is being asked is what would happen when it is possible to attribute different levels of blame to individual drivers (which in practice is likely to be the case)?

It is important to emphasise that the intuitive objection to the desert principle in this illustration is not for technical reasons. For example, envisage a sophisticated video monitoring system that is able to calculate what levels of responsibility might be ascribed to whom in regard to the cause of a motor vehicle accident, the results of which are then relayed to any desert paramedics arriving at the scene. I am therefore assuming that levels of desert can be decided upon.[4] In this context, the contention is that the principles of need fulfilment and giving priority to the worst-off will tend to 'trump' any alternative decision not to treat victims.

Nevertheless, despite the above 'trump-cards' being used in motorway pile-ups I also argue that within different situations other principles are often seen as justifiably playing a more prominent role. For example, regular cash payments from the state allow much greater room for, say, desert and reciprocity principles. This is for a number of reasons. First, comparing relative needs often, by itself, seems morally significant. If someone is bleeding to death from a car accident then her needs are more urgent and acute than someone who is claiming, say, Child Benefit to supplement her other income. Therefore, it might be more reasonable to ask in the latter case whether the person deserves the benefit. Whereas in the former, appealing to desert seems less appropriate when it is conceded that the needs ought to be attended to as a matter of urgency because of their acuteness.

However, it is possible to make room for other principles without having to focus on the acuteness of needs. Although persuasive in the above circumstances given large disparities in urgency, it is not decisive when making a distinction between the above policies of health care and social security provision. It could be, for example, that the injuries sustained in a road accident (being relatively minor) generate less acute needs than that of, say, a poverty-stricken social security claimant. Yet it is often thought reasonable to meet the former's needs without having to consider whether she deserves the treatment or not, and at the same time argue in the latter case that it is not reasonable to refuse the same consideration at least. This is not I contend because the road accident generates needs that, say, could be paid for by the victim, but that this position is morally justifiable whether the victim pays for her treatment or not. How is this plausible?

Again, I believe some of the explanation is found in the way values can be understood as being in conflict with each other. According to certain ethical positions, what the above situation might produce is a pro tanto moral dilemma (that is a dilemma that is not solved by any single philosophical system). Pro tanto dilemmas are those occurring after the philosophical arguments are 'in' so to speak. These can be contrasted with prima facie dilemmas that may appear at first sight as dilemmas but are solvable by reference to particular philosophical systems, leading

---

4   This argument also raises questions about the meaning of responsibility and how this may (or may not) relate to issues of moral agency. See, for example, my arguments in Smith (2002a, 113–168). Suffice it to say here, the video monitoring system would be able to support a desert principle related to acts that are attached to persons but without implying a deeper moral culpability. The job of the desert paramedics would be one of translating the computation producing a priority list as to who should be treated first.

to either only one choice being made or a number of choices being allowed but without producing a moral dilemma.

If pro tanto dilemmas occur in the above contexts then meeting the needs of a reckless driver (whether these needs are the result of serious or minor injuries) contains both moral gains and losses. The driver might be thought of as undeserving in relation to her behaviour whilst still having needs that ought to be met. It could also be argued that moral gains and losses are produced from not meeting the needs of an undeserving claimant. In either case, the principles of need and desert are understood as pulling in opposite directions and yet are both valued. According to some commentators the mature ethical response in relation to this dilemma is acknowledging that the 'solution' is not to jettison one principle in favour of the other, but to reject the idea that moral decision-making principles exist. Instead, both values are taken to each specific situation and intuitive judgements are made accordingly, the argument being that these values conflict at 'ground-level' and we should expect decision-making to reflect this (for example see Dancy, 1993, 109–115). Consequently, there is no monistic solution to these dilemmas – they are dilemmas that de facto occur and ought to be incorporated within the complex moral world human beings occupy.

The above incorporation can come in many different forms. At one end of the spectrum (that is the most soluble) values can be placed in a lexicographic ordering, exemplified in John Rawls's, *Theory of Justice* (1971, especially see 42–5). The value of individual freedom is often understood as conflicting with the value of distributive equality. However, Rawls solves this by guaranteeing certain freedoms (acting as a first principle) after which a further distributive principle comes into play (acting as a second principle) but without having to refer to the first. Turning again to the desert paramedics example above, they might decide (if lexically inclined) that if everyone is equally to blame then treatment ought to be distributed according to need. This strategy is effectively placing desert as a first value after which (if fulfilled) need operates as a second independent principle.[5]

At the other end of the spectrum (that is the least soluble) conflicting values are viewed as incommensurable. For Joseph Raz: 'A and B are incommensurate if it is neither true that one is better than the other nor true that they are of equal value.' (Raz, 1988, 332). Therefore, it is not possible to lexically rank values given they are not comparable. Instead, qualitatively different losses and gains are experienced depending upon what choices are made. Distributing according to desert or need could therefore be seen as based on values *so* different that it is not possible to even compare values and situations and make judgements accordingly. As with the strong intuitionists/dilemma proponents we are left with moral losses and gains whatever option we choose.

Finally, somewhere in the middle of the spectrum, it is possible to 'trade-off' values suggested by Barry for example (Barry, 1995, 5–7). Here, one value is diminished for the sake of another but without sacrificing entirely the first. Consequently, a

---

5   I still contend, however, that for most people this solution in this circumstance is no more morally persuasive than using desert to trump need altogether.

certain balance of conflicting values is achieved which again is intended to reflect our moral intuitions.

Personal Identity and Policy Debate

I have argued elsewhere that engaging in the above debates concerning dilemmas and value-conflict can throw considerable light on how social policy is variously justified (for example see Smith, 1998, 234–242; Smith, 2005b). However, part of the reason why and how dilemmas and value-conflict are produced, I believe is connected not only with the different ways values conflict, amongst a set of ethical commitments held by a particular position. It also concerns how persons themselves (in relation to their environment, circumstances and personal identity) are variously viewed. For example, one of the reasons we may decide to treat the victim of a road accident (regardless of whether she deserves the treatment in relation to her behaviour or not) is precisely because she is viewed as a victim. More specifically, being defined a victim then provides a reason to suspend judgment in relation to her deservedness. For example, as a victim it could make her an object of pity that then may readily lead to a sympathetic response ensuring that the meeting of her needs trump any desert claims.

Nevertheless, my final point is that although this latter position has considerable moral appeal in the road-accident case, there may be many other cases where it does not. The main contention is that the lack of appeal in these cases cannot only be argued for philosophically, but also accounts for why many groups who are usually classified as victims often militantly reject being defined in this way. Instead, these groups are keen to stress their ability to survive *and* thrive through particular conditions and circumstances – regardless of how they were caused (also see my arguments in Smith, 2002a; Smith, 2002b; Smith, 2005a). This, by implication, requires us to acknowledge two distinct but related sets of moral concerns and their derivation. First, acknowledging that the positive identity of those who belong to disadvantaged groups is derived from the moral significance of *being* different, and that this difference is a basis for personal development and making contributions to the welfare of others. Second, acknowledging that the fair or unfair treatment of such groups is derived from the moral significance of *claiming* just distributions, and that this requires a redistribution of resources from the better-off to the worst-off (also see Smith, 2002b, 47–60). I believe that recognising both these moral domains (as separate but related) has profound implications for how moral relations between persons are viewed and responded to, which in turn also has a profound impact on how policy and practice is, and ought to be, implemented.

References

Barry, B. (1995), *Political Argument* (London: Harvester Wheatsheaf).

Blakemore, K. (2003), *Social Policy: An Introduction*, 2nd edn (Buckingham: Open University Press).

Dancy, J. (1993), *Moral Reasons* (Oxford: Blackwells).

Freeden, M. (1994), 'Political Concepts and Ideological Morphology', *Journal of Political Philosophy*, **2**(2), 140–164. [DOI: 10.1111/j.1467-9760.1994.tb00019.x].

Goodin, R.E. (1988), *Reasons for Welfare: The Political Theory of the Welfare State* (Princeton, New Jersey: Princeton University Press).

Goodwin, B. (1994), *Using Political Ideas*, 3rd edn (Chichester: John Wiley and Sons).

Gowans, C.W. (1987), *Moral Dilemmas* (New York: Oxford University Press).

Habermas, J. (1990), *Philosophical Discourse of Modernity* (Cambridge: Polity Press).

Lewins, F. (1992), *Social Science Methodology: A Brief Critical Introduction* (Melbourne: Macmillan Publishing).

McIntosh, M. (2000), 'Feminism and Social Policy' in Pierson and Castles (eds).

Parfit, D. (1987), *Reasons and Persons* (Oxford: Clarendon Press).

Pateman, C. (2000), 'The Patriarchal Welfare State' in Pierson and Castles (eds).

Pierson, C. (1990), *Beyond the Welfare State? The New Political Economy of Welfare* (Cambridge: Polity Press).

Pierson, C. and Castles, F.G. (eds) (2000), *The Welfare State Reader* (Cambridge: Polity Press).

Plant, R. (1991), *Modern Political Thought* (Oxford: Blackwell).

Popper, K.R. (1968), *The Logic of Scientific Discovery* (London: Heinemann).

— (1972), *Objective Knowledge* (Oxford: Oxford University Press).

Rawls, J. (1971), *A Theory of Justice* (Oxford: Oxford University Press).

Raz, J. (1988), *The Morality of Freedom* (Oxford: Clarendon Press).

Smith, S.R. (1997), 'Disarming the Ideological Conflict between the Centre-Left and the New Right: The Implementation of UK Social Security Policy', *Journal of Political Ideologies*, **2**(1), 79–97.

— (1998), *The Centre-Left and New Right Divide? Political Philosophy and Aspects of UK Social Policy in the Era of the Welfare State* (Aldershot: Ashgate Publishing).

— (1999), 'Arguing Against Cuts in Lone Parent Benefits: Reclaiming the Desert Ground', *Critical Social Policy*, **19**(3), 313–334.

— (2002a), *Defending Justice as Reciprocity: An Essay on Social Policy and Political Philosophy* (Lampeter: Edwin Mellen).

— (2002b), 'Fraternal Learning and Interdependency: Celebrating Difference Within Reciprocal Commitments', *Policy and Politics*, **30**(1), 47–60. [DOI: 10.1332/03 05573022501566].

— (2005a), 'Keeping a Distance in Compassion-Based Social Relations', *Journal of Moral Philosophy*, **2**(1), 69–88.

— (2005b), 'Equality, Identity and the Disability Rights Movement: From Policy to Practice and From Kant to Nietzsche in More than One Uneasy Move', *Critical Social Policy*, **25**(4), 554–576. [DOI: 10.1177/0261018305057060].

Smith, S.R. and O'Neill, M. (1997), 'Equality of What And the Disability Rights Movement', *Imprints: A Journal of Analytical Socialism*, **2**(2), 123–144.

West, D. (1996), *An Introduction to Continental Philosophy* (Cambridge: Polity Press).

Wilensky, H.L. (1975), *The Welfare State and Equality* (Berkeley: University of California Press Books).

Chapter 2

The Lure of 'Facts' in Asylum Appeals: Critiquing the Practice of Judges

James A. Sweeney

Introduction

In common language we often complain that something works 'in theory', but not 'in practice'. The refugee status determination (RSD) process in the UK is much the same. However, this chapter also looks at 'theory' and 'practice' in a rather different sense too.

Immigration judges focus overwhelmingly upon questions of 'fact' and, specifically, asylum seekers' 'credibility', to the exclusion of more legal-definitional issues (Clayton, 2004, 398; Thomas, 2006, 79). The suggestion made here is that by doing so, immigration judges are lured away from thinking theoretically. Dealing with 'facts' appeals to a sense of the 'practical', where asylum decisions can be justified on grounds of plain common sense (Weston, 1998, 88).

The aim of this chapter is to use the example of immigration judges to show the practical problems that flow from attempting to take complex decisions whilst in denial of their theoretical context. The Chapter proceeds in four parts; First, the RSD process itself is sketched, in order to introduce the topic and to explain the importance of focusing upon asylum appeals. Second, the legal elements that constitute the definition of a refugee are introduced, in order to see the interplay between (apparently common sense) questions of credibility and fact on the one hand and (apparently more difficult) questions of law on the other. This part continues by showing that there is a marked tendency to over-simplify the RSD process by emphasizing the former at the expense of the latter. Third, the 'common sense' approach of immigration judges is outlined and critiqued. Unreported legal 'determinations' obtained by the author through his volunteer work with failed asylum seekers provide the data for this section. Particular attention is paid to the way in which immigration judges assess the believability of alleged persecutors' actions. Finally, the theoretical complexity of thinking about facts is demonstrated. Although it seems that immigration judges are lured away from thinking theoretically, they are still engaged in the inherently theoretical process of reasoning from general (legal) principles to actual practice. However, theory is not just a tool for being critical of the practice of immigration judges. Alain de Botton's popular philosophy book, *The Consolations of Philosophy*, showed how great philosophical works might have some practical benefit to the way we live and view our everyday lives (de Botton,

2001). Following Alain de Botton's lead, legal theory is shown to provide some 'consolations' for immigration judges.

The Importance of Asylum Appeals

Immigration judges (formerly 'adjudicators') sit in the Asylum and Immigration Tribunal (AIT). The AIT replaced the Immigration Appeal Tribunal (IAT) on 4 April 2005 (see Hooper, 2005; Thomas, 2005). The AIT deals with appeals against (among other things) the Home Secretary's initial decision to refuse asylum. Around 80 per cent of initial decisions result in a refusal to recognise refugee status (Home Office, 2005, 3). The quality of initial decisions has been strongly criticised (Home Affairs Committee, 2004, 3 et seq.; Clayton, 2004, 13; National Audit Office, 2004). The Home Office is now working with the United Nations High Commissioner for Refugees (UNHCR) to improve the initial decision-making process (UNHCR, 2005). In the meantime, overwhelmingly negative initial decisions of dubious quality give rise to many asylum appeals. The implications of a negative decision, namely any combination of detention, removal, and voluntary return (encouraged by the forced destitution of failed asylum seekers, now including those with families), exacerbate the demand upon the appellate bodies as failed asylum seekers attempt to challenge the decision in their case (see Gibney and Hansen, 2003; Phuong, 2005).

Further rights of appeal from the AIT are heavily circumscribed. As well as legal rules about exactly what can be appealed, there are very tight time limits and public funding for legal advice in asylum cases has been cut (Hooper, 2005; Thomas, 2005). This means that the first stage of the appeal process is often the first and only substantive hearing the asylum seeker will have (Asylum Aid, 1999, 72).

Most of the asylum-seeking respondents who participated in this research were in the bottleneck created by this state of affairs; they had made an unsuccessful appeal against an initial decision but were unable to take the case further. However, they took issue with many of the statements made by the adjudicator or immigration judge in the first stage of the appeal. Parties to the case are given a written copy of the determination (in English), but determinations are not easily available for study by NGOs or academics (Electronic Immigration Network, 2006).

Clearly this has some methodological implications for the present study. I have been reliant upon written determinations supplied by failed asylum seekers I have met though volunteer work with 'The Harbour Project North East'. The organisation works with destitute failed asylum seekers until they voluntarily return to the state from which they have claimed asylum or are removed there. The sample therefore cannot be fully representative because the determinations supplied are necessarily negative decisions. Nevertheless, since it is established that the vast majority of asylum applications initially fail, the relatively small number of determinations discussed here can be taken as examples from within an objectively verified trend.

Over-simplifying the RSD Process

The Refugee Definition

Under the 1951 Geneva Convention Relating to the Status of Refugees, known as either the 'Geneva' or the 'Refugee' Convention, an asylum seeker must show they have a 'well founded fear' of persecution for one of a number of grounds (Article 1A(2) Refugee Convention, as amended; see Hathaway, 1991; UNHCR, 1992; Clayton, 2004). Article 33(1) of the Refugee Convention prohibits states expelling or returning someone to another state where they might suffer persecution. This, known as the principle of 'non-refoulement', is what compels states to grant asylum to those on its soil who meet the Convention definition of a refugee (Clayton, 2004, 346).

In addition to the obligations flowing from the Refugee Convention, the immigration judge must also separately consider whether the UK's obligations under the 1950 European Convention on Human Rights (ECHR) are engaged. An EU directive has been adopted that will provide a unified European definition of a refugee, taking into account the Refugee Convention, the ECHR, and existing EU Law (EU Qualification Directive; Lambert, 2006). It came into effect on 10 October 2006.

The activities of immigration judges when they apply elements of the refugee definition in asylum appeals can be seen as classic instances of legal reasoning. The same can be said for the interpretation of the relevant articles of the ECHR, or the EU directive. The decision maker must apply abstract legal rules to the case at hand and, in so doing, will have to interpret those rules. The issues at stake are easily recognised as questions of 'law'. This type of legal reasoning is perhaps a paradigm example of the philosophical process of reasoning from abstract (legal) norms to actual practice. Such reasoning is considered far from a matter of 'common sense'; John Barnes, then Vice President in the Immigration Appeal Tribunal, stated that it involves 'specialist legal knowledge in this arcane jurisdiction' (Barnes, 2004, 350).

The reality of the RSD process is that these difficult legal definitional questions are only rarely discussed. The bulk of the 'determination' is often given over to what are labeled 'findings of fact and credibility', and the application of asylum law to them is downplayed.

Facts and Proof

Asylum seekers must show that they have a 'fear' of persecution; this is about proving that something may transpire in the future. Since we cannot, with any degree of certainty, know what will happen in the future, this issue is a difficult one to resolve.

It is generally accepted that 'fear' in this context has both subjective and objective elements (see Hathaway, 1991; UNHCR, 1992; Clayton, 2004). The subjective element (that is actually fearing persecution) is often relatively straightforward. The more complex process is examining whether the subjectively held fear is objectively 'well-founded'.

The standard of proof in respect of both elements of fear is meant to be low (see Gorlick, 2002). Neither the strict 'beyond a reasonable doubt' criminal standard nor the lesser 'on the balance of probabilities' civil standard applies. According to the leading case of *Sivakumaran* there must simply be 'a reasonable likelihood' or a 'serious possibility' that the applicant's fear will materialise if they are returned. It is important to the argument made below that proving past events should be considered part of the process of determining a well-founded fear to this standard, rather than a pre-requisite step (*Kaja*, 1995; *Karanakran* 2000).

It is worth briefly considering how the apparently low standard of proof applied to elements of the appellant's testimony can be used against them in a rather insidious way. Take the case of 'A', who I met at the Harbour Project in January (2005). His appeal was heard in November 2004. 'A' is a homosexual man from the Democratic Republic of Congo (DRC). His case involved, amongst other things, allegations that he was raped whilst in custody for political activities in the DRC. In respect of the rapes, the adjudicator stated:

I accept that those rapes took place on the lower standard of proof ('A' case, para. 29).

By coupling the findings with a re-statement that a low standard of proof has been used, the adjudicator instantly casts doubt on whether the rapes actually took place. This is troubling because, for 'A', instead of the lower burden of proof making it easier for him to establish the material facts, it implies that he has not *conclusively* established that the rapes ever took place. Ultimately the case failed because the adjudicator found that the rapes did not form a 'systematic campaign of persecution' ('A' case, para. 29), and that although the UK presented some comparative advantages for a homosexual, there was no real impediment to his returning to the DRC.

In summary, there is a common recognised legal threshold for proving material facts and prospective risk. Both these intimately connected factors help to determine whether an asylum seeker's fear is 'well-founded' within the terms of the Refugee Convention.

Credibility and Over-simplicity

In looking at the question of 'fear' the applicant's testimony is given pre-eminence (Hathaway, 1991, 83) because asylum seekers tend only rarely to have corroborative evidence (UNHCR, 1992; Thomas, 2006, 81, para. 196; Weston, 1998, 87). With little scope for corroboration, the immigration judge looks to the personal credibility of the applicant to assess whether the material facts are proven to the requisite standard (Thomas, 2006, 81). Although the credibility of the applicant, such as whether they have deliberately misled the decision-maker, is a relevant consideration, the personal credibility of the appellant and the proof of material facts (leading to a well-founded fear) become conflated. This is often expressed as determining whether the evidence presented by the appellant 'is credible' (Thomas, 2005, 473).

This can be seen in 'B's case, which was heard in November 2004. I met 'B', a human rights activist from Russia, at the Harbour Project in Autumn 2005. We shall examine the reasoning in this case further below. At this stage we need to see the effect of disputing the 'credibility' of the appellant's testimony. After a lengthy and unsystematic account of the main witnesses' evidence the adjudicator begins his 'findings of fact' at paragraph 66 by stating:

> that the appellant's story has been largely consistent and in many respects is consistent with the objective evidence. I however have to look at whether it is reasonably likely she was involved as claimed as consistency does not equate to it *being credible* ('B' case, para. 66, emphasis added).

Thus, the matter of proving material facts becomes a credibility issue. Instead of merely finding that the material facts are not proven to the required standard, the adjudicator's conclusions become a stinging attack on the personal credibility of the asylum seeker and her husband:

> As with all of the appellants [sic] evidence I only have her word to go on. She and her husband in my judgement are witnesses upon whose word I can place no reliance for the reasons I have already given…

> I had the benefit of seeing appellant [sic] and her husband giving evidence and being cross-examined at length. I formed the view that this account of repeated detention ill-treatment and harassment as a result of human rights involvement has been fabricated. I do not accept any of the incidents to which the appellant has made reference occurred are reasonably likely to be true [sic] ('B' case, paras 81–2).

There is no further heading as to findings in terms of the Refugee Convention, but para. 83 continues:

> The question I must ask myself is what is reasonably likely to happen to her on her return to Russia. I do not accept it is reasonably likely anyone will be interested. She left the country using her own passport on a properly issued Visa and will be able to return. The appellant has failed to establish that she is a refugee ('B' case, para. 83).

This finding is rather imprecise, but can be interpreted as follows. The first sentence is a reference to Article 33(1) of the Refugee Convention (the principle of non-refoulement). The second sentence suggests that, because of the aforementioned findings of fact, there is no well-founded fear of persecution and so the principle of non-refoulement is not engaged. The third sentence probably goes to the question of whether there are any other impediments to the appellant's return (but incorrectly assumes that refugees never flee with valid documentation (UNHCR, 1992, para. 47). The fourth sentence clearly suggests that the paragraph as a whole can be taken as a finding on the application of the Refugee Convention to facts of the case.

The application of European human rights law to the facts is similarly brief at paragraphs 84–6, where the adjudicator attempts to summarise the applicable law but, without relating it to the substance of the case at hand, simply concludes that:

> Given the findings I have made it is clear the human rights appeal must fail ('B' case para. 86).

The only 'findings' thus far made are those in respect of the 'credibility' of the appellant's account so it is assumed that, in the light of these findings in respect of the material facts, no further legal issues need to be examined.

The 'B' determination fits the pattern suggested above by concentrating upon the 'credibility' of the appellant's account of material facts to the virtual exclusion of prospective risk (or the application of any other legal elements of the refugee definition).

In addition to minimising legal analysis, this approach presents an over-simplified view of what decisions on the 'credibility' of the appellant's account entail. Firstly, the conflation of personal credibility and the proof of material facts such as in the 'B' case obscures that these factual findings are nevertheless legally complex. As suggested above, 'pure' credibility, that is to say the *personal credibility of the appellant*, will be an issue in some cases (*Kingori*; Weston 1998, 87; see s8 Asylum and Immigration (Treatment of Claimants) Act 2004). However, findings on the *credibility of the account* also involve the proof of material facts giving rise to a 'well-founded fear of persecution'. Not all conclusions on the material facts are reflective of the appellant's credibility, and the question of a well-founded fear should be fully considered in any case. The 'credibility of the account' thus involves complex legal-definitional questions, but it is presented a non-specialist form of reasoning; the apparently more straightforward and familiar business of identifying a liar.

Secondly, unpicking the material facts alleged by the appellant in their testimony focuses all our attention on the account of *past* events and, by doing so, provides a false contrast between proving past events and proving prospective risk (notwithstanding that in legal terms they are both composite elements of the same test of 'well-foundedness'). Although the difficulty of proving something in the future will transpire is recognised it seems that, by contrast, determining past events is somehow simpler. Even a tentative exploration of legal theory shows that thinking about facts is never this simple.

By focusing so much upon the 'credibility' of the account, immigration judges have thus presented an over-simplified version of the RSD process. It appears to be a non-legal inquiry into past events. This in turn paves the way for intuitively appealing common sense decisions, rather than any form of 'specialist' legal reasoning.

'Common Sense' and Credibility

Types of Credibility Decision

Writing in a practitioner-focused journal, Amanda Weston identified three broad types of credibility finding in asylum appeals (Weston, 1998, 88). Firstly, immigration judges frequently point to perceived 'internal inconsistencies' as undermining the appellant's credibility. This might be where the appellant gives different accounts of their story at different times. Clearly such behavior might justifiably undermine the credibility of the asylum seeker. Conversely, in his candid reflection upon his time as an adjudicator Tony Talbot has also added that a 'perfectly logical and consistent account [was] often more likely to raise [his] suspicions of a 'packaged story' than an account which reflects all the oddities and quirks of real 'life' (Talbot, 2004, 29).

This is a good point, but also raises an awkward problem: An inconsistent story is unlikely to be believed, but then neither will a consistent one.

Asylum Aid and Amnesty International have criticised the over-use of internal inconsistency to deny refugee status, especially where a peripheral inconsistency is taken to undermine the core of the case (Hathaway, 1991, 85; 1999, 30; Gorlick, 2002, 12; Amnesty International, 2004, 20). There are many reasons why refugees may give several different accounts over time, particularly in cases involving rape or torture. Moreover, there are sound academic and medical explanations of why both the memory recall of traumatised witnesses and their ability to give an account of events, is impaired (Scheppele, 1994; Cohen, 2003). The well-known 'Henderson guide' to asylum appeals provides some useful authority for arguing that asylum seekers should at least have the opportunity to address any perceived inconsistencies in their testimony (Henderson, 2003).

As I suggested above, so called findings of fact and credibility tend to be rooted in an isolated examination of past facts rather than linking them to the proof of prospective risk. The appeal of the internal inconsistencies argument is linked to the assumption that such facts are conclusively provable. Internal inconsistencies grate with the apparent certainty that characterises past events, in contrast to the more nebulous idea of prospective risk. Moreover, these inconsistencies are clear to anyone who reads the account of the case. The judge, therefore, appears to play only a minimal role in actually settling the case; the inconsistencies speak for themselves.

A second category of credibility finding relates to what Weston terms 'external inconsistency' (Weston, 1998, 88). Here the asylum seeker's account might seem at variance with the available objective evidence about the country of origin. Where it does not match, the truthfulness of the account and therefore the appellant's personal credibility are undermined.

Again, there is clearly some force to this sort of argument. Indeed, Weston argues that understanding the background and context is the 'only way' that an adjudicator can avoid the dangers of subjectivity (Weston, 1998, 88). However, there is a problem with arguing that if the events described by the appellant are not clearly in line with the formal 'objective evidence' then they cannot be true. Firstly, the Home Office relies heavily upon reports produced by its own 'Country Information Policy Unit', but these reports have been criticised for painting a more positive outlook of the conditions in countries that they cover than is actually the case (IAS, 2003; Good, 2004, 362; IAS, 2005). Secondly there is a tension because an important purpose of the appellant's testimony is to provide further evidence about the country of origin and, in particular, their relationship to it (Hathaway, 1991, 86). Immigration judges should not underestimate the capacity of asylum seekers to provide new and interesting material that could contribute further to an understanding of the context, in addition to what is presented in the Home Office's own reports. The same caution should be expressed when dismissing expert reports commissioned by appellants (Good, 2004; Jones and Smith, 2004, cf. Barnes, 2004).

The real difference between the asylum seekers' evidence and the Home Office reports is that the former must be assessed by the immigration judge, whilst the latter is already deemed 'true'. This tips the scales in favor of the 'objective' evidence and, at the same time, reduces the scope of the immigration judge actively to engage with both sources. In other words, once again, the supplied 'objective' evidence that immigration judges merely present is allowed to outshine evidence that requires interpretation and analysis by them.

These first two types of finding clearly have a place in the consideration of asylum appeals; the problem is with relying upon them to too great an extent. Both appeal to some kind of easily verifiable, tangible, problem with the appellant's story. Both downplay the active decision-making of the immigration judge in favor of apparently allowing the facts to speak for themselves.

The third and final type of finding that Weston identified is where immigration judges cite the 'inherent implausibility' of the facts as described (Weston, 1998, 88). These sorts of findings can be made without reference to any other tangible evidence. They are so plain, so obvious, that no further explanation is needed; common sense points to the same conclusion as reached by the immigration judge.

For example, in the case of 'B' the adjudicator quickly dismissed the appellant's husband's account (described at para. 42) of escaping from some police officers who were beating him:

> I do not accept it is reasonably likely the appellants [sic] husband was able to escape from his abduction in the manner claimed. It is inherently implausible that whilst lying on the ground and being kicked and beaten by three armed officers one of whom pulled a knife on him he would be able to get up and escape through the woods whilst they shot at him. It is my judgement that this element of the appellants [sic] husband's claim has been fabricated and he was never abducted ('B' case, para. 69).

These are the most troubling sort of findings on an appellant's credibility. As is often the case where 'inherent implausibility' findings are made (Weston, 1998, 88), the finding in this case is poorly reasoned. It does not explain what is implausible. What if the police officers enjoyed watching their victim run away, scaring him with gunfire? Having beaten and humiliated him, they might not have intended actually to kill him. He would nevertheless be terrified for his life, and unable to account for his survival. This is just speculation, but where speculation is possible there is nothing 'inherent' about the findings.

The finding thus depends upon unstated assumptions about the motives, and 'efficiency', of persecutors. These assumptions are not self-evident, but are made by the judge.

In the next section we shall examine these types of finding further and argue that they are cleverly cloaked in the language of obviousness and objectivity, but tend actually to be rooted in the subjective views of the immigration judge. That is to say that on the face of it, they allow the facts to 'speak for themselves' much in the same way as the internal and external inconsistencies arguments. However, the immigration judge has played an integral role in actively constructing the notion of what might be termed a 'reasonable persecutor', against which implicitly to judge the 'credibility' of the behavior described by the appellant.

Inherent Implausibility and the 'Reasonable Persecutor'

In law the idea of the 'reasonable man' or 'reasonable person' is often used by judges as an analytical tool, particularly in the determination of liability in negligence (Mullender, 2005, 681; see, for example *Hall v Brooklands Auto Racing Club* [1930]). The question is whether by his allegedly negligent act or omission the defendant falls below the standard expected of the 'reasonable person'. If he did not behave like the 'reasonable person' then we will impose liability upon him. The idea of the 'reasonable person' is designed to bring some objectivity to the process of determining liability. It appeals to community norms about the level of care we owe to each other.

The approach of the immigration judge to constructing a 'reasonable persecutor' has a very different effect. If the alleged persecutors fall short of the standard to be 'expected' of a 'reasonable persecutor' then the story is disbelieved. However, there can be no community benefit from arriving at a generally agreed minimum level of persecution that we expect of alleged persecutors. Unlike the 'reasonable person', they do not live up to community norms. This argument is not merely a normative one suggesting that we ought not to construct a standard against which to judge the efficiency of persecutors, it suggests that the process by which we have arrived at the notion of a 'reasonable person' cannot apply to the 'reasonable persecutor'. Thus, instead of appealing to a collectively constructed sense of what we expect from a persecutor, we shall see that the findings tend to be based upon the immigration judge's impression of how the persecution could have been better executed.

We can now return to 'B's case (the Russian human rights activist). She has claimed asylum in the UK with her husband and two young children. She alleges having suffered persecution by the authorities including the murder of her brother, several arrests and beatings for both she and her husband (one of which was discussed above), the kidnap and return of one her children and ultimately, a failed attempt to kill her in a car 'accident' in which her cousin died. These actions were allegedly taken after she helped her late brother, also a journalist, to store some sensitive material about corruption and other unlawful activities during an electoral campaign.

The facts of the case as presented in the determination are complex, not least because the adjudicator is unable to establish whether key figures in the case are in fact siblings or cousins ('B' case, para. 21). Nevertheless, it is possible to identify some key elements leading to the adjudicator's ultimate refusal of the application for asylum, which we saw above. Most significant for this part of the Chapter is the way in which the adjudicator casts doubt upon 'B's account of the car 'accident'. As well as citing the 'inherent implausibility' of surviving the accident relatively unscathed, the adjudicator states at para. 71:

> I do not accept it is reasonably likely that if the police were chasing them to create some kind of accident that they would not then stop to ensure that their aim had been achieved ('B' case, para. 71).

In this rather chilling finding the adjudicator is assuming that in order for the appellant's story to be believable the persecutor must have acted with a 'reasonable' degree of 'efficiency'. Apparently a 'reasonable', normal, unexceptional persecutor would not have allowed 'B' to survive the accident. Before unpicking the implications of this assumption further, however, we shall examine another case.

The case of 'C' was heard by an immigration judge under the new appeal structure in July 2005. I met 'C' in January 2006. 'C' is a school teacher from Iraq, who arrived in the UK in March 2003. Part of the decision in 'C's case hinged upon whether the immigration judge believed his account of hiding from his feared persecutors at his brother's house in Iraq for a short time, prior to claiming asylum in the UK. In respect of this part of the case, the immigration judge again uses the 'reasonable persecutor' model. At para. 40 the immigration judge states:

> I think that the Appellant began to embellish his account... I agree with the Secretary of State that his account of the efforts being made by the INA, the Ba'*a*th Party and the families of his friends to find him between the time he ran to his brother's and left the country, is far-fetched. I agree that surely one of them would have followed his brother from the family home in an effort to find the Appellant. I think this element of his account is greatly exaggerated ('C' case, para. 40).

Apparently a 'reasonable persecutor' would have found the appellant and therefore the story must be false. It should be noted here that, unlike 'B's case, in dismissing the appeal this determination does examine other matters going to the question of well-founded fear in addition to the material facts asserted ('C', paras 42–7). Nevertheless, like the 'B' case above, this case also highlights the means by which the judge chooses to consider alleged material facts. The model of a 'reasonable persecutor' is not a stable means of assisting this consideration.

Firstly there can be no such thing as a 'reasonable persecutor'. In substantive terms people involved in persecution cannot be said to observe normal rules of reasonableness (Hathaway, 1991, 81; Clayton, 2004, 399). The 'reasonable person' expresses the bare minimum we would expect from unexceptional people. The inventive capacity for cruelty displayed by persecutors makes constructing a cross-cultural standard of their expected minimum level of competence as persecutors very difficult (as well as undesirable) (on cross-cultural reasonableness see Henderson, 2003, 2 citing *Kasolo*). If there is no objective or reasonable standard that we expect from persecutors, then it would seem that the immigration judge is simply arguing that with hindsight the persecution could have been handled more efficiently. It is an impossibly high standard to require that to be believable the alleged persecutor must be described as having behaved with clinical 'efficiency', because if they did so then the appellant could not have escaped them to claim asylum in the UK in the first place.

Secondly, there is a logical problem that relates to exactly what is being proved. J.L. Montrose's classic discussion of the laws of evidence discussed the necessity of distinguishing between 'brute facts' and 'propositions of fact'. A brute fact could be a mathematic statement such as 'two plus two equals four' (Montrose, 1954, 534). In the reasonable persecutor cases the judge will usually be dealing with propositions of fact. Montrose argues that there is a further distinction between a *particular* proposition of fact and a *general* proposition of fact (Montrose, 1954, 534). A particular proposition of fact would assert the past or present existence of a particular fact, such as the particular asylum applicant having been persecuted in precisely the way described. A general proposition of fact would be more akin to a scientific law, such as Pythagoras' Theorem.

In the 'reasonable persecutor' cases the immigration judge mistakes the type of fact that is actually being established. The asylum seeker does not claim that *all* persecutors would behave in the way that they described. Such a general proposition of fact would be a weak one to make based on their alleged individual experiences. To take their argument as such overstates the case that they are trying to make and by doing so the immigration judge instantly undermines the argument's strength. Further, the immigration judges seem to make a general proposition of fact that persecutors *always* act in a particular 'reasonable' way (or, more accurately, *never* act in the way described). For the same reasons, this argument is weak; methodologically speaking the judges do not have the data that could prove such a conclusion.

Finally, the 'reasonable persecutor' approach does not convincingly justify to the appellant the conclusion that has been reached in their case. It attacks their personal credibility without convincing reason and so the finality of the decision is not accepted and further appeals ensue. Thus, it is unsatisfactory from the perspectives of both the appellant and the efficiency of the RSD process.

The 'reasonable persecutor' technique thus fails in its apparent aim of revealing an obvious conclusion that speaks for itself. It may appeal to a shared sense of what is reasonable, but it is actively constructed by the immigration judge according to their impression of how the persecution in the case at hand could have been 'improved'.

The notion of the 'reasonable persecutor' (albeit not it these terms) has been identified in the initial decisions on asylum made by the Home Office (Henderson, 2003, 2; Amnesty International, 2004, 22; Smith, 2004, 25). The IAT has cautioned against 'speculating' on how persecutors behave (*Toro*, para. 15) and the Henderson guide has emphasised this case to lawyers engaged in asylum appeals (Henderson, 2003, 386), but its impact on the reasoning of initial decision-makers and immigration judges seems minimal.

Unpicking the Lure of Facts

This section unpicks the lure of facts upon which the preoccupation with credibility is based and shows that by focusing upon them immigration judges are far from avoiding complex theoretical questions; they have merely recast them in a way that makes them more difficult to recognise. However the recognition that we can think theoretically about facts is shown to provide some 'consolations' to immigration judges.

Understanding Lawyers' Approach to Facts

The determination of credibility is clearly about the establishment of 'facts'. This process of establishment, through the courts, is in an important sense 'rational'.

The rational judicial process has replaced other methods of determining 'facts', for example trial by battle, where the 'facts' are determined by divine guidance or some other arbitrary method (Montrose, 1954, 527). Although the court system is certainly rational in this sense rationality does not, and cannot, result in the knowledge of absolute 'truths' (Thomas, 2005, 476). However the power games employed by lawyers and judges when they are able to label some views as 'not credible' and others as legal 'findings of fact' feed this false impression of privileged access to 'truth' (Muller-Hoff, 2001).

In their credibility findings it seems that immigration judges have taken the products of rational procedures too far and lost sight of the idea that legal 'facts' can never be proved absolutely true or false in court, just more or less likely to be true or false. Instead they search for simple ways to show conclusively that events did or did not transpire. This has a great deal to do with legal education.

William Twining observed that legal theorists have tended to concentrate upon the activities of the higher courts (Twining, 1980, 13). Since the higher courts tend to deal with 'hard' questions of law, questions of fact, which are typically determined at first instance, are systematically excluded from legal education and theory. Fact-handling skills, argues Twining, are therefore taught less intensively to lawyers (where they are taught at all) than rule-handling skills (Twining, 1980, 21). This feeds through to tribunals such as the AIT, which are no less populated by lawyers.

Why are fact-handling skills so rarely taught? Twining suggests that the determination of facts is seen as a matter of ordinary inductive logic which is external (or prior) to legal education (Twining, 1980, 22). This would explain why immigration judges are prepared to explain their credibility findings as matters of common sense; thinking about facts is something that lawyers (wrongly) tend to think is far easier than the rest of their practice. If one has acquired the difficult and prestigious skills required of a lawyer, then one must be more than equipped to make decisions about facts.

Twining has argued that issues of fact and evidence are, however, an important aspect of understanding law (Twining, 1980). They raise important theoretical questions not normally on the agenda of legal theorists. The exclusion of 'facts' from the idea of (legal) 'theory' is precisely why immigration judges do not recognise the theoretical milieu in which concentrating upon the 'credibility' of the appellant's account places them. This, in turn, explains why judges would seek to obscure their role in 'constructing' rather than 'knowing' the truth.

Constructivism, Subjectivity and the 'Consolations' of Theory

It has been described as 'an astonishing accomplishment' that courts operate perennially as if factual judgments were 'clear and solid' (Scheppele, 1994, 92). The approach of immigration judges is based on this (unknowingly) positivistic conception of facts.

Anthony Good has observed this tendency in immigration judges' approach to expert evidence (Good, 2004). Disagreement about the role of experts in asylum cases, he argues, derives from differing perceptions about the nature of facts. For lawyers, they are 'philosophically unproblematic' (Good, 2004, 375). For the experts themselves "facts' are always products of a particular theoretical approach, and 'truth' is at best provisional and contested' (Good, 2004, 377).

The problem is that the positivistic way in which facts are viewed in law generally and in asylum appeals in particular is at odds with the way that 'facts' really operate in law. Legal facts, properly understood, are a study in *constructivism in practice*. Social scientists have long argued that the phenomena of daily life are socially constructed (Sarbin and Kitsuse, 1994, 3). The establishment of legal 'facts' exemplifies the process of constructing meaning and significance. The 'facts' established by immigration judges are actively constructed *by* them from the competing narratives presented *to* them.

Given the law's inherent dependence on a practically constructivist theory of facts, problems ensue when judges attempt to deny or obscure the importance of their construction of events. As I suggested above the centrality of the appellant's account is clearly recognised, but I would add that the role of the judge in constructing (rather 'finding') knowledge is consequently underestimated.

Each of the three types of credibility finding discussed above can be understood as having at its heart a defensive attempt to obscure the judges' active construction of knowledge subsequently to be presented as a legal fact. In the 'internal inconsistency' decisions the judges' findings are based upon inconsistencies that are objectively verifiable by reading the material presented to the judge. The 'external inconsistency' decisions make perhaps the clearest use of 'objective material'. Even the 'inherent implausibility' findings are cloaked in references to what it is (apparently objectively) reasonable to believe. The decision is thus rationalised in terms of the objectively verifiable; matters that are at least normally more accessible and understandable than complex legal reasoning. The conclusion is reached on consideration of evidence that is presented as being so clear that anyone would have to agree with the immigration judge. Given the grave consequences of refusing refugee status to an asylum seeker who makes their application whilst in the UK, it is unsurprising that judges seek to be unequivocal in their commitment to the certainty of their decision.

The 'objective' point of reference seems required in order to defend against accusations of 'subjectivity', and where 'subjectivity' is linked to uncertainty. But if we recognise that facts are inherently contestable and that judges will inevitably have a role in constructing them, they can afford to be a little less defensive. This is the 'consolation' of my approach; it is important that judges are aware of their own enculturation and attempt to understand its impact upon their decision making (Clayton, 2004, 399), but they should not feel the need to deny their role in constructing knowledge. A less defensive approach that acknowledged the full complexity of determining, or constructing, facts in asylum appeals would have less use for the 'reasonable persecutor' arguments criticised above. If it is understood that the judge constructs knowledge, then more care can be taken in choosing the tools to effect that construction.

Conclusion

At face value concentrating upon facts in asylum appeals seems like a good idea. It seems like an expedient, practical approach to dealing with the case-load without further reference to asylum and refugee law. I have argued that, by contrast, engagement with the facts is an infinitely theoretical exercise – albeit one that lawyers are not trained to recognise. However, as well as criticising the apparent over-simplification of the RSD process I have argued that there are 'consolations' to recognising its theoretical complexity.

The approach taken by immigration judges *seems* to avoid having to make the philosophical move from the generally accepted definition of a refugee to the case at hand by introducing a pre-requisite common sense examination of the facts. In legal terms this pre-requisite step is awkward because although expressed in terms of the 'credibility' of the account, findings of fact are meant to be formally considered alongside the legal question of proving a well-founded fear of persecution. Moreover, there are several additional general normative propositions that are implied by the judges' approach to credibility findings, and which still have to be applied to the case at hand; principally, that asylum seekers are identifiably truthful and consistent, and that persecutors go about their business with a reasonable degree of efficiency.

On the view presented here, thinking about facts is never a practical alternative to the philosophical exercise of reasoning from the general to the particular but an alternative *form* of such reasoning. Thus, thinking about facts is theoretically resonant from the outset and, as such, should be undertaken alongside other forms of moving from the normatively general to the specific. Identifying one's own engagement in making the move from the normatively general to the particular is perhaps as difficult as making it. However, most decisions involve some element of this process so it is better to recognise it than to seek apparently 'practical' ways of avoiding it. Attempts to avoid theory by, for example, dealing in facts, are doomed to failure because theory will resurface elsewhere. Taking the 'consolations' of theory, such as given above, is preferable to an irrational and ultimately unsuccessful attempt to avoid it altogether.

Acknowledgements

Many thanks indeed to the asylum seekers who allowed me access to their 'determinations'. Thanks also to my colleagues at the Harbour Project, especially Perry Vincent, Paul Rintoul (who I first heard use the term 'reasonable persecutor') and Lauren McKinley; to Ann Sinclair at Newcastle Law School; to John Dean at the Electronic Information Network for his advice on access to asylum determinations; and finally to Judith Keyworth.

The law is stated as at June 2006.

References

Asylum Aid (1999), *Still No Reason At All: Home Office Decisions on Asylum Appeals* (London: Asylum Aid).

Barnes, J. (2004), 'Expert Evidence – The Judicial Perception in Asylum and Human Rights Appeals', *International Journal of Refugee Law*, **16**(3), 349–357. [DOI: 10.1093/ijrl%2F16.3.349].

Clayton, G. (2004), *Textbook on Immigration and Asylum Law* (Oxford: Oxford University Press).

Cohen, J. (2001), 'Questions of Credibility: Omissions, Discrepancies and Errors of Recall in the Testimony of Asylum Seekers', *International Journal of Refugee Law*, **13**(3), 293–309. [DOI: 10.1093/ijrl%2F13.3.293]

De Botton, A. (2001), *The Consolations of Philosophy* (London: Penguin).

Franks Committee (1957), 'Report of the Committee on Administrative Tribunals and Enquiries' (Cmnd 218, 1957).

Gibney, M. and Hansen, R. (2003), 'Deportation and the Liberal State: The Forcible Return of Asylum Seekers and Unlawful Migrants in Canada, Germany and the United Kingdom', *New Issues in Refugee Research, Working Paper 77*, UNHCR Evaluation and Policy Unit, Switzerland.

Good, A. (2004), 'Expert Evidence in Asylum and Human Rights Appeals: an Expert's View', *International Journal of Refugee Law*, **16**(3), 358–380. [DOI: 10.1093/ijrl%2F16.3.358].

Gorlick, B. (2002), 'Common Burdens and Standards: Legal Elements in Assessing Claims to Refugee Status', *New Issues in Refugee Research, Working Paper 68* (Switzerland: UNHCR Evaluation and Policy Unit).

Hathaway, J. (1991), *The Law of Refugee Status* (London: Butterworths).

Henderson, M. (2003), Best Practice Guide to Asylum and Human Rights Appeals, (London: Immigration Law Practitioners' Association in association with the Refugee Legal Group).

Home Office (2005), 'Asylum Statistics: 4th Quarter 2005 United Kingdom'. http://www.homeoffice.gov.uk/rds/pdfs06/asylumq405.pdf, Accessed on June 27 2006.

Hooper, L. (2005), 'The New Asylum Court System', *The New Law Journal*, **155**(7175), 682–683.

House Of Commons Home Affairs Committee (2004), Second Report of Session 2003–04, Volume I, 'Asylum Applications' (HC 218–I).

Immigration Advisory Service (2003), Research and Information Unit, 'Home Office Country Assessments: an Analysis'.

Immigration Advisory Service (2005), Research and Information Unit, 'Submission to APCI: An Analysis of Home Office Country Reports'.

Lambert, H. (2006), 'The EU Asylum Qualification Directive, its Impact on the Jurisprudence of the United Kingdom and International Law', *International and Comparative Law Quarterly*, **55**(1), 161–192. [DOI: 10.1093/iclq%2Flei070]

Montrose, J.L. (1954), 'Basic Concepts of the Law of Evidence', *The Law Quarterly Review*, **70**, 527–555.

Mullender, R. (2005), 'The Reasonable Person, the Pursuit of Justice, and Negligence Law', *The Modern Law Review*, **68**(4), 681–695. [DOI: 10.1111/j.1468-2230.2005.00556.x].

Muller-Hoff, C. (2001), 'Representations of Refugee Women – Legal Discourse in Europe', *Law, Social Justice & Global Development*, **1**. http://www2.warwick.ac.uk/fac/soc/law/elj/lgd/2001_1/muller1/, Accessed on June 27 2006.

National Audit Office (2004), Report by the Comptroller and Auditor General, Session 2003–2004, 'Improving the Speed and Quality of Asylum Decisions' (HC 535).

Phuong, C. (2005), 'The Removal of Failed Asylum Seekers', *Legal Studies*, **25**(1), 117–141. [DOI: 10.1111/j.1748–121X.2005.tb00273.x].

Rhys Jones, D. and Smith, S.V. (2004), 'Medical Evidence in Asylum and Human Rights Appeals', *International Journal of Refugee Law*, **16**(3), 381–410. [DOI: 10.1093/ijrl%2F16.3.381].

Sarbin, T. and Kitsuse, J. (eds) (1994), *Constructing the Social* (London: Sage Publications).

— (1994), 'A Prologue to Constructing the Social' in Sarbin, T. and Kitsuse, J. (eds).

Scheppele, K.L. (1994), 'Practices of Truth Finding in a Court of Law: The Case of Revised Stories' in Sarbin, T. and Kitsuse, J. (eds).

Smith, E. (2004), *Right First Time? Home Office Interviewing and Reasons for Refusal Letters* (London: Medical Foundation for the Care of Victims of Torture).

Talbot, T. (2004), 'Credibility and Risk: One Adjudicator's View', *Immigration Law Digest*, **10**(2), 29–31.

Thomas, R. (2005), 'Evaluating Tribunal Adjudication: Administrative Justice and Asylum Appeals', *Legal Studies*, **25**(3), 462–498. [DOI: 10.1111/j.1748-121X.2005.tb00679.x].

— (2006), 'Assessing the Credibility of Asylum Claims: EU and UK Approaches Examined', *European Journal of Migration and Law*, **8**(1), 79–96. [DOI: 10.1163/157181606776911969].

Twining, W. (1980), 'Taking Facts Seriously' reprinted in Twining, W. (ed.).

— (1990), *Rethinking Evidence: Exploratory Essays* (Oxford: Blackwell Publishing).

UNHCR (1992), Handbook on Procedures and Criteria for Determining Refugee Status under the 1951 Convention and the 1967 Protocol relating to the Status of Refugees (HCR/IP/4/Eng/REV.1).

UNHCR (2005), 'Press Release, 'UNHCR Issues UK Asylum Report as Numbers Plummet', http://www.unhcr.org.uk/press/press_releases2005/pr11March05.htm, Accessed on March 29, 2006.

Weston, A. (1998), '"A Witness of Truth" – Credibility Findings in Asylum Appeals', *Immigration and Nationality Law and Practice*, **12**(3), 87–89.

Treaties/Legislation

1950 European Convention on Human Rights
1951 Convention relating to the Status of Refugees
Nationality, Immigration and Asylum Act, 2002
Asylum and Immigration (Treatment of Claimants, etc.) Act, 2004
EU Qualification Directive (Council Directive 2004/83/EC of 29 April 2004, OJ 30
    September 2004, L 304/12.23)

Cases

Hall v Brooklands Auto Racing Club [1930. H. 3471.].
Karanakaran (*Karanakaran v Secretary of State for the Home Department*) [2000]
    All ER 3,449 [2000] INLR 122 [2000] IMM AR 271.
Kaja [1995] IMM AR 1.
Kasolo [1996] (*Majorie Kasolo v The Secretary of State for the Home Department*)
    Appeal number: 13,190–HX–70,731–95 (01/04/96).
Kingori (*R v Secretary of State for the Home Department ex parte Kasolo, aka
    Mpyanguli*) [1994] IMM AR 539 (CA).
Sivakumaran (*R v Secretary of State for the Home Department ex parte Sivakumaran*)
    [1998] AC 958.
Toro (2002) (*Maria Fanny Toro De Pino v Secretary of State for the Home Department*)
    Appeal number: [2002] UKIAT06539–HX/14,589–2,002 (14/02/03).

N.B. The asylum seekers who allowed me to use their unreported determinations in
this research agreed to do so only if they remained anonymous. I cannot therefore
supply appeal references for these cases. However I have, for the purposes of
validating the academic integrity of the Chapter, and on condition that they are not
made available to anyone else, supplied copies of the determinations to the editor of
this volume.

Other

Electronic Immigration Network (2006), personal e-mail correspondence with John
Dean, editor.

Chapter 3

From Eclecticism to Orthodoxy in Practice: Can Theory and Practice Merge in Probation?

Francis Cowe, John Deering and Maurice Vanstone

Introduction

Evidence-based practice is now well established in probation work, but its potential has been limited by the fact that the current top-down model of accredited programmes ignores the individualised context of practice in the social world. This chapter outlines an alternative model in which ideas have to be worked out and tested through a collaborative relationship between the academy and the agency which is mutually interdependent and critically reflexive. It is recognised that such an approach requires no less rigorous attention to issues of epistemology and ontology, so academics not only need to hold on to these concepts but also need to learn to apply knowledge or at least facilitate its application by recognising that knowledge creation happens in the field and is tested in the field on real lives. For their part, practitioners need not only to be curious about the effects of their interventions in people's lives but also committed to the processes of evidence-based practice and accountability.

An Historical Overview

Only in recent years has the Probation Service experienced the full weight of a political accountability which, if not threatening its existence, endangers its primacy in the role of supervising offenders in the community. Until the publication of the National Statement of Objectives and Priorities (Home Office, 1984) it had lived its life as a semi-autonomous organisation in a benign political environment which allowed its methodology and theoretical basis to be shaped by a mixture of current theories, philosophies, religious and moral trends and individual interests. Whilst it is not the purpose of this chapter to rehearse a detailed history of probation – that has been done elsewhere (King, 1969; Bochel, 1976; McWilliams, 1983, 1985, 1986, 1987; Vanstone, 2004) – nevertheless an awareness of the historical context is critical to understanding how this process has occurred. Essentially, it is a history that can be divided into three periods: first the religious with its emphasis on salvation and redemption; second, the quasi-professional with its normative aspiration; and third, the politically accountable with its shift to evidence-based practice and correction, along with an ideology of 'punishment in the community'. Of course, these phases are not so distinct, but thinking about the history in this way provides a helpful framework for understanding how the practice of rehabilitative effort with offenders has been fashioned.

The first, although dominated by Christianity and charity giving which had embraced the secular base of social work as worthwhile activity (Young, 1976; McWilliams, 1983; Bowpitt, 1998; Vanstone, 2004) was characterised by a struggle between science and religion and, as McWilliams (1983) has demonstrated, science would eventually prevail because the fledgling science of psychology was readily available to assist in the development of assessment techniques required for classifying offenders (Rose, 1996). As Garland's (1985) analysis of the differences between what he terms the *Victorian and Modern Penal Complexes* reveals, the Victorian preoccupation with the crime rather than the individual was superseded by a new interest in the nature of the individual offender and normative adaptation of punishment to personality with the effect that during the early years of the twentieth century, institutions (for example, Borstal) and experts multiplied and psychology exerted an increasing influence on probation practitioners. Training based on the social sciences began as early as the 1920s and during the next 20 years practitioners were exposed to a hotchpotch of theories which included psychoanalysis, eugenics and mental hygiene (Ayscough, 1929). Ultimately, the result of such training was a casework approach premised on a medical model of treatment which prevailed well into the 1970s (Hardiker, 1977) until the cumulative effect of philosophical, ideological and research based criticisms (Hooper, 1952; Wootton, 1959; Folkard et al., 1974, 1976; Bean, 1976; Brody, 1976; Bottoms and McWilliams, 1979) eclipsed it in favour of a policy of diversion from custody. By then the era of political accountability and punishment in the community loomed on the horizon. That era will be examined in more detail below, but first it is important to be aware of both the previous ideological and theoretical practice history and the practice model that has become dominant at the era's zenith.

Through the Service's history, it is possible to discern the operation (or promotion) of a number of different models of practice with varying ideological and theoretical underpinnings and, until recently, no apparent connection to any official policy directive or research evidence (Senior, 1984; Raynor, 1985; Vanstone, 2004): rather, they seem the result of the autonomy enjoyed by probation services throughout most of their history. There is not enough space in this chapter to describe them all,[1] but the most relevant to the themes of this chapter are: *Rehabilitation* which was associated closely to the development of casework which traditionally involved the *expert* diagnosing the problems of the *client* (Senior, 1984); *Non-Treatment* or *personalist* which in response to the critiques of the treatment model promoted the notion of unconditional help within collaborative relationships founded on principles of respect for people and an acceptance of the legitimacy of their view of their world (Bottoms and McWilliams, 1979); *New Rehabilitation* which consolidated itself in

---

1   Interested readers can find a full description in Vanstone (2004a).

the wake of what has been described as the *What Works* movement, and is associated with *Offending Behaviour* programmes (McGuire and Priestley, 1985), cognitive-behavioural groupwork (Ross et al., 1988), and a modification of the *Non-Treatment Paradigm* which made the provision of help consistent with the reduction of harm and relevant to criminogenic need (Raynor and Vanstone, 1994) all conducted within an enforcement framework.

The Emergence of Theory and Political Accountability

What was to become an era of evidence-based practice and political accountability had three elements: research; a shift to work with more serious offenders; increased governance of the Service itself. Because of a wealth of critical commentary the story of What Works is well known by those with an interest in probation, but for those who are less familiar it followed a period in which the idea that little could be done about people's offending had gained considerable currency as the result of pessimistic research finding in North America and the UK (Folkard et al., 1974, 1976; Martinson, 1974). In the late 1980s other studies provided counter-evidence of the positive impact of cognitive-behavioural programmes on the subsequent levels of re-offending by high risk offenders (for example, Raynor, 1988 and Ross, Fabiano and Ewles, 1988). In the UK, the revival of optimism stimulated by these studies led to the institutionalisation of evidence-based practice in the *Pathfinder Project* (Home Office, 1998).

Perhaps less well documented is what happened to the caseloads of probation officers and its impact on the nature of probation practice: in effect, it involved probation officers increasingly having contact with higher risk offenders through the introduction of parole in 1967 and alternatives to custody, namely Community Service and Day Training Centres, in the early 1970s (Vass, 1990; Vanstone, 1993). The third element, the unprecedented government interest in the work of the Service, began with the Statement of National Objectives and Priorities (Home Office, 1984), gathered momentum with the publication of a series consultative papers and White Papers on the direction and shape of policy, philosophy, language and practice (Home Office, 1988, 1988a, 1990, 1990a) and two Criminal Justice Acts in 1991 and 1993 premised on a hybrid justice, culminating in the introduction of National Standards which for the first time prescribed the nature and process of probation supervision, enforcement and pre-sentence assessment (Home Office, 1992, 1995, 2000).

Practice and Theory – The Arguments for Change

Given this history, two questions arise. First, why might a closer relationship between theory and practice (and practitioners and academics) be mutually beneficial and how might it be achieved? On the first question, the point is that practitioners, academics and those subject to probation supervision will benefit because both practice and theory will be better placed to develop in a mutually informed manner. Furthermore, such a relationship should enable a fuller exploration of the ethical dimensions of probation practice than has perhaps been the case in the past. Not only is this likely to be more conducive to effectiveness, ethically it is preferable for the relationship between a state agency and an individual to be constructed in this way. The second question is addressed below in the form of a proposed new model covering the relationship between practice and theory.

Whatever view may be held about the origins and purpose of the Service (see, for example, May 1991, Vanstone, 2004a), there seems general agreement that it sought to carry out its work on the basis of a legally-based relationship founded on mutual respect; however, this idea has been threatened over the last few decades. The reasons for this are complex, but include the demise of rehabilitation and the rise of attitudes towards offending that emphasise personal responsibility and punishment rather than any socio-economic context (for example see Hudson, 2002).

By the 1990s this process had accelerated and since then successive governments have pursued criminal justice policies based upon what has been called 'populist punitiveness' (Bottoms, 1995) – in other words, 'tough' rhetoric combined with policies shaped more by their popular appeal than their rationality, ethical foundation or potential effectiveness. Tonry (2004, 1) has argued that despite claims to be interested only in What Works, the Labour Government, because of its 'determination, always and on all issues, no matter what the evidence may show, to be seen as 'tough on crime'', has chosen only to base policy on empirical evidence of effectiveness in non-controversial areas.

Such thinking influenced the preceding Conservative Government's decision to abolish the requirement for probation officers to train as social workers (Ward and Spencer, 1994) and change the probation order to a sentence in its own right in the Criminal Justice Act, 1991. Both decisions began a process of changing the relationship between the Service and those it supervised which was reinforced by the introduction of National Standards for the supervision of offenders under community sentences in 1992. Progressively, they limited the discretion of probation officers with regards to non-compliance with the terms of a community sentence and contributed to the notion (endorsed by probation minister Paul Boateng in the 2000 National Standards) of the Probation Service as a 'law enforcement agency' (Newburn, 2003, 156). Admittedly, whilst the Labour Government has invested heavily in accredited programmes (Home Office, 1998a) and many practitioners have responded with enthusiasm and commitment to effective helping, programmes have been backed up by a rigid system of enforcement and breach. The result has been pressure on practitioners to emphasise authority and control in their relationships with probationers.

All of this has been seen by some theorists as forming part of the changes to western societies within late-modernity. Some years ago, Garland warned of the collapse of the 'solidarity project' and the emergence of a more divisive criminal justice system and society (Garland, 1996; 2001) in which the 'otherness' of offenders and the 'need to punish' are emphasised. As previously argued, this has been characterised by neo-liberal governments since the late 1970s placing emphasis on the need of the individual citizen to take control of, and responsibility for, their behaviour. This 'responsibilisation' agenda is premised on the notion that all citizens are rational and free actors, capable of determining their own behaviour and shaping their own destiny. Transgression leads therefore to exclusion and the categorisation of those who transgress as a dangerous group who forfeit the rights of citizenship. Rose argues that this process has seen the re-vitalisation of personal responsibility to the extent that major issues such as poverty and wealth distribution have been subsumed into new categories of the 'included' and the 'excluded' in society, alongside the re-emergence of communitarianism incorporating individual moral codes of conduct and responsibilities towards others (Rose, 2000, 323). So, the 'included' are able to take part in civil society but the 'excluded' are denied the benefits of society whilst being increasingly subject to control by state and other agencies according to the risk they may pose to others. In this process, Rose argues, workers in the criminal justice and welfare systems have become 'control workers' with a consequential change in their relationship with those they purport to help.

However, whilst Rose's analysis may help the reader to understand general trends, essentially it remains a macro level argument that fails to take full account of not only the motivation, values and practice of individual practitioners, but also their understandings of the Probation Service (indeed, many in practice may not recognise Rose's view of their behaviour). Moreover, it obscures the fact that there has been a debate about probation values within and without the Service over a considerable period. Rutherford (1994, 3) for example, has argued that those working within the criminal justice system fall into one of three broad 'value categories': those seeking the 'punitive degradation' of offenders; those seeking to manage the system efficiently; those with 'liberal and humanitarian values'. Another commentator has delineated a range of probation values which includes respecting those supervised 'as unique and self-determining individuals' and believing that 'purposeful professional relationships can facilitate change in clients' (Williams 1995, 12–20). Without contradicting Williams, others have espoused the idea that probation values should be based upon the notions of restorative justice, community justice and human rights, and warned that a commitment to public protection could lead to an authoritarian service. This possibility may arise if the Service, as a state agency, came to do 'whatever is necessary' to individual offenders to protect the public, without due consideration of their human rights and to responses proportionate to their offending or the potential harm they may pose (Nellis, 1999; Nellis and Gelsthorpe, 2003). This is particularly the case where preventive measures are considered, such as extended prison sentences and post-custody supervision provided for within the Criminal Justice Act, 2003. In contrast, Farooq (1998) whilst seeing the change from an unquestioning social welfare approach to one which deals more explicitly with enforcement and public protection as inevitable and correct, nevertheless argues that probation officers need to continue to mediate between offenders and society, balancing the 'conflicting' interests of the individual, the courts, the Home Office and the wider community (Farooq, 1998). More recently, Lewis has argued that rehabilitation as pursued by the Labour Government is one based upon a managerialist approach which considers it useful only as far as it has the potential to reduce re-offending in some individuals (Lewis, 2005).

Despite this debate, however, political and ideological forces have resulted in the Probation Service being viewed as a law enforcement agency, aiming to punish offenders and reduce re-offending while retaining the aim of rehabilitation. Whilst aspects of this (that is, notions of free will and personal responsibility) can be seen to be attractive and can fit into ideas of empowerment, in this chapter it is argued that to push responsibilisation to current levels in an unequal society is to locate all responsibility for offending within the individual and to refute any possibility of the impact of social, economic and environmental factors on crime. Of course, the situation is complex and the Labour Government has pursued some policies aimed at reducing poverty and promoting social inclusion (see, for example Joseph Rowntree Foundation, Social Exclusion Unit, 1998), but even then there is some evidence that some of the success achieved may have not benefited young men (many of them offenders) without childcare responsibilities (Institute for Fiscal Studies, 2004)

Perhaps a preferable approach to the issue of individual responsibility is to balance it with the duty of the state to seek to provide for the basic needs of all its citizens; within such an approach rehabilitation would be more rights-based. Lewis (2005, 124–125) identifies five principles which might underpin such an approach, namely: the duty of the state to provide help to allow offenders to become full members of society and to make a contribution; the principle of proportionality which would not allow for longer sentences for the purposes of rehabilitation than could be justified by the nature of the offence or the culpability of the offender; voluntary engagement in the process help and rehabilitation, as opposed to coercion (while recognising the difficulties of this within the criminal justice system); the use of prison as a last resort; the need to place rehabilitation within a social policy approach that makes opportunities for social inclusion available to all, irrespective of whether they commit offences. None of this, however, is viable without acknowledgement of the importance the professional relationship in relation to the efficacy of supervision. What little research there is suggests that officers can affect compliance and reconviction rates by working in a 'pro-social manner' (Trotter, 1999) and that offenders relate their ability to desist from offending to the quality of the relationship they have with a supervisor, seeing it as active and participative (Rex, 1999, 371). As Rex puts it, 'engagement seemed to be generated by the commitment, both personal and professional, shown by workers'. Similarly, Hopkinson and Rex (2003) argue that proper engagement of the supervisor with the offender is an essential pre-requisite of successful probation supervision, and call for the promotion of supervisor skills and for a debate about (and proper definition of) what the move from 'supervisor' to 'case manager' actually means. Brown (1998) confirms the quality of the supervisory relationship and 'knowing who to turn to' as key factors in success in terms of compliance and re-offending as defined by probationers. Moreover, Farrall (2002, 73) although critical of much of the content of probation intervention, still stresses the need for supervisors and offenders at the very least to engage in a helping process based an agreed set of criteria and a 'productive working relationship'.

The importance of achieving quality of the kind described above is given added weight by evidence that some practitioners may be demoralised, de-professionalised and lacking in commitment (Mair, 2004, 30–31). Less pessimistically, Farrow (2004) in a small study carried out in two Probation Areas in England, found that experienced practitioners *had* become disillusioned with the Service as an organisation, but nevertheless still retained a basic commitment to the job. The main reasons for this were the downplaying of traditional skills, and the domination of cognitive-behaviourism, which was seen as placing less emphasis on personal commitment and the personal relationship.

This might not be seen as so important perhaps if current probation methods and programmes were seen to be a complete success. However, some of the first completed reports on the 'Think First' Programme show mixed results, with significant improvement in reconviction rates for programme completers over non-completers, but with completion rates of only 28 per cent. Raynor (2004, 208) cites Ong et al. (2003) and Roberts (2004) in concluding that completion could be improved by 'better targeting, by better case management to motivate offenders, by supporting them through the programme and helping with other problems in their lives' and the attention paid to Basic Skills and the work of partnership agencies may be regarded as encompassing at least some of these issues. In addition, in their Home Office Study Harper and Chitty (2004, 75–76) report that the 'Reasoning and Rehabilitation' and 'Enhanced Thinking Skills' programmes may be effective with medium-high risk offenders, but that the evidence is 'mixed and limited' with many programmes suffering from implementation problems and low completion rates. Others criticise the evangelical nature of the accredited programmes initiative and argue that it was implemented for reasons linked to neo-liberal thinking and not effective research and evaluation (Kendall, 2004). While accepting that cognitive-behaviourism might be seen as 'rescuing' rehabilitation, Kendall claims that psychological models of intervention such as this fit into the responsibilisation agenda, which has the aim of a self-controlling society and which is increasingly punitive for those who subsequently 'fail' and offend (Kendall, 2004, 78–79).

The current situation therefore, differs from most of the history of the Service in a number of ways: firstly, the links between theory and practice are more explicit than at any time in its history in that accredited programmes are based on cognitive behaviourism and meta-analyses of their effectiveness (McGuire, 2001); second, the Service is now highly centralised and subject to close control of its procedures and practices; third, it is now officially an agency of enforcement and punishment in which the ethical dimension of its practice has been insufficiently debated. There is a need, therefore, to move away from a too-rigid link between cognitive-behaviourism and practice, brought about by a top-down process linked to centralisation and managerialist practices. Aspects of accredited programmes clearly have the potential to be effective with the 'right people', but at times they seem driven more by political ideology than understanding of the links between theory and practice. One possible consequence of this is that if accredited programmes are seen in the future to be insufficiently effective and, therefore, fall out of political fashion their positive potential may be obscured. The situation is made more uncertain by the creation of the National Offender Management Service (NOMS) in June 2004. Intended as an overarching body that would merge the functions of the probation and prison services, NOMS aims to bring 'contestability' and a market approach to criminal justice, by making possible a situation in which the Probation Service would have to compete to provide services with the voluntary, private and not-for-profit sectors. Although not in its final form at the time of writing (June 2006) the possibility now exists for probation areas to close down if they fail in the future to 'attract enough business' from the NOMS commissioning process (Home Office, 2004; NOMS, 2005).

A shift of the kind envisaged should not be mistaken as a call for a return to a mythical golden age in which professional autonomy ruled, the relationship between the probation officer and his or her 'client' was one of complete mutual respect and officers had complete discretion to decide on the range and types of intervention to be used to achieve rehabilitation, including whether or not to enforce any probation order – discretion and freedom of this kind, although having the potential for good practice, created idiosyncratic practice with its attendant dangers of unfair and discriminatory treatment. Instead, it should be viewed as part of an argument that practice and research need to come together to facilitate the development of ethical practice that has its roots in an empirically based approach to rehabilitation and reduction of re-offending, based in the realities of practice. How then should this be achieved?

The Future and Possibilities for Change?

The Home Office Circular (PC 95/2005) further demonstrates the continuing existence of a centralising tendency present in both knowledge acquisition and the dissemination of information. Increasingly research has to demonstrate a connection to policy aims to gain funding and approval. Practice requires research that is accessible, of local relevance and open to scrutiny and externality. The tensions between top-down and bottom up approaches reflect wider value debates about the nature and ownership of both knowledge (epistemology) and our relationship with the world (ontology) of practice: those who lay claim to knowledge also lay claim to power. Donald Cressey (cited by Gendreau and Cullen, 2001) suggested as far back as 1958 that those who run intervention programmes and evaluate them seemed to ensure that the results of the research could be interpreted as 'conclusive' if they favoured a particular programme and 'inconclusive' if they did not. Knowledge production in the applied fields would not appear to be a value free endeavour!

Probation has tended towards the large scale study and a meta-analytical approach which devalues and ignores the benefits that can be drawn from single case evaluations (Kazi, 1998; 2003) including more qualitative studies. Whilst outcomes and targets are core to good research and evaluation, an exclusive fixation with them by organisations can undermine local research effort. Ironically, the world of practice or at least the hierarchical structures which shape practice have driven a wedge between theory and practice – a situation more often associated with an 'ivory tower' approach in higher education. Practitioners and managers are rarely involved in research projects and areas appear to wait for research findings to come to them (usually from the Home Office) and senior policy makers with considerable academic or practice credentials have been lost (Gendreau et al., 2002). This position can be reversed in the long-term if research and practice are recognised as two sides of the same coin, but only if practitioners and researchers question the extent to which the current top-down model of probation knowledge building remains 'scientific' and open to critical scrutiny and argue for its replacement with a more appropriate social research model.

The accepted social research model has its roots in traditional 'scientific' enquiry that Polgar and Thomas (1998, 5) have described as having three core constituents: firstly, scepticism (all ideas and practices can be open to doubt and analysis); second, determinism (casual relationships, which can be uncovered, behave in a way which if known can lead to an understanding of rules and laws); third, empiricism (observation and verification of the world can lead to enhanced understanding of that world). Usually the 'scientific' model involves a process of observation, hypothesis and generation of theory by individuals or groups either within or between different disciplines, and although some modes of enquiry may be more or less favoured for their scientific rigour by different schools of thought it is not premised upon a particular type of enquiry (qualitative or quantitative). Thus, the centralisation of research and the production of a top-down centralist model may not be conducive to this model (and may be anti-scientific) because the focus of exploration is prescribed by political and managerial concerns and healthy scepticism is reduced. If we accept Foucault's (1977) assertion that knowledge and power are interwoven in organisational structures, then the tying of research to State policy making functions and ministerial oversight may seriously limit alternative and legitimate perspectives, locate knowledge and power away from the local within government functions and risk blurring the distinction between political policy-making and the dissemination of research findings. What Works research has taken place at the local level, but the centre has determined the research agenda and retained data analysis and publication of results to itself. As Pawson and Tilley (1997) argued realistic evaluation is about a *model building* approach that asks: 'What Works, for whom in what circumstances?' Neither political nor ideological frameworks can guarantee the delivery of practice relevant research and, as Roberts (2006, 3) has recently suggested there are considerable dangers in uncritically accepting What Works research based on 'expert' (Home Office) evidence.

Maruna (2000) argues that narrow frameworks for theory and practice limit the ability of practitioners and researchers to generate acceptable alternative hypotheses and are unhelpful in exploring efficacy in practice; rather, he suggests engagement with individual service users and not 'grand theory' as the key to understanding how change is facilitated. However, the predominance of any theoretical (or policy) perspective is problematic as one cannot a priori determine the nature and basis of the casual relationships that will be discovered in the field nor the perspectives that best explain these. The removal of knowledge from its locus in practice has produced an 'iron cage' of policy making which limits the shape, content and publication of findings centred on practice focused research. The epistemological danger is that 'knowledge' becomes not a product of enquiry but rather a matter of policy choice. Moreover, once policy development drives research publication the ethical process of knowledge development can too easily be forgotten. Self critical, ethical research processes which reveal their results are critical to a collaborative inquiry that both delivers new insights into 'offenders' and challenges our assumptions about the nature of practice and the values inherent in our understandings of the practice.[2]

An alternative model to the top-down, centralised research that currently epitomises probation discourse would respond to the above whilst acknowledging the policy demand to balance the managerial needs of the organisation and those of practitioners and service users, recognising that these may at times be in conflict. It could be built upon a local collaborative model between higher education institutions and local probation areas which feeds national research projects that mutually inform each other. Probation research requires a critically reflexive context that promotes peer scrutiny. However, before describing the model it is important to acknowledge the influence of Pawson and Tilley (1997); Kazi (1998, 2003), Fox (2003) and the authors' history as probation practitioners turned academics. Moreover, in the spirit of the suggested model acknowledgment will be made of its potential shortfalls.

Practitioners are not necessarily good at research. Despite good intentions it remains the case that practitioners who research on their own are likely to be poorly equipped and lack sufficient resources. Consequently, they are more likely to be doing research as a 'bolt on' to other major tasks, and may have a limited range of methodologies and theoretical perspectives to draw on. Furthermore, support for projects and the dissemination of findings may be highly dependent on a few key individuals, and both impetus and commitment may be lost if staff move on. Conversely, 'expert' research may be high quality in terms of design, methodology and academic credentials, but may suffer from a lack of knowledge about the current content and context of practice. Practitioners may not value or engage with its findings because of a failure to involve them or value their perspective and expertise; it may be expensive; it may obscure the individual's needs and motivations; dissemination of findings may be constructed in ways which are better suited to journal publications and government policy than application and understanding in the world of practice. As Fox (2003, 83) has argued, it may be that instead of 'practitioners [...] disregarding research evidence, the fault lies with the model of research which has been developed in academia'.

Neither a centralised top-down model nor a bottom-up practitioner model appears capable of meeting both the needs of practice and the requirements of scientific scrutiny in applied fields. However, separating practice out from the source of enquiry is essentially problematic as it both ignores the benefits that research methods can bring to practice and can encourage a belief that practice can be a value or theory neutral endeavour. Fox (2003) rejects three dualisms that expert models tend to promote, namely researcher versus researched, research versus experience, theory versus practice. These dualisms appear to have been at the heart of some What Works research and ignore the fact that practice knowledge about particular individuals in particular sets of circumstances; that is, it occurs in an open system with local influences on both its content and context. Meta Analysis (see for example, Bonta and Andrews, 1994) is important and accreditation panels can be useful; however the Probation Service has mistakenly assumed that by extrapolating

---

2   Readers interested in exploring the growing tension between research and policy making may be interested to read 'Criminal Justice Matters' no 62. Winter 2005/06.

general principles from such analyses a general heuristic can be applied to all situations. This creates the suspect assumption that the accreditation of programmes written by 'interventions experts' in a centralised location will have local currency and ownership. Such approaches risk creating a hegemonic approach to knowledge creation and practice prescription, which ignores difference and individual service user variables, and assumes that one size fits all (Fox, 2003). That is not to say that the results of local studies should not be the subject of national debate and part of wider meta-analysis. However, knowledge and its context are local and contingent, and understanding the content, context and mechanisms of practice are essential to the development of a collaborative research model (Kazi, 2003, 30–31).

If research findings are not generated in the contexts in which they will be applied, or at least related to practice in ways which allow practitioners to comment on What Works (or not) and why, then knowledge generation is no more than the appropriation of the practice and experience of workers and service users in order for those who have power to impose their own interpretations (policies) on reality. A collaborative model of research could reverse this trend and assist the Probation Service in establishing itself as a learning organisation that pursues excellence at the local and national level. Moreover, it would challenge practitioners, researchers and policy-makers to develop new collaborative relationships in developing practice focused knowledge.

A New Model

The proposed model would have four key elements, namely: *real scepticism* which is open and not prescribed in its limits or cynical in its application; *openness* to a range of disciplines that might offer insight into possible causal relationships underpinning human action and interaction; *collaborative commitment to observation and verification* closely linked to practitioners and service users, and the localities in which it is applied; *a self critical reflexive* approach to knowledge generation and underlying assumptions about theories and values, even if at times it might undermine individual researcher or practitioner preferences or the political exigencies of defined organisational purpose(s).

The advantages of a collaborative model are numerous. It would encourage a range of perspectives on practice and promote an explicit commitment to a holistic discourse of practice development. Indeed, Pawson and Tilley (1997) have already suggested a realist approach that would fit well with such a model and Kazi (2003) has included single case evaluation as a practical and rigorous method that can be applied in the field. Key to such research design is the desire to find out why some interventions work with some people and not others – an approach that current What Works research has tended to ignore and which is important given poor completion rates on accredited programmes to date (for example, see Raynor, 2004). Such an approach would also allow for other perspectives such as offender desistence and restorative justice to possibly emerge naturally.

A collaborative realist approach would not be prescriptive in its methodological boundaries and would (as a matter of priority) seek to support research that is scientifically rigorous and demonstrates a commitment to the above principles. To paraphrase Pawson and Tilley (1997, 214) the aim is to encourage understanding that certain inputs will work for certain subjects in certain conditions. It is important, therefore, to observe practice through a range of lenses each of which reveals different characteristics and creates multiple perspectives. The current What Works approach tends to depend on a single lens and the danger is that this may limit understanding of what is being looked at. As Pawson and Tilley (1997, 218) note:

> The division of expertise requires a teacher-learner relationship to be developed between researcher and informant […] the research act, then involves 'learning' the stakeholders theories, formalising them, 'teaching' them back to the informant, who is then in a position to comment upon them, clarify and further refine the key ideas. Such a process, repeated over many evaluations, feeds into the wider cycle of 'enlightenment' between the research and policy fields.

Current practitioner-researcher formations ignore the potential learning that individual researchers and practitioners might gain from both service users and each other about why some things work and others do not. They appear to have designed out feedback mechanisms that allow for hypothesis revisions emanating from practice. It assumes a particular view of learning in which the master leads or directs the pupils rather than facilitates students' own endeavour. Probation research may have much to gain by engaging more fully (and locally) with its staff and service users in finding out What Works. In addition to measuring the efficacy of interventions, the collaborative research model would be useful, for instance, in responding to a desire to improve performance in a particular area, or evaluating a local crime problem, a service user need, or victim concerns. However, it assumes a close relationship between the social and human sciences, and the drawing together of academics, practitioners, managers and policy makers is essential in order to balance the four key elements described above.

As noted, probation as an organisation has become more politicised and centralised. The research model suggested here challenges apparent research hegemony, requiring practitioners and local policy makers to exercise choice over how they wish to develop the probation knowledge base and their professional identity. With the advent of NOMS a defining choice has to be made as to whether to develop facilitative relationships with higher education institutions that enable, evaluate and critique policy and practice developments or whether to prescribe What Works on policy rhetoric. The proposed model includes critique as a two way process, informing and shaping the development of future research and practice and a self awareness that alternative perspectives and methodologies may be employed. Moreover, the Case Manager role as suggested by NOMS may offer fertile opportunities for a more robust and critical practice (NOMS, 2005a). The development of research and evaluation of practice as core to NOMS and the Case Manager role would allow for a timely and responsive approach to risk assessment, design of interventions and the development of a critical and flexible organisational culture.

Furthermore, the model might test out the commitment of higher education institutions and NOMS to developing a relevant and high quality service that meets the needs of practice. It also critically begs the question as to how far policy-makers and researchers can maintain their morally separate agendas and credentials. There is a place for 'blue skies' and 'removed expert' research too; however, this should complement and not replace a theory building approach which recognises that knowledge for practice can only be tested out in practice (Pawson and Tilley, 1997, 85). The integration of academic and practice expertise has the potential to develop more user friendly research paradigms that are respectful of diversity. This is not a new phenomena, but a more consistent two-way transfer of knowledge and practice experience could lead to 'added value' in developing an understanding of What Works by increasing awareness of the mutual benefits and encouraging case managers to be proactive and imaginative in their responses to offending and offending related behaviours. In a world of partnership and contestability higher education institutions are well placed to enable organisations to evaluate the impact of policy on practice, and research findings emanating from a collaborative approach are likely to be 'owned' and have immediate potential to feed into performance enhancement.

Conclusion

What kind of future is there for evidence-based practice? Perhaps a realistic answer is that at this point we cannot be certain because at a time when proposals for the privatisation of community supervision are in prospect, the signs are not good. Yet with its rich history of experience in this field the Probation Service remains best placed to respond to current challenges. Clearly, its days as an unchallenged moral good are long gone, but because of recognition of the importance of evidence of effectiveness its potential to contribute to the reduction of offending within a non-punitive framework has never been greater. To survive in the tough new world of increased governance and a political consensus around punitive populism, it has to be an innovative, flexible and a just organisation at the same time as being rational and accountable (Raynor and Vanstone, 2002). An important key to unlocking the door to that achievement is a coherent theoretical foundation based on the kind of collaborative research model outlined in this chapter which effectively informs practice.

References

Ayscough, H. (1929), *The Probation of Offenders* (London: William John Hewitt).

Bean, P. (1976), *Rehabilitation and Deviance* (London: Routledge and Kegan Paul).

Bernfeld, G., Farrington, D. and Leschied, A. (eds) (2001), *Offender Rehabilitation in Practice: Implementing and Evaluating Effective Programs* (Chichester: Wiley).

Bochel, D. (1976), *Probation and After-care: Its Development in England & Wales* (Edinburgh: Scottish Academic Press).

Bonta, D. and Andrews, J. (1994), *The Psychology of Criminal Conduct* (Cincinnatti: Anderson Publishing).

Bottoms, A. (1995), 'The Philosophy and Politics of Punishment and Sentencing' in Clarkson and Morgan (eds).

Bottoms, A. and McWilliams, W. (1979), 'A Non-Treatment Paradigm for Probation Practice', *British Journal of Social Work*, **9**(2), 159–202.

Bottoms, A., Rex, S. and Robinson, G. (eds) (2004), *Alternatives to Prison: Options for an Insecure Society* (Cullompton: Willan).

Bowpitt, G. (1998), 'Evangelical Christianity, Secular Humanism, and the Genesis of British Social Work', *British Journal of Social Work*, **28**(5), 675–693.

Brody, S. (1976), *The Effectiveness of Sentencing* (London: HMSO).

Brown, I. (1998), 'Successful Probation Practice' in Gibbs (ed.).

Chui, W. and Nellis, M. (eds) (2003), *Moving Probation Forward. Evidence, Arguments and Practice* (Harlow: Longman).

Clarkson, C. and Morgan, R. (eds) (1995), *The Politics of Sentencing Reform* (Oxford: Clarendon Press).

Cressy, D. (1958), 'The Nature of Effective Correctional Techniques, Law and Contemporary Problems', *Prison Service Journal*, **81**(3), 711–754.

Evaluation. *HORS*, **24** (London: HMSO).

Farooq, M. (1998), 'Probation, Power and Change', *Vista*, **3**(3), 208–220.

Farrall, S. (2002), *Rethinking What Works With Offenders* (Cullompton: Willan).

Farrow, K. (2004), 'Still Committed After All These Years?, Morale in the Modern—Day Probation Service', *Probation Journal*, **51**(3), 206–220. [DOI: 10.1177/026 4550504045898].

Folkard, M., Fowles, A., McWilliams, B., Smith, D., Smith, D. and Walmsley, G. (1974), *IMPACT. Intensive Matched Probation and After-Care Treatment, Volume 1. The Design of the Probation Experiment and an Interim*.

Folkard, M., Smith, D. and Smith, D. (1976), *IMPACT. Intensive Matched Probation and After-Care Treatment, Volume 11. The results of the experiment*.

Foucault, M. (1977), *Discipline and Punish:, The Birth of the Prison* (London: Penguin).

Fox, N. (2003), 'Practice-based Evidence: Towards Collaborative and Transgressive Research', *Sociology*, **37**(1), 81–103. [DOI: 10.1177/0038038503037001388]

— (1985), *Punishment and Welfare: A History of Penal Strategies* (Aldershot: Gower).

Garland, D. (1996), 'The Limits of the Sovereign State', *British Journal of Criminology*, **36**(4), 445–471.

— (2001), *The Culture Of Control* (Oxford: Oxford University Press).

Gendreau, P., Goggin, C., Cullen, F. and Paparozzi, M. (2002), 'The Common Sense Revolution and The Correctional Policy', in Maguire, M. (ed.), *Offender Rehabilitation and Treatment : Effective Programmes and Policies to Reduce Re-offending* (Basingstoke: John Wiley and Sons).

Gibbs, A. (ed.) (1998), *Proceedings of the Probation Studies Unit Second Colloquium* (Oxford: Oxford Centre for Criminological Research).

Hardiker, P. (1977), 'Social Work Ideologies in the Probation Service', *British Journal of Social Work*, **7**(2), 13–54.

Harper, G. and Chitty, C. (2004), 'The Impact Of Corrections On Re-offending: A Review of What Works', *HORS*, **291** (London: Home Office).

Home Office (1984), 'Probation Service in England and Wales: Statement of National', *Objectives and Priorities* (London: Home Office).

— (1988), 'Punishment, Custody and the Community', Cm. 424 (London: HMSO).

— (1988a), *Tackling Offending. An Action Plan* (London: HMSO).

— (1990), 'Supervision and Punishment in the Community', *A Framework for Action Cm,* **966** (London: HMSO).

— (1990a), *Partnership in Dealing with Offenders in the Community. A Discussion Paper* (London: Home Office).

— (1992), *National Standards for the Supervision of Offenders in the Community* (London: Home Office).

— (1995), *National Standards for the Supervision of Offenders in the Community* (London: Home Office).

— (1998), 'Effective Practice Initiative'. *'National Implementation Plan for the Supervision of Offenders', Circular,* **35** (London: HMSO).

— (2000), 'The Accredited Programmes Initiative', *Probation Circular 60/2000* (London: Home Office).

— (2000), *National Standards for the Supervision of Offenders in the Community* (London: Home Office).

— (2003), *The Heart Of the Dance. A Diversity Strategy for the National Probation Service for England and Wales 2002–2006* (London: Home Office).

— (2004), *Reducing Crime, Changing Lives* (London: Home Office).

— (2005), 'Quality Assurance for Research', *Probation Circular 95/2005* (London: Home Office).

Hooper, W. (ed.) (1952), *Lewis, C.S. Undeceptions Essays on Theology and Ethics* (London: Geoffrey Bles).

Hopkinson, J. and Rex, S. (2003), 'Essential Skills in Working with Offenders' in Chui and Nellis (eds).

HORS, **36** (London: HMSO).

Hudson, B. (2002), 'Punishment and Control' in Maguire et al. (eds).

Institute for Fiscal Studies (2004), *Poverty and Inequality in Britain: 2004* (London: Institute for Fiscal Studies).

Joseph Rowntree Foundation, 'Progress on Poverty 1997 to 2003–4', *Joseph Rowntree Foundation* [website] (published online 24 August 2005)http://www.jrf.org.uk/knowledge/findings/socialpolicy/043.asp.

Kazi, M. (1998), *Single Case Evaluations by Social Workers* (Aldershot: Gower).

— (2003), *Realist Evaluation in Practice* (London: Sage).

Kendall, K. (2004), 'Dangerous Thinking: A Critical History of Correctional Cognitive Behaviouralism' in Mair (ed.).

King, J. (1969), *The Probation and After-care Service,* 3rd edn (London: Butterworth).

Lewis, S. (2005), 'Rehabilitation: Headline or Footnote in the New Penal Policy?', *Probation Journal,* **52**(2), 119–135. [DOI: 10.1177/0264550505052645].

Maguire, M., Morgan, R. and Reiner, R. (eds) (2002), *The Oxford Handbook of Criminology,* 3rd edn (Oxford: Oxford University Press).

Mair, G. (2000), 'Creditable Accreditation?', *Probation Journal,* **47**(4), 688–671.

— (2004), 'Introduction: What Works and What Matters' in Mair (ed.).

— (2004), *What Matters In Probation* (Cullompton: Willan).

Martinson, R. (1974), 'What Works? Questions and Answers about Prison Reform', *The Public Interest* Spring No. 5: 22–54.

Maruna, S. (2000), *Making Good, How Ex Convicts Reform and Rebuild their Lives* (Washington: American Psychological Society).

May, T. (1991), *Probation: Politics, Policy and Practice* (Milton Keynes: Open University Press).

McGuire, J. (2001), 'What Works in Correctional Intervention? Evidence and Practical Implications' in Bernfeld et al. (eds).

McGuire, J. and Priestley, P. (1985), *Offending Behaviour: Skills and Stratagems for Going Straight* (London: Batsford).

McGuire, J. (ed.) (2002), *Offender Rehabilitation and Treatment: Effective Programmes and Policies to Reduce Re-offending* (Chichester: Wiley).

Martinson, R. (1974), 'What Works?, Questions and Answers about Prison Reform', *The Public Interest*, Spring, No. 5: 22–54.

McWilliams, W. (1983), 'The Mission to the English Police Courts 1876–1936', *Howard Journal of Criminal Justice*, **22**(3), 129–147.

— (1985), 'The Mission Transformed: Professionalism of Probation Between the Wars', *Howard Journal of Criminal Justice*, **24**(4), 257–274.

— (1986), 'The English Probation System and the Diagnostic Ideal', *Howard Journal of Criminal Justice*, **25**(4), 241–260.

— (1987), 'Probation, Pragmatism and Policy', *Howard Journal of Criminal Justice*, **26**(2), 97–121.

National Offender Management Service (2005), *Restructuring Probation to Reduce Re-Offending* (London: NOMS). And: National Offender Management Service (2005a), *The NOMS Offender Management Model* (London: NOMS).

Nellis, M. (1999), 'Towards the Field of Corrections: Modernising the Probation Service in the Late 1990s', *Social Policy*, **33**(3), 302–323.

Nellis, M. and Gelsthorpe, L. (2003), 'Human Rights and the Probation Values Debate' in Chui et al. (eds).

Newburn, T. (2003), *Crime and Criminal Justice Policy*, 2nd edn (Harlow: Longman).

Pawson, R and Tilley, N (1997) *Realistic Evaluation* (London: Sage).

Polgar, S. and Thomas, S. (1998), *Introduction To Research In the Health Sciences* (Edinburgh: Churchill Livingstone).

Raynor, P. (1985), *Social Work, Justice and Control* (Oxford: Blackwell).

— (1988), *Probation as an Alternative to Custody* (Aldershot: Avebury).

— (2004), 'Rehabilitative and Reintegrative Approaches' in Bottoms et al. (eds).

Raynor, P. and Vanstone, M. (1994), 'Probation, Practice Effectiveness and the Non-Treatment Paradigm', *British Journal of Social Work*, **24**(1), 387–404.

— (2002), *Understanding Community Penalties: Probation, Change and Social Context* (Buckingham: Open University Press).

Rex, S. (1999), 'Desistence From Offending: Experiences of Probation', *Howard Journal of Criminal Justice*, **38**(4), 366–383. [DOI: 10.1111/1468-2311.00141]

Roberts, R. (2006), 'Editorial', *Criminal Justice Matters* Winter 2005/6:62.

Robinson, G. and McNeill, F. (2004), 'Purposes Matter: Examining the "Ends" of Probation' in Mair (ed.).

Rose, N. (1996), 'Psychiatry as a Political Science: Advanced Liberalism and the Administration of Risk', *History of the Human Sciences*, **9**(2), 1–23. [DOI: 10.11 77/095269519600900201].

— (2000), 'Government and Control', *British Journal of Criminology*, **36**(4), 321–339. [DOI: 10.1093/bjc%2F40.2.321].

Ross, R., Fabiano, E. and Ewles, C. (1988), 'Reasoning and Rehabilitation', *International Journal of Offender Therapy and Comparative Criminology*, **32**(1), 29–35. [DOI: 10.1177/0306624X8803200104].

Rutherford, A. (1986), *Growing Out of Crime* (Harmondsworth: Penguin).

— (1994), *Criminal Justice and the Pursuit of Decency* (Winchester: Waterside).

Senior, P. (1984), 'The Probation Order: Vehicle of Social Work or Social Control?', *Probation Journal*, **31**(2), 64–70. [DOI: 10.1177/026455058403100209].

Social Exclusion Unit (1998), *Bringing Britain Together: A National Strategy for Neighbourhood Renewal CM4045* (London: The Stationery Office).

Tonry, M. (2004), *Punishment and Politics: Evidence and Emulation in the Making of English Crime and Control Policy* (Cullompton: Willan).

Trotter, C. (1999), *Working With Involuntary Clients* (London: Sage).

Vanstone, M. (1993) 'A missed opportunity re-assessed: the influence of the Day Training Centre Experiment on the Criminal Justice System and Probation Practice', *British Journal of Social Work* 23, 1, 213–229.

— (2004), 'Mission Control: The Origins and Early History of Probation', *Probation Journal*, **51**(1), 34–47. [DOI: 10.1177/0264550504041376].

— (2004a), *Supervising Offenders in the Community: A History of Probation Theory and Practice* (Aldershot: Ashgate Publishing).

Vass, A. (1990), *Alternatives to Prison: Punishment, Custody and the Community* (London: Sage).

Ward, D. and Spencer, J. (1994), 'The Future of Probation Qualifying Training', *Probation Journal*, **41**(2), 95–98. [DOI: 10.1177/026455059404100206].

Williams, B. (1995), *Probation Values* (London: Venture Press).

Wootton, B. (1959), *Social Science and Pathology* (London: George Allen & Unwin).

Young, P. (1976), 'A Sociological Analysis of the Early History of Probation', *British Journal of Law and Society*, **3**(1), 44–58. [DOI: 10.2307/1409798].

Chapter 4

Scepticism and Belief: Unravelling the Relationship between Theory and Practice in Counselling and Psychotherapy

Sheila Spong

There is no evidence to date that theory is actually relevant to the delivery of effective psychotherapy (Clarkson, 2000, 308).

Introduction

In this chapter I discuss some questions about theory and practice in counselling and psychotherapy,[1] outlining three types of relationship between theory and practice and examining the implications of each for therapy. These relationships are: theory as a direct representation of practice reality; theory as models or metaphors for practice and theory as an explanatory framework for clients. In response to the question: 'What do counsellors need from theory?', I conclude that an effective relationship-based practice requires *pragmatic belief*.[2]

Pragmatic belief is important to counselling in three main ways: theoretically, phenomenologically, and professionally. Here, I am predominately discussing theoretical pragmatic belief, which requires the counsellor to hold in tension the belief needed for therapy to be effective and the scepticism required to maintain openness to alternative interpretations. It involves engaging with a given theoretical perspective as a credible and coherent way of framing the client and his[3] world, whilst at the same time being able to regard this perspective as just one of many potentially helpful possibilities. Theoretical scepticism is essential to enable counsellors to resist the temptation to engage in the authoritarian forms of practice that otherwise can arise from the adoption of expert forms of knowledge.

This is paralleled when a counsellor adopts a position of pragmatic belief with regard to the client's phenomenological world: she combines a full acceptance of the

---

1   I use counselling/counsellor and psychotherapy/therapist as synonymous. Any exceptions to this usage are indicated in the text.

2   I am not making reference here specifically to philosophical pragmatism.

3   For ease of reading I have chosen to refer to the counsellor as 'she' and the client as 'he' in this chapter.

validity of the client's perspective with the awareness that there may be alternative, equally valid frames of reference. Professional pragmatic belief involves adopting a position of both belief and scepticism in relation to the institution of counselling. In this way the counsellor seeks to maintain a critical perspective on counselling as a social practice whilst maintaining with integrity a commitment to the therapeutic process. This requires her to look beyond counselling theory, making connections to social theory and avoiding the confinement of a disciplinary cul-de-sac.

The current movement towards forms of integrative and eclectic practice informed by post-modern ideas (Hollanders, 2000; Frie, 2003) is particularly helpful in making visible tensions of scepticism and belief with regard to theory and practice. I will discuss here several factors especially salient to counselling and psychotherapy which have implications for the ability of practitioners to adopt a flexible, pluralist approach based on pragmatic belief. These include the structure and location of counselling training, the dominance of the common factors approach to integration and the pressure to move towards evidence-based practice.

Theory

Before I continue, it may be useful to consider what I mean by 'theory'. In their Dictionary of Counselling, Feltham and Dryden define theory as 'conceptualisation of and explanation for the ways in which people function and malfunction, and in which counselling helps or cannot help' (Feltham and Dryden, 1993). This definition lacks the emphasis on objectivity and prediction seen in, for example, Corsini's definition of theory in psychology: 'a body of inter-related principles and hypotheses that explain or predict a group of phenomena and have been largely verified by facts or data' (Corsini, 2002, 994). The more general nature of Feltham and Dryden's definition indicates the differentiation of counselling from psychology, reflecting the lack of a dominant paradigm in the discipline and marking the tension between science and phenomenology within counselling. I have adopted Feltham and Dryden's broad definition of theory, although below I also discuss the usefulness of differentiating between 'theory' and 'model'.

What Do Counsellors Need or Want from Theory?

The theoretical basis of counselling is highly contested but this is not necessarily reflected in way in which counsellors are inducted into their profession. Counsellor training is usually based around immersion in one main theoretical perspective, though it may incorporate some familiarity with and critique of other dominant approaches. This does not necessarily facilitate the development of a sophisticated approach to understanding the nature or the status of theory. Individual practitioners understand the theoretical frameworks they learn in differing, developing and multiple ways, not all of which include a well-developed critical awareness. Three such ways in which counsellors may relate theory to their practice are discussed below, namely a search for a true representation of reality, the provision of metaphors and possibilities for the practitioner and an explanatory system for the client to believe in. I briefly explain these and then consider the implications of each for practice.

A Search for a True Representation of Reality

Counsellors may at times treat theory as an accurate representation of reality. This can provide the practitioner with a great deal of personal security in her work. Her understanding of clients is built about a firm foundation of knowledge and she can determine with some confidence the most helpful interventions. She can gain a personal satisfaction from having learnt a useful and graspable body of knowledge, and can acquire professional status based upon this. For the individual practitioner, then, there are advantages in relating to theory as if it accurately represents reality. The history of counselling and psychotherapy demonstrates, however, that different groups believing in the truth of competing traditions can also lead to the fragmentation of the profession (Clarkson, 2000).

Given the multiplicity of conflicting counselling theories it is difficult to grant each or any of them the status of 'knowledge', even if one were to adopt a sufficiently positivist perspective to permit such an understanding of theory. It is, perhaps, more appropriate to treat the 'theory as representative of reality' approach as an example of 'belief'. The 'belief' relationship to theory is most immediately apparent in proponents of single therapeutic traditions but can also be manifested in other ways. For example, the movement towards developing integrative approaches to counselling through the search for those factors which are common to all successful therapy, can also manifest a truth orientation (Hollanders, 2000). The move towards evidence-based practice based on empirical research is frequently oriented towards discovering which theory tells us 'the truth' about the best answers to given types of human problems.

The contemporary reduction in overt 'Schoolism' (Clarkson, 2000) means that the notion that any theory offers a privileged truth representation which can sufficiently represent the complexities of human experience is perhaps less common now than was the case in earlier decades of development of the therapeutic professions. However, even where practitioners do not explicitly adopt a stance that their theoretical perspective expresses unchallengeable truths, they may behave as if this were the case (Mahrer, 2004). Where the profession is organised around theoretical orientation, as for example in UKCP (the United Kingdom Council for Psychotherapy), shared language, identity and communication structures can foster a strong group identity, with limited interaction between theoretical orientations. In these circumstances, theoretical certainty can develop as a habit as well as act as a security for the counsellor (Clarkson, 2000).

There are two groups of practitioners who are particularly likely to adopt a 'true believer' stance in relation to a given theoretical orientation (Feltham, 2005). First, there are those new practitioners who during the uncertainty and disorientation of learning to become a counsellor adopt unquestioningly the ideas taught to them. This can, perhaps, be expected amongst novices as a transitional stage in the learning process (Kitchener and King, 1981; Skovholt and Ronnestad, 1995).

Secondly, counsellors often invest substantial resources in their training and in their own therapy. Those who train in a therapeutic approach because they have found it helpful in their own lives – in counselling the transition from client to practitioner is perhaps more common than in many professions – may find it particularly difficult to adopt a critical stance in relation to that approach. Even where the experience of undergoing therapy is not the predicating factor to becoming a counsellor, the therapy requirement common to many trainings means that many trainees will have undertaken a financially and emotionally demanding engagement with their theoretical orientation, in addition to the commitment involved in the training course. The investment involved in these activities may encourage the development of a belief orientation, making it more difficult for the counsellor to be critical of her theoretical perspective. The effect of this is to restrict the extent to which she can develop her practice by listening deeply to clients (Feltham, 2005) as she will find it difficult to become aware of aspects of her client's experience which do not fit her pre-determined framework. In addition to limiting the professional growth of the practitioner, this has the effect of emphasizing and exacerbating the power differential between the two parties in the therapeutic relationship (Proctor, 2002) as the counsellor positions herself as the holder of privileged knowledge.

Theory as Providing Metaphors and Pictures of Possibilities

The position that theory is intended to offer an accurate representation of reality may be rejected on the ontological and epistemological grounds that there is no single knowable reality, or on pragmatic grounds that we have not yet, and are unlikely in the future to reach a point of fully understanding human nature and human change. In either case, a counsellor may see adopting a theoretical orientation, not as a commitment to the truth of this theory, but rather as one way of framing the therapeutic experience which may provide useful guide to her actions. In this view, theory provides a framework for understanding human beings and their relationships, a guide to help the practitioner choose between a multitude of potential interventions and an indication of when the relationship is troubled. Three useful and intersecting ways of conceptualising this version of theory are: 'models of usefulness' as described by Mahrer (2004); theory as metaphor; and theory versus practice-based knowledge.

Models of usefulness   Alvin Mahrer differentiates between 'theories of truth' and 'models of usefulness', arguing that psychotherapists tend to make truth claims for theory, even when claiming to reject this as a position. I will not reiterate here arguments about the relativist epistemological claims that truth is not the appropriate validation criterion for psychotherapeutic theory: these are explored elsewhere (Polkinghorne, 1992; Gergen, 1994; Erwin, 1997). Instead, I suggest that such arguments about epistemology, though important for the discipline, should not be allowed to divert attention away from the ways in which practitioners use theory. If counsellors see their theoretical perspective as one possibility amongst many, to be used where and when it is helpful, this has two effects. First, a position that there is no theoretical perspective which uniquely represents reality[4] encourages the practitioner to remain acutely alert to new experience, to the lived relationship and to the client's shifting frame of reference. Secondly, it acts as a partial counter-balance to the authority of the therapist: holding that only that which is useful to the client has validity in therapy encourages humility in the therapist, challenging the justification for autocratic or paternalistic interpretation from the counsellor as she is not assumed to know best. There are sufficient examples of abusive relationships in therapy (Masson, 1990) for this to remain a central concern for the profession. Resting validity on usefulness simultaneously empowers the client and frees the counsellor to adopt and be comfortable in a position of not knowing.

Theory- and practice-based knowledge Theory, as a coherent and systematic series of linked propositions, is only one form of knowledge in a practice-based discipline. At least as important as theory is practice-based knowledge, which is developed by experienced practitioners in their repeated day-to-day interactions. Polkinghorne (1992) describes practice-based knowledge as tacit and fragmented rather than systematically and publicly described; and as validated by its usefulness rather than by its derivation. Counselling combines practice-based and abstracted forms of knowledge into a discourse of therapeutic change.[5]

The relationship between theory and practice-based knowledge is complex. In counselling and therapy the main theoretical traditions are derived from the day-to-day experience which forms practice-based knowledge. Over time, this has become increasingly abstracted. The work of Rogers (1967); Freud (1973), Beck (1976), Maslow (1998), and Ellis (1962) has developed in this way.[6] There is always the possibility for such practice-based knowledge, codified and passed on by practitioners committed to a particular approach, to become calcified into absolutist discourses of truth, leading to the schisms which have characterised the psychotherapeutic world (Clarkson, 2000).

The Schoolism that has developed from the 'setting' of practice-based knowledge into systems which are treated as universalistic truths has however been challenged by the contemporary movement towards integrative and pluralistic practice. This is particularly the case with pluralistic forms of practice which involve a re-ordering of the status of theory and practice-based knowledge, in that the practitioner may move, not only between theoretical frameworks, but between incommensurable[7] paradigms that are chosen and drawn on according to the therapist's practice experience.

---

4   This does not imply that all theories are equally plausible or useful.

5   'Discourse' here includes a range of practices as well as the way these are constructed in language.

6   Behavioural therapy is possibly an exception to this, having developed from learning theory. However, therapy that is *primarily* behavioural in character is generally excluded from definitions of counselling, though not necessarily from psychotherapy.

7   By 'incommensurable' I mean that the paradigms are logically incompatible and not fully translatable from one to the other; I am not able here to join the debate on the different meanings of incommensurable in the philosophy of social science.

Theory as metaphor An alternative conceptualisation of 'pictures of possibility' for the therapist is the notion of theory as metaphor, in which it is emphasised that it is by its very nature an abstraction and so cannot accurately represent reality. Where theory is seen as metaphor it offers a reminder that any metaphor involves selectivity – decisions about which characteristics are significant in the comparison – and there is an assumption that all the parties to the communication understand that selectivity. Morgan has reiterated the distortions inevitable in metaphor: 'The man is a lion. He is brave, strong and ferocious. But he is not covered in fur and does not have four legs, sharp teeth and a tail' (Morgan, 1986). Any vision of the person, whether as information processor, self-actualiser or repository of forgotten early relationships, can offer no more than partial insight. Conceptualising theory as having a metaphorical nature alerts us to this partiality: to what is left out and what is given particular emphasis. It reminds us to consider when the metaphor is illuminating and when it makes the vision of the client opaque. Each counsellor can, as an essential part of her personal and professional development, ask what aspect of her own self has led to the choice of this metaphor rather than that one, assaying the relevance of a particular metaphor to a particular client.

The commonalties between these three ways of seeing theory in counselling practice are first, that theory does not have a privileged position in relation to other forms of knowledge in practice; secondly, that theory is adjudged in terms of its helpfulness rather than on truth criteria; and thirdly, an assumption that theory cannot be representative of reality.

Theory as an Explanatory System for the Client to Believe In

The discussion above is concerned with the usefulness of theory to the *practitioner*: that below is particularly related to the importance of theory to the *client*. Jerome Frank (1961) suggested that the effectiveness of psychotherapy was due to a significant extent not to its theoretical accuracy or the particular procedures used, but rather to the client's and the therapist's belief in the process. The combination of the provision of an explanatory framework, a sense of hope and the enactment of rituals or procedures undertaken within a culturally approved social framework, enable the client to feel and act differently. Frank's ideas have been very significant in the development of the common factors approach to integration (Hubble, Duncan and Miller, 1999a), but for the practitioner there are problems arising from a conflicted relationship to theory. The important issue here is that the *client* needs to believe that the theoretical framework effectively reflects his reality and that the practice techniques are valid ways of promoting change. Whether or not the *practitioner* also needs to believe in the particular therapeutic approach is a more difficult question. Frank suggests that this is the case. However, if meta-theoretical factors are as powerful as has been claimed (Hubble, Duncan and Miller, 1999b; Snyder, Michael and Cheavens, 1999) it would be only a naïve counsellor who maintained an uncritical belief in any theoretical position. The informed practitioner will be aware that it does not matter too much which theoretical framework she adopts as it is only a catalyst for the meta-theoretical factors of hope, belief and participation. Not only would the level of *understanding* of the theoretical framework differ between the two parties to the counselling relationship but so would their *belief* in it. The practitioner needs to be committed to the therapeutic system to work effectively but the client needs to believe in its efficacy. Within a value-based profession with a commitment to authenticity and honesty (Totton, 1997; Holmes and Lindley, 1998; Strawbridge, 1999), it would be untenable for the counsellor to encourage the client towards an unquestioning belief (however therapeutic that might be) she herself does not share.

A Helpful Relationship between Theory and Practice

I have suggested that there is no single theoretical framework for counselling which is widely accepted as an accurate representation of how people are and how they change, and it is debateable on both pragmatic and epistemological grounds whether there can be. In addition, where a counsellor holds a 'true believer' approach to her theoretical orientation, her superior knowledge-base privileges her perspective over that of the client. This increases the risk of subverting the helping relationship into an authoritarian relationship that is damaging to the client's self-understanding and to the therapeutic process.

For these reasons it may be particularly helpful for a counsellor to understand that in adopting a particular theoretical perspective, she is taking a position – one of many possible positions – the function of which is to guide her in developing the therapeutic relationship, to facilitate her in communicating effectively with colleagues and to arouse the client's hope and belief in the potential of change. This is consistent with empirical research that suggests that there is no counselling approach which is more effective overall than any other (Luborsky, Singer and Luborsky, 1975), and also with evidence that the theoretical position the counsellor adopts is likely to change across time (Skovholt and Ronnestad, 1995; Horton, 2000). Adopting a pluralist approach to theory implies that that it is helpful for the counsellor to be able to sensitively shift between theoretical perspectives according to her own strengths, the client's preferences and needs, the issues brought or the practice context in which the meeting takes place.

Choosing which theoretical perspective to draw on at any one time requires a counsellor who is adequately grounded in more than one approach and able to manage the complexities and contradictions that this entails. Choosing effectively relies on theoretical breadth, a mature, confident practice-based knowledge, well-informed supervision, and an ability to remain well-tuned to signals from the client. The counsellor needs to be sufficiently committed to each perspective she may adopt to be able to carry the client into a position of belief and hope for change, without falling into a 'belief' relationship to a single perspective. Practice-based knowledge supports the counsellor in responding sensitively to the client, helping her to judge how strongly to suggest that a given approach is useful for this client/counsellor dyad, with this issue, at this time. The impetus of the counsellor's suggested approach needs to be strong enough to provide the client with a useful framework to understand what is happening for him and begin to move towards change. However, the counsellor needs also to remain aware that she is only sharing in one of many possible frameworks which could help the client. It is by no means necessarily 'true' and indeed may not prove to be helpful; this will only be seen in time. This fusion of scepticism and belief is an important but difficult balance to maintain: the therapist needs to be able to generate the client's trust in her judgement about the validity of a conceptual framework without falling into the trap of implying that she knows best. In short, the counsellor needs to be believable without becoming autocratic in her knowledge.

As noted at the beginning of this chapter, this fusion of scepticism and belief in relation to theory can be paralleled with a position that is very familiar to counsellors in relation to their clients. Real listening to the client requires a deep commitment to the sense and value of what is being said, and an immersion in the client's phenomenology. At the same time, the counsellor retains what can be described in person-centred terms as an 'as-if' position: she is immersed but not absorbed; she retains an ability both to be utterly present and to have a meta-view, understanding that there are other possibilities and perspectives. Acknowledging the client's world view as valid and simultaneously seeing it as partial, personal and situated requires the same fusion of scepticism and belief as does the relationship to theory I am suggesting.

A Fusion of Scepticism/Belief in Contemporary Counselling

Next I will explore three factors which impact on the potential for counselling to achieve a fusion of scepticism and belief in relationship to theory. These are the nature of counselling training, the particular form taken by the integrative movement in counselling, and contemporary developments of professionalisation and evidence-based practice.

The Nature of Counselling Training

Tradition-based training   From the beginnings of psychotherapy, training was based in institutions attached to particular schools and sub-schools of thought, each dedicated to the continuance of a particular tradition. Although this has facilitated in-depth training involving immersion in one particular school of thought, it has not been the best system for developing a critical and comparative view of a range of therapies, especially given the history of tension and vituperation between rival theoretical approaches (Tallis, 1998).

In addition to this, theory-specific training means that the therapist has made her considerable emotional and financial investment to that School rather than to the therapeutic profession in general. As discussed above, the more time, energy and money an individual has devoted to becoming qualified and skilled to practise in a distinctive way, the more difficult she will find it to challenge the fundamental postulates of that approach. With significant practice experience, therapists do move away from their first theoretical orientation (Orlinsky and Rannestad, 2005), but it is unclear how far the key principles of their early therapy learning experiences remain intact and unquestioned at some level in therapists, even when their expressed affiliation changes.

More recently, the increase in counselling training based with the university system has begun to alter this picture, as within the higher education system there tends to be less institutional commitment to a given theoretical position and a greater emphasis on developing comparative and critical thought. However, unlike some other professions (such as clinical psychology or social work) standard training practice remains focused on learning a single approach (either a 'pure' theoretical approach or a form of integration). Although there may be some awareness of, and comparison with, alternative theoretical perspectives included in counselling training, novice practitioners tend to be closely allied to one approach and may initially lack any substantial knowledge of other approaches or the skills of critical appraisal with which to consider these.

The core theoretical model   The learning of a single approach has become institutionalised in counselling through the notion of the 'core theoretical model'. The British Association for Counselling and Psychotherapy (BACP: the main professional body for counsellors in the UK) requires that individuals and training courses seeking accreditation are able to identify a core theoretical model. This means that to achieve accreditation a counsellor needs to be able to demonstrate that her activity with clients is coherent and explainable within a theoretical framework, whether this is a single theoretical tradition or a specified integrative approach. Similarly, training courses which seek BACP accreditation are required to teach a core theoretical model.

On one hand this is a very practical way for the professional body to manage the proliferation of therapeutic approaches, none of which is demonstrably better than the others (Luborsky et al., 1975; Tallis, 1998). On the other hand the message it gives out is rather confusing: it suggests that having a *commitment* to a particular theoretical position is more important than the *content* of the model. If *any* core theoretical model is acceptable,[8] then the question is left as to why it is important to identify one model, rather than two, or many. The requirement for practitioners and courses to adopt a core theoretical model has been criticised by Feltham (1997) on various grounds including an absence of evidence for its impact on practice, but more significant for the argument here is that the commitment by a therapist to a core theoretical model encourages counsellors to adopt an unwarranted truth-based relationship to theory which is neither empirically nor epistemologically supported.

The structure of training   The current structure (or lack of structure) for training in counselling is a third factor affecting the ability of counsellors to adopt a pluralist approach to practice. There are broad differences between psychotherapy training and counselling training in that psychotherapy training tends to be longer and it may require more hours of personal therapy than does counselling training: the following comments apply specifically to counsellor training.

There is so much variation in training practices within counselling that it is difficult to generalise, but it is, perhaps, reasonable to say that despite recent increases

---

8   I am not aware of any requirements concerning the plausibility of the accounts given by a theoretical perspective.

in the percentage of counsellor training courses that are accredited by BACP there are still many training courses that are not accredited by any institution, and that counselling courses exist at a very wide range of academic levels, with widely varying requirements for therapy and practice.

A common model for counselling training is a two to four year part-time course, usually taught one day a week. Often admission criteria are concerned with the students' personal characteristics rather than previous academic achievements. Courses necessarily focus heavily on personal development work and skills work as well as developing theoretical understanding and associated competencies. For all of these reasons – short courses, many academically inexperienced students, crowded curricula – counselling courses often have little time available to equip new practitioners to consider ideas beyond the mainstream of practice. In particular, trainee counsellors are not always facilitated in discovering the connections between counselling theory and ideas from other disciplines about human nature and human change (Feltham, 1997), and new practitioners emerging from their courses may not be well equipped to understand the contested nature of the theory they have learnt.

Counselling training and theoretical certainty   To summarise then, contemporary psychotherapy and counselling theory overwhelmingly originates in practice-based knowledge, which then becomes abstracted to varying degrees and taught as the theoretical basis for new practitioners. However, tradition-based training, emphasis on the core theoretical model and the typical focus and structure of courses all combine to exacerbate the certainty-seeking developmental tendency of learners. In this way there is a risk that the situated, practice-based nature of the knowledge base is lost, and the training will produce counsellors by whom the conceptual underpinnings of counselling are accepted as truth with little recognition of the constructed and competing nature of theory. This risks new practitioners starting their practice relying on a rigidly applied conceptual framework which is so taken for granted that the assumptions which underpin it become almost invisible.

Proliferation, Pluralism and Integration

There seems to be something about therapy practice which leads to the proliferation of theoretical approaches. Hubble, Duncan and Miller (1999b) claimed some years ago that there were probably more than 200 models of therapy and doubtless that has increased since. Colin Feltham suggests three reasons for the multitude of therapeutic approaches: an economically driven tendency to the reinventing and re-branding of counselling as a product; a disciplinary narrowness which means that old ideas about human nature are rediscovered under new names; and, as discussed above, oversimplification in training and counsellor development which leads to counsellors who are 'immersed in belief rather than remain[ing] open to experience' (Feltham, 2005, 18). All these factors are underpinned, I suggest, by the search to find theory-as-truth, which has led to the addition of many integrative models to the tally of therapeutic approaches, each of which seeks to uniquely represent human nature.

The proliferation of therapeutic approaches can be seen as problematic by those who are looking for a best type of therapy. Hubble and his colleagues (1999b) for example, suggest that the lack of theoretical agreement undermines respect for the practice of therapy and damages the standing of the profession when it is struggling for recognition in a climate of evidence-based practice. However, an alternative perspective is that the multitude of therapeutic modes is consistent with an acknowledgement of the complexities and contradictions of human experience. Ceasing to strive for the perfect way of dealing with human distress can free the counsellor to adapt her work to suit her own beliefs, strengths and desires and those of the client, and to emphasise practice-based knowledge rather than abstracted theory by acknowledging the partial, utility-based knowledge of counselling theory. The generous multiplicity of theory is then seen, not as vacuousness but as strength, appropriate for therapy where it is understood as a reflective process based on inter-personal relationship, rather than as a technical activity to be applied to clients.

Pluralist practice and the integrative movement   The development of multiple integrative models is one expression of a movement which challenges the previous division of the therapeutic community into theoretically discrete and conflicting schools (Hubble et al., 1999a; Clarkson, 2000; Hollanders, 2000; Lapworth et al., 2001). This rejection of division could, however, be further transformed by the development of a more pluralist approach to counselling theory, offering an alternative to the increasing fragmentation that is inherent in the continued growth in 'new' types of integrative model.

Integration in counselling theory takes several forms: perhaps the most frequently cited is the common factors approach which seeks to discover super-ordinate elements of counselling, that is those elements that are common to all types of therapy (Hubble, Duncan and Miller, 1999a; Lapworth, Sills and Fish, 2001). In this way it is hoped to explain the so-called 'Do-do bird verdict', that is the finding of much empirical research that regardless of the theoretical approach adopted, different models of counselling have broadly similar degrees of success (Luborsky, Singer and Luborsky, 1975). In the search for 'common factors', the development of new knowledge arises from a synthesis of practice-based knowledge and an empirical exploration of the validity of meta-concepts. Here the approach to knowledge involves the search for a closer approximation to truth, which supersedes the fragmented and incomplete truths of the separate traditions.

An alternative that is salient to this argument is the post-modern or pluralist approach, which adopts a position of not-knowing, rejecting the notion of a universal truth. The practitioner develops her therapeutic framework in a spirit of pragmatism, using practice-based evidence about which explanatory frameworks are likely to be helpful to particular clients in which contexts. Here is an interesting iterative relationship between theory-based and practice-based knowledge: the individual pragmatically draws on theoretically-based frameworks to suit the circumstances of his or her intuitive knowledge of self and of practice. Permitting this stance is a post-modern meta-theoretical perspective which is accepting of the concurrence and potential validity of competing truth claims. Without the rejection of absolute truth claims implicated in the post-modern position, a form of practice described here would be theoretically untenable. Inevitably, post-modern approaches to truth are themselves subject to critique on the basis of being, by definition, without foundation or certainty. However for the purpose of the argument made here it is sufficient to note that the possibility of multiple truths permits the development of a pluralist approach not based on hierarchical truth claims.

Whilst considering the increasing prominence of integrationist and pluralist perspectives, it is interesting to note the typical pattern of individual theoretical development over time. With increasing years of experience, the practice of psychotherapists tends to converge across theoretical orientations. As psychotherapists' practice matures, they seem to be less bound by theory and develop a more intuitive approach to their work, driven by practice-based knowledge (Skovholt and Ronnestad, 1995), though these changes in what they actually do according to observers ('theory-in-action') are not always reflected in changes in their reported theoretical orientation ('espoused theory') (Horton, 2000). More recently, work by Orlinsky and Rannestad (2005) has suggested that, as their careers progress, most therapists increasingly describe their orientation as including elements of more than one therapeutic tradition. What seems to be occurring is that as the therapist becomes more experienced, the pluralist and integrative potential of practice-based knowledge softens the separation of theoretical traditions.

Contemporary Developments: Professionalisation and Evidence-Based Practice

The third issue which is significant for the development of pluralist approaches to practice is the contemporary shift towards evidence-based practice, linked to the greater professionalisation of counselling (Bower and King, 2000; Mace and Moorey, 2001). Practice is increasingly being driven by empiricism and this has raised some fundamental questions about the nature of knowledge in counselling.

There is heightened pressure within the National Health Service and other funding agencies for evidence, not only that counselling is an effective form of help, but that a particular model or technique offers the *most* effective help for a particular type of problem or client (Roth and Fonagy, 1996; Rowland and Goss, 2000; DoH, 2001; Mace and Moorey, 2001). At the same time there is increasing momentum for counselling to become more thoroughly professionalised, and so to gain status and resources (House and Totton, 1997). This requires counsellors to move from the liminal position they have adopted within many organisations and conform to the agenda of major funders. These inter-dependent forces of professionalisation and the development of an evidence base for counselling have surfaced an enduring tension between two very different ways of understanding the nature of counselling.

The main thrust of this argument is that although it is possible and useful to systematically assess the outcomes of counselling when it is seen as an intervention for mental health or other discrete problems, there is a dimension to counselling which cannot be subjected to this type of scrutiny. Totton (2004) and Rowan (2004) are both advocates of this position. Totton, for example, differentiates between two different and equally valid activities, which he sees as currently conflated into one. He refers to these as 'expert systems' and 'local knowledge' therapies. Expert systems therapy focuses on symptom removal, requiring the therapist to have available techniques which, when applied in therapy, will be efficacious and so will have measurable outcomes. Because expert systems therapy is dependent on the language and knowledge of the counsellor, Totton suggests this type of work is intrinsically limited to that which is already known by the therapist and so it cannot be taken beyond symptom removal to a development of deeper understanding beyond theory. In other words, it is theory-dependent. Local knowledge therapy, in contrast, is concerned with personal growth and self-exploration. Totton describes it as a 'practice of truth', in that the client is facilitated in finding his own truth, rather than adopting the language or conceptual framework of the therapist.

Totton's proposed division of therapy into two distinct activities offers a solution to the pressures on counselling to conform to a medical model of evidence-based practice but the loss to counselling is substantial. The full subtlety and complexity of counselling is reliant on the interplay between the client's phenomenological world and systems of knowledge that originate outside the client. It is not only the type of knowledge system that is important, but also the way in which it is used. The tentative and sensitive *offering* of (theoretically-based) alternative ways of constructing the client's experience can be revelatory and growthful for a client, whilst using the same theoretical base to seek to *impose* a solution can be counterproductive. Furthermore, local knowledge therapies are grounded in value positions and models of human functioning just as much as expert system therapies, though these may not be explicit. The taken-for-granted assumptions of humanistic counselling (an example of a 'local knowledge' approach) can be as authoritatively communicated as those of any other type of therapy. A pluralist approach to counselling theory allows the therapist to draw on both expert systems and local knowledge therapies, using the interplay between them to help the client to explore different ways of understanding and experiencing himself and his history.

This important debate questions the very purpose and identity of therapeutic practice, and highlights the problematic relationship between theory and practice. The idea that theory can be converted into a testable form of practice fails because theory cannot be reduced to factors capable of being empirically tested. Experienced, skilled practitioners develop a flexible, intuitive knowledge which combines with multiple theoretical perspectives and enables them to draw on a range of forms of therapeutic knowledge to develop a fusion of relationship and technical aspects of their work.

Conclusion

In this chapter I have argued that the most fruitful relationship between theory and practice in counselling is built upon a tension between scepticism and belief which facilitates the development by practitioners of a pluralist stance. For the counsellor to achieve this I suggest she will:

1. have a highly developed practice-based knowledge so she trusts her own judgement as to an appropriate and potentially helpful theoretical framework for the client;
2. have an acutely sensitive awareness of the client's response to the theoretical framework she is proposing;

3. construct relationships in which the (inevitable) power differential between the two participants in the counselling is acknowledged and minimised in order to facilitate the challenging of the counsellor's own preferred or proposed theoretical frameworks;
4. be familiar with more than one way of conceptualising human development and human problems;
5. be comfortable with being in a state of not-knowing and with a non-hierarchical approach to different constructions of knowledge;
6. be able to achieve in practice a way of managing different theoretical frameworks in such a way that the experience of the counselling makes overall sense to the client.

For the counselling profession as a whole to move towards productively managing the scepticism and belief dualism it will need to:

1. encourage an approach to training which allows for adequate development in more than one theoretical approach;
2. ensure that training and continuing professional development pay attention to the development of a critical approach to the application of theory;
3. move away from the requirement for a core theoretical approach;
4. ensure that counsellors in training are exposed to a range of theoretical perspectives from outside the disciplines of counselling and psychology.

By making visible this tension between scepticism and belief we are best able to manage it without slipping into a more comfortable, but less challenging and ultimately less helpful, position of authority and certainty.

References

Beck, A.T. (1976), *Cognitive Therapy and the Emotional Disorder* (New York: International Universities Press).

Bower, P. and King, M. (2000), 'Randomised Controlled Trials and the Evaluation of Psychological Therapies' in Rowland and Goss (eds).

Clarkson, P. (2000), 'Eclectic, Integrative and Integrating Psychotherapy or Beyond Schoolism' in Palmer and Woolfe (eds).

Corsini, R. (2002), *The Dictionary of Psychology* (New York: Brunner-Routledge).

Department of Health (DoH) (2001), *Treatment Choice in Psychological Therapies: Evidence Based Clinical Practice Guidelines* (London: NHS Executive).

Ellis, A. (1962), *Reason and Emotion in Psychotherapy* (Secaucus, NJ: Lyle Stuart).

Erwin, E. (1997), *Philosophy and Psychotherapy* (London: Sage).

Feltham, C. (1997), 'Challenging the Core Theoretical Model' in House and Totton (eds).

— (2005), 'Are We Over-Selling Ourselves?', *Counselling and Psychotherapy Journal*, **15**(9), 16–19.

Feltham, C. and Dryden, W. (1993), *Dictionary of Counselling* (London: Whurr).
— (ed.) (1999), *Controversies in Counselling and Psychotherapy* (London: Sage).
Frank, J. (1961), *Persuasion and Healing: a Comparative Study of Psychotherapy* (Baltimore: Johns Hopkins University Press).
Frank, J. and Frank, J. (1991), *Persuasion and Healing: a Comparative Study of Psychotherapy*, 2nd edn (Baltimore: Johns Hopkins University Press).
Freud, S. (1973), *Introductory Lectures on Psychoanalysis* (London: Penguin Books).
Frie, R., ed. (2003), *Understanding Experience: Psychotherapy and Post-modernism* (Hove: Routledge).
Gergen, K. (1994), *Realities and Relationships: Soundings in Social Construction* (Cambridge, MA: Harvard University Press).
Hill, D. and Jones, C. (eds) (2003), *Forms of Ethical Thinking in Therapeutic Practice* (Maidenhead: Open University Press).
Hollanders, H. (2000), 'Eclecticism/Integration: Some Key Issues and Research' in Palmer and Woolfe (eds).
Holmes, J. and Lindley, R. (1998), *The Values of Psychotherapy* (London: Karnac).
Horton, I. (2000), 'Principles and Practice of a Personal Integration' in Palmer and Woolfe (eds).
House, R. and Totton, N. (1997), *Implausible Professions: Arguments for Pluralism and Autonomy in Psychotherapy and Counselling* (Ross-on-Wye: PCCS Books).
Hubble, M.A., Duncan, B.L. and Miller, S.D. (eds) (1999a), *The Heart and Soul of Change: What Works in Therapy* (Washington, DC: American Psychological Association).
— (1999b), 'Introduction' in Hubble et al. (eds).
Kitchener, K.S. and King, P. (1981), 'Reflective Judgement: Concepts of Justification and their Relationship to Age and Education', *Journal of Applied Developmental Psychology*, **1**(2), 89–116. [DOI: 10.1016/0193-3973%2881%2990032-0].
Kuhn, T.S. (1970), *The Structure of Scientific Revolutions* (Chicago: University of Chicago Press).
Kvale, S. (1992), *Psychology and Post-Modernism* (London: Sage).
Lapworth, P., Sills, C. and Fish, S. (2001), *Integration in Counselling and Psychotherapy* (London: Sage Publications).
Luborsky, L., Singer, B. and Luborsky, L. (1975), 'Comparative Studies of Psychotherapies: Is it True that "All have Won and All Must Have Prizes"?', *Archives of General Psychiatry*, **32**(1), 995–1008.
Mace, C. and Moorey, S. (2001), 'Evidence in Psychotherapy: A Delicate Balance' in Mace et al. (eds).
Mace, C., Moorey, S. and Roberts, B. (2001), *Evidence in the Psychological Therapies: A Critical Guide for Practitioners* (Hove: Brunner-Routledge).
Mahrer, A. (2004), *Theories of Truth, Models of Usefulness* (London: Whurr Publishing).
Maslow, A. (1998), *Toward a Psychology of Being* (New York: John Wiley and Sons Inc).

Masson, J. (1990), *Against Therapy* (London: Fontana).

Morgan, G. (1986), *Images of Organisations* (London: Sage).

Orlinsky, D.E. and Rannestad, M.H. (2005), *How Psychotherapists Develop: a Study of Therapeutic Work and Professional Growth* (Washington, DC: American Psychological Association).

Palmer, S. and Woolfe, R. (eds) (2000), *Integrative and Eclectic Counselling and Psychotherapy* (London: Sage).

Polkinghorne, D. (1992), 'Post-Modern Epistemology of Practice' in Kvale, S. (ed.).

Proctor, G. (2002), *The Dynamics of Power in Counselling and Psychotherapy* (Ross-on-Wye: PCCS Books).

Rogers, C. (1967), *On Becoming a Person* (London: Constable).

Roth, A. and Fonagy, P. (1996), *What Works for Whom?* (New York: The Guilford Press).

Rowan, J. (2004), 'Three Levels of Therapy', *Counselling and Psychotherapy Journal*, **15**(10), 20–25.

Rowland, N. and Goss, S. (eds) (2000), *Evidence-based Counselling and Psychological Therapies* (London: Routledge).

Schroder, T. (2005), 'Interesting Times with Challenging Clients: On Listening to Practitioners' Experiences', Paper at British Association for Counselling and Psychotherapy, research conference (Nottingham).

Skovholt, T.M. and Ronnestad, M.H. (1995), *The Evolving Professional Self* (Chichester: Wiley).

Snyder, C.R., Michael, S.T. and Cheavens, J.S. (1999), 'Hope as a Psychotherapeutic Foundation of Common Factors, Placebos and Expectancies' in Hubble et al. (eds).

Strawbridge, S. (1999), 'Psychotherapy as Enabling and Empowering' in Feltham, C. (ed.).

Tallis, F. (1998), *Changing Minds: The History of Psychotherapy as an Answer to Human Suffering* (London: Cassell).

Totton, N. (1997), 'Not Just a Job: Psychotherapy as a Spiritual and Political Practice' in Totton, N. (ed.).

— (2004), 'Two Ways of Being Helpful', *Counselling and Psychotherapy Journal*, **15**(9), 5–8.

Chapter 5

Applying Theories in Care Management to Practice

Lana Morris

Introduction

The unified assessment process within care management being implemented in Wales is aimed at addressing tensions within the care management system. Students on the BA (Hons) Social Work programme are required to demonstrate how they develop and utilise the theory and skills required for assessments within care management processes. This chapter will explore some of the methodological considerations in applying theory to the assessment role within care management. The focus will be on the unified assessment process to explore tensions between the eclecticism of theories offered to social work students and the tensions created through an assessment process which, it is argued, perpetuates a reductionist functionalist position. This position leads to an insufficient consideration of values, critical evaluation and deploys front-line knowledge to second place within the assessment process. Moreover it fails to account for social workers' emotional experience of their relationship with service-users. In short, the procedural aspect of assessment becomes more important than the quality of the assessment itself as the former seeks to meet the structural needs of an organisation in accruing information rather than meeting the actual needs of service-users.

The chapter will also consider how students utilise theory to support their development of creativity and expertise within care management in an attempt to move from this reductionist functionalist perspective of care management, to one which reflects holism. By applying a reductionist functionalist approach, social work is at risk of being reduced to techniques bound by procedures (also see Adams et al., 2005, 14) rather than recognising the complexity of human situations and seeing the service-user as '(w)holistic' and multidimensional. To be able to provide a (w)holistic assessment, students should be supported to develop creativity within social work practice. Creativity rests upon developing complex levels of knowledge and understanding, self-confidence and the ability to move away from the above proceduralism.

The chapter begins with a brief overview of the care management system, its theoretical underpinnings and the recent developments of a unified assessment process. It explores the nature of the process of assessment in terms of how assessment frameworks can contribute to a reductionist functionalist approach, focusing more on attaining resource outcomes rather than meeting service-user need.

It then describes some of the students' experiences in respect of the tensions between competency; being based on attainment of 'traditional expertise' (for example through the *National Occupational Standards of Social Work*) and creativity; being based on using reflective and reflexive processes (Fook, 2002, 34) to transform practice (that is the social worker as artist rather than technician). It also includes anecdotal comments from students' experiences of unified assessment within their practice learning opportunities. Finally, the chapter will consider the interface between theory and practice within the context of care management; how theory enhances understanding and enables some prediction of process or outcome; how it enables social work students to formulate strategies for intervention (O'Hagan, 1996, 10); and how theory can be creative and imaginative in order to develop creative-practice rather than procedural-driven practice. The chapter will conclude with considerations for enabling students to demonstrate competency, creativity and engagement in transformative practice.

Care Management

Since the NHS and Community Care Act, 1990, the emphasis on assessment and care management has dominated the way in which students perceive the social work role; almost to the exclusivity of being a 'care manager' social worker, rather than a social worker who undertakes a care management function. This reflects Parton's notion (1998, 80) that social workers have shifted from a case worker role which draws upon therapeutic skills, to case managers who assess risk and need and operationalise individualised packages of care. Moreover, Hanvey and Philpott (cited in Thomas and Pierson, 1995, 358) argue that care management has created the most change in relation to the nature of social work, moving it from a profession which provided therapeutic intervention as a core activity, to one which focuses on assessment and risk minimisation. In addition, McLaughlin (2007, 2) notes varied conceptual understandings of social work and that social work is more than what social workers do. This implies that social work should not be reduced to just the roles and responsibilities of social workers, although social workers tend to be defined by them (for example see *The Garthwaite Report* 2005); but should be recognised as something which is ambiguous and evolving in parallel with how society develops in terms of its values and culture. In this context, theories have an important place in considering how the world is viewed and how social workers use theories to make sense of social work, particularly in relation to moving from a reductionist functionalist position to wholisitic perspective as outlined above.

To carry out assessment effectively, students as social work practitioners need to be confident and competent in using a multitude of skills. Some key principles of care management is to place the need of service-users and carers before those of service providers (Audit Commission, 1992, 2); to develop effective partnerships and stakeholders from other professional disciplines (Quinney, 2006, 28), and to recognise how organisational culture affects the way in which they, as practitioners, are expected to carry out assessments within a framework which requires a multidisciplinary approach. However, these aspects of care management are fraught with competing claims from various sources:

1. The principles upheld by social workers within the Code of Ethics and Code of Practice and how these are demonstrated within their relationships with service-users and other stakeholders.
2. The theoretical principles of social work theories and the interface between theory and practice.
3. The way in which agencies determine and interpret government policy and how this is operationalised for social workers to undertake the required tasks.
4. Individual and user/carer experiences and aspirations of care management, that is, what they understand the assessment process to be, their prior knowledge or experience of it, and how their needs are assessed.
5. How the social worker operates within a multidisciplinary, multi-agency or Inter-professional framework.

The above indicates that social workers have to understand the knowledge behind social work principles, concepts and values and carry out the 'doing' of social work; understanding this 'doing' as an abstract concept, albeit operating within a professional practice context. However, this approach within and to social work is seen as contributing to the lack of unity in the understanding of applying social work theories to practice. Chan and Chan (2000, 545) identify three reasons for this problem. First, there is no unified consensus regarding the understanding of social work theories. Second, theory and practice are often artificially separated and not seen as mutually informing. Third, the relationship between theory and practice and the effect of social and cultural context on that relationship is rarely considered. The practice context becomes the arena in which social workers demonstrate their 'profession', through evidencing their competence as a social work practitioner. However, as social work is recognised as a profession (Horne, 1987, 3; and, 2004, 4), it is also driven by certain principles and values that are derived from theory, practice and legislative frameworks.

Consequently, government policy guidelines propose principles underlying assessment frameworks and leave limited scope for the individual practitioner to develop the 'doing' of assessment as local authorities, not the practitioner, are responsible for interpreting and implementing policy. So, whilst practitioners are reliant upon their professional value base, expertise, skills, commitment and principles, they are susceptible to the agency's interpretation of the assessment process. This is evidenced through the way in which service-users needs are identified, often via complex eligibility criteria which include risk assessment. Fook (2002) suggests that social workers experience competing tensions in their practice. One being that to maintain professional elitism, social workers are reliant on the state to exert professional power. However, in order to retain professional power, social workers are socialised to comply; professional autonomy and control is lessened as professional knowledge is represented in terms of a managerial interpretation of practice. This is illustrated through the way in which care management reforms have been implemented, that is:

> ... to provide a top-down assessment and care management system which reduced the scope of professional discretion so as to standardise responses to need and control demand according to resources available (Ellis, Davies and Rummery, 1999, 262).

In short, the objectives of care management are focused on systems which can be perceived as being controlled via a functionalist process. One illustration of this is through the design of assessment forms by local authorities. The forms are usually based on how the service determines the identification of need. Within this organisational context the practice of social work ignores developments in the theory of need-assessment by failing to draw on theory to design forms. This atheoretical approach to practice has been criticised as it reduces social work to a mere 'activity', but is both ambiguous and inconsistent in practice situations (Preston-Shoot and Agass, 1990, 6). Moreover, there is a lack of engagement with front-line social workers when designing these forms and as part of the process of determining how the needs of service-users should be assessed. This suggests that the assessment process lacks 'partnership', as well the application of theory, at a functional level. In other words, it suggests a taken-for-granted acceptance of competency-based approaches that are reductionist in character – that is competencies are judged according to outcomes achieved, but with the latter being reduced to questions concerning what are the available resources, not how needs are conceptualised as related to service-users. Gorman (2005, 164) and Adams (1998) explore how this approach also reduces the practitioner's ability to deploy frontline knowledge, and in their use of critical evaluative skills and upholding social work values. Similarly, Preston-Shoot and Agass (1990, 5) argue that whilst theory should be crucial to outcomes, social workers are either ambivalent or lack confidence in applying theory to their work as they are uncertain of its relevance within their organisational context.

In addition, the functional character of social work is reinforced in two other ways; first, the emphasis on competency based education is derived from behaviourism – 'identifying what individuals should ultimately do' (Melton, 1994, 286), and functional analysis – 'the use of the agency function and function in professional role to give focus, content and direction to social work processes ... [which] assures accountability to society and agency' (Smalley, 1967, 151, cited in O'Hagan, 1996, 6). Given this, social work is specifically addressed at assessing and measuring for the purpose of competence in outcomes, as distinct from developing a worker's capacity for critical reflection. Hence, the purpose of assessment becomes the evidence for social workers demonstrating concrete and measurable outcomes which are predominantly resource-led, rather than via a critical and theoretical engagement that links need-assessment with practice. Moreover, this process may encompass the social worker's application of her professional value-base, skill and ethical considerations but these are secondary, and in some cases aspirational, rather than inherent to the assessment process. For example, Nocon (1996, 40) identifies that the process and outcome of community care is problematic as there is no 'method' to establish to what extent needs have been met and objects achieved. This implies that there is no theory upon which to establish a method.

Community Care and the process of care management also identifies that assessment of need can be carried out by other professionals. *Caring for People: Community Care in the Next Decade and Beyond* (DoH, 1989) recognised both the expertise of individual practitioners, whilst at the same time requiring joint-working with other professionals such as nurses, Occupational Therapists and General Practitioners. The notion of partnership and multidisciplinary team work has taken increasing precedence and has been further enshrined in recent UK legislation which enables pooled budgets between health and social care (for example Health Act, 1999; Health and Social Care Act, 2001), and so supposedly returning to the focus of the service-user being central to the assessment process. Under this unified assessment process 'partnership' is a key function of assessment and delivery of resources.

However, one of the many tensions identified within these joint working arrangements is when two or more models of care are introduced. These tensions in turn may reflect polarised positions on delivering care in respect to the different practitioners' identities, expertise and skills, but are tensions that are often masked given the pressure to work collaboratively. This pressure in turn produces atheoretical practice as genuine theoretical disputes and debates become excluded from the critically reflective process. There is though an advantage of joint working arrangements and the development of multidisciplinary teams as it at least allows social workers the opportunity to explore the roles of allied professionals. It is also timely in that a growing body of academic literature has considered the various concepts of multidisciplinary and interprofessional work and theories pertinent to joint-working. For example, McLaughlin (2007, 147) notes that attempts at creating a common framework and common methodology resolves issues of a 'uni' disciplinary primacy, where one body of knowledge and theory dominates over others. In this way, complex hybrid theories might be evolving from and impacting upon practice, despite organisational pressure which may consider theory either as unimportant or as problematic in respect to achieving consensus over practice within a multi-disciplinary context.

The Unified Assessment Process

The unified assessment process is a way of further concretising the standardisation of the assessment process within the care management framework. For example, the *National Assembly for Wales Consultation Document* (2001) outlined a Single Assessment and Care management system which would address the aims of improving health in Wales and forms part of the National Assembly for Wales' response to the *National Service Framework for Older People*. In 2002, further guidance, *Health and Social Care for Adults: Creating a Unified and Fair System for Accessing and Managing Care* (2002: 2005) shifted terminology of a single assessment process to a unified assessment process, which placed emphasis on a coordinated and streamlined approach to assessment and care management. The unified assessment process was implemented for older people in April 2005 and outlined specific requirements of the assessment process. The guidance also explains the core principles of the unified assessment and care management system for all adult groups. Jane Hutt states in the foreword:

> The key feature is a Person Centred approach to managing care. The service-user is at the centre of the whole process. Additionally, whichever agency an individual first approaches for help will need to ensure that the individual is responded to in a joined up manner and not passed inappropriately from one agency to another. Assessments will be proportionate to a person's needs and individuals will not have to repeat the same information on numerous occasions to care professionals (WAG, 2002).

A further feature is that there is a clear duty and responsibility on the National Health Service and local authorities to ensure effective multi-agency working. In short, the approach to assessment and planning care is that it begins with the service-user's perspective of their situation. The aim of the service-user and professional working together is to look at the strengths and abilities of the service-user. The role of the service-user is supposedly moved from one in which professionals solely determine their eligibility for help to one where the service-user gathers, organises and evaluates information about their own needs and circumstances (2002, 9). Furthermore, it is the most appropriate professional who has skills in assessment, multidisciplinary working and the circumstances of a specific service-user group who should carry out the assessment, rather than a delegated professional body charged with the responsibility of assessment. In this context, social workers are not exclusive in the role of undertaking the assessment and care management process.

To summarise, the unified assessment process purports to enable three key principles: first, the service-user is central via a Person-Centred Approach; second, a coordinated approach from the professionals is postulated to further partnership via alignment and integration across all agencies providing health and social care within adult services. Third, the assessment process aims for greater cohesion of common understanding of various professional disciplines through developing a 'shared culture' of the assessment process, where partnership working is key to developing a shared culture.

However, again there are a number of tensions in respect of the three features identified. The concept of Person-Centred Approach is one which is derived from counselling theory and is aligned to therapeutic work based on Carl Rogers' work (1961). Its premise is that the client knows best and has the potential to resolve their own problems and is supported via the counsellor creating three core conditions; acute empathic understanding, where the practitioner recognises and responds to another's feelings without necessarily having those feelings; congruence, where the practitioner is willing and able to be open, genuine and not manipulative; and unconditional positive regard, where the practitioner worker combines acceptance and a non-judgemental attitude when working with the service-user. On the face of it then, this suggests that social workers are being driven by government policy to return to the therapeutic relationship with service-users, and seen as a traditional 'core' activity of social workers in the 1960s and 1970s. But this approach also seems at odds with the current managerial regime as explored above, with the focus of the agency being on the outputs of the practitioner as reduced to matching needs to available resources.

In addition, the person-centred approach requires time to develop the relationship with the service-user and to enable the service-user to work in partnership with the professional, which also conflicts with the procedural models and timescales within which social workers demonstrate their outputs. Finally, service-users also need to be sufficiently motivated to respond to this type of approach, which is difficult given these organisational and resource constraints. In short, the contention here is that the assessment process if perceived as functionalist and reductionist, will not lend itself to the principles of a Person-Centred Approach.

Nevertheless, one advantage of the Unified-Assessment process may be the centralisation of multi-agency collaboration and development of a shared culture. Joint training of health and social work professions can enable partnership working, albeit recognising some of the difficulties experienced in delivering collaborative practice such as 'divisive language, professional possessiveness, professional identity and the issue of responsibility for initiating contact with other workers' (Hornby and Atkins (2000, 5). Moreover, examples of partnership indicate that people with a flair for boundary crossing are not necessarily staff occupying key positions (Adams, 2005, 112). One of the features of partnership working is the need for practitioners to have real, authentic knowledge of locality, which is often best obtained through front-line working. Moreover, Sarason and Lorenz (1998, 95) argue that this knowledge should arise through curiosity rather than be passively obtained. The point being that the role of theory could enable practitioners to develop their curiosity as well as deepen their existing knowledge.

Further advantages of partnership working across various stakeholders are that it enables a more streamlined approach to service delivery; it consolidates the opportunity for multidisciplinary and joint working, and it provides an opportunity for a new breed of workers entering the social work and social care profession. The new consultation document on social services for the next 10 years in Wales, *Fulfilled Lives, Supportive Communities* also emphasises partnership working as the key concept in increasing the quality and consistency of service provision.

The underlying theories of partnership working can therefore be explored in training to enable social work students to consider the advantages and disadvantages of partnership working. Examples of these theories include systems theories that focus on the way objects are interdependent and interrelated so that they function as a single unit. Systems theories were popular in social work in the 1970s as it was seen to offer an opportunity to develop a singular social work approach. However, as a theory it was also criticised for encouraging merely an abstract understanding of unitary method, and so lacked practice guidance to social workers (Howe, 1987, cited in Thomas and Pierson, 1995, 372). In response to this, systems theory has been further applied through the use of eco-maps – a tool used to explore someone's social situation. Another theory derived from systems theory is ecological theory which analyses reciprocal connections and personal and social interrelationships in its consideration of wider support networks. Examples of ecological theory can be found in the *Framework for the Assessment of Children in Need and their Families* (DoH, 2000).

Students as Practitioners

But given the above developments in theory and its application to practice, how do we facilitate social work students learning, so as to utilise social work theories and skills given this complexity of the theory-practice interface, and within the context of the unified assessment and care management process? Moreover, how do social work educators explore with students the tensions between the now orthodox model of expertise (being based upon competencies) and that of creativity (based upon critically reflective and reflexive skills acquired through expansive and transformative learning)? How do social work educators engage students in creative thinking when the process of assessment and care management assumes a singular 'truth' with interventions being derived from a reductionist functionalist perspective? Finally, given the ambivalence of theory as noted by social work academics and the lack of consensus on the definition of social work as explored above, how do we ensure that social work students recognise the value of theory and the recognition that theory(ies) underpin their interventions?

Many social work students are already practitioners with substantial experience within local authorities, and undertake forms of assessment without question as it is deemed the central part of their social work role. The institutionalisation of care management as a perceived singular function of the social worker is one which is challenged early on within their social work training, but one which also merits greater debate. As already highlighted, theory is crucial in assisting students to understand networks of concepts and how theory moves from the abstract, to the 'doing' of social work.

Other students come with little or no experience of the statutory sector and enter the profession with either the minimum requirement of six weeks supervised social care experience, or have had substantial social care experience outside of the statutory sector. They may therefore enter the programme with limited skills or knowledge in the area of care management. These 'direct entry' students have commented on feeling deskilled and overwhelmed in relation to the care management process and do not always recognise from the outset that the skills they bring into the professional training arena are (a) transferable and (b) can be further developed. Moreover, these students are also likely to associate the term 'social worker' with that of the role of a care manager, primarily due to the way in which the social work role is described by practitioners and some literature aimed at encouraging students into the social work profession. It can be argued that this narrowing focus of the definition of social work and the social work role is an outcome of wider contemporary debates concerning the role of the social work practitioner and the lack of consensus from social workers as to what distinguishes social work from other professions (Thompson, 2005, 2). Equally the accepted assumption by students that the care management function is the 'only' role they undertake diminishes the multi-faceted role of the practitioner. It gears students learning towards an assessment within the context of care management and via form-filling, rather than broadening thinking to consider the various theories and their merits which could be applied to assessment.

Consequently, despite assessment being a key task in delivering and practicing social work (Parker and Bradley, 2003, 2; Baldwin and Walker, 2005, 36) and one which is central to student education, many students struggle with the proposition that there are others ways of producing an assessment which do not rely on agency forms or templates. That there are different types of assessment; that they can be informal or formal, and fluid in terms of need evolving over time or highly structured and time-focused as with child protection (Brandon, 1994). In short, that assessment does not end through the presentation of a written care plan.

In response, a range of theories can be explored to assist students to develop complex thinking – that is moving from a singular position that assessment seeks out the 'truth' of the service-users situation, to one in which they recognise there is a multidimensional picture of the service-user, including dialogue with and observation of service-users' individual actions. This engagement with complex thinking is initially a challenge for students, given there is no singular theory that can come 'off the peg' to 'fix' the situation and tutors are not able to give a 'fixed' answer. It is commonly reported by students and educators alike that students often feel thwarted or frustrated in trying to understand the relevance of some theories explored within the academic setting. For example, and as noted earlier, systems theory is not always considered when carrying out an assessment as at first glance it assumes interconnections between social systems, rather than providing a basis for understanding individual relations. However, when considering family relationships, life events and circumstances and the pattern of systems occurring in an individual's life, as a body of theory it merits further investigation from the student as to what social patterns can be altered in an effort to achieve problem resolution. For example, Doel (2006, 35) highlights the value of understanding systems for effective group work where individual group members are helped in their understanding of the 'internal self' as it relates to 'external systems' and social contexts. Other theories which can be used similarly include humanist psychology, which recognise that humans will deviate from 'the good' when circumstances prevent them from reaching their potential. Thompson (2005, 66) explores how the social work task, when using this theory is to 'liberate people from these barriers so that their natural goodness can flow through'. The point being here that if these theories are applied to practice it will enhance the critically reflective process.

To summarise so far, a new social work student can therefore enter the profession with the singular idea that the social worker's primary role is the care manager function. So students may initially see social work as performing a functional role where theory is not evident within practice, and hence an atheoretical position is assumed. Moreover, we have found that this assumption is sometimes supported by practice learning agencies. For example, one student relayed a conversation she had with a team manager whilst she was on a 20-day practice learning opportunity at the beginning of her social work training. When she asked what theories were used in the local authorities children's team she was told: 'We don't use theory here, that's a classroom activity.' Another student on a 20-day practice in a statutory adults service asked the same question to a qualified social worker and was told: 'Theory is not important, the speed and efficiency of the assessment it paramount in order to achieve performance targets.' Such comments may well reflect the 'reality' for practitioners within the agencies and supports the notion that theory is still perceived as confined to the classroom and has no relationship on or in practice. This could however become a serious stumbling block for some agencies and practitioners as they need to demonstrate the understanding of theory and its interface with practice, as required through the *National Occupational Standards for Social Work and Code of Practice for Social Care Workers*. The question to be addressed here is whether a learning culture which explores the theory and practice relationship could be sustainable within this type of atheoretical organisational context?

Values, Competency and the Stifling of Creativity

In addition to the above, there is a tension between establishing an appropriate value base for social workers, as reflected in national occupational standards and codes of practice, whilst performing what is understood as a 'competent function' by the organisation social workers are employed. For example, 'developing trust' is enshrined in one of the Codes of Practice for Social Care workers, but is often perceived by students as problematic particularly where, in some cases, local authorities demand that assessments be completed within five working days. So questions asked by a recent in-take of students included: 'how do you develop trust, respect and empowerment when you are expected to have completed an assessment and care plan within such a short period of time? How do you demonstrate which theory you've applied when you've only got five days to get the assessment done?' Moreover, if they fail to conform to this expectation this might lead to questions about the student's competence, which means that the student also has to consider and reconcile their feelings about the theories they have explored and *the degree to which* they can test out these theories within the practice environment. So, if the agency is ambivalent or dismissive about theory in practice, as described above, it is likely to produce tensions for the student who has to demonstrate to their assessors how they have used theory in the practice environment. It is within this context that issues concerning how a student might be creative in their work are especially salient.

As already noted, the care management process has become more unified, and with some good reason, particularly in relation to a shared assessment form with allied professionals such as District Nurses and Occupational Therapists. For example, this should prevent service-users from having to repeat information about their background to the various professionals they might see. However, there remains a central concern that the reductionist functionalist approach outlined above will stifle creativity in social work practice. For example, the application of private sector organisational theories and business management models to the profession as a way for making it more efficient, accountable and needs-focused has been criticised as contributing to increased individual paperwork, leading to less contact time with service-users. More specifically, the implementation of scientific management theories 'removes the decision-making on how to perform a role from the worker' (Harlow, 2004), thereby leading to an undermining of the practitioner's confidence and autonomy in decision-making, and so leaving them at the whim of senior managers. As a result, practice is often measured against team and organisation performance targets aligned more to efficiency gains than the meeting of human or 'soft needs' – for example interaction, interpersonal dialogue, reflection and being Person-Centred.

The main contention here is that as social work is inherently a human activity, the application of business management models produces further tensions for the practitioner who has to respond to theses efficiency goals but also respond to a person 'in need'. Moreover, these models have facilitated emotional distance between the worker and the service-user partly because of restrictions in their professional autonomy (as noted by Fook, 2002), but also because there is less time with service-users to provide creative interpersonal interactions and relationships. The reductionist approach to social work so far identified is one which fails to account for the emotional experience of the social worker and service-user (Trethivick, 2005). In response, Thompson (2005, 103) argues that social workers should not put up with the ways in which problems, demands, frustrations and disappointments of the work manifest, but learn what he calls 'resilience', through developing a commitment to make a success of social work, and devise coping skills and support networks. More specifically, resilience in social work is attributed to managing the emotional, physical and mental pressures from the work itself (Thompson, 2005, 102), and the way in which creative relationships are developed between the agency and worker, the worker and the service-user, and the cultural and socio-political context of social work (also see Nash et al., 2005, 58). Therefore, the ability to be resilient given the pressures within social work and in training is one which students need to develop. But how is this done, given the above issues and tensions?

Responding through Multidimensionality

One way of responding to the above is through knowledge of social work theories in understanding and delivering care management. A range of expertise and skills are required in order to undertake a basic assessment of need and these skills are informed in part through theory. Social work education needs to provide 'enough' of a conceptual framework combined with the skills and pragmatism of applying it to practice, as well as a forum for debate concerning the relationship between theory and practice. In addition, social work research needs to demonstrate how it integrates theory with practice and the ways in which theory and practice influence each other. However, as Dominelli highlights (2005, 231), social work research is weak in this respect as it often fails to adequately theorise. Arguably, both the advantage and disadvantage of social work is that it has few 'purist' theories and models which are derived from social work itself, but uses a range of theories from other disciplines and interprets them within the context of social work practice. For example, task-centred case work is widely recognised as a purist model within social work in that it is one which has been developed within the context of social work. Whereas, attachment theory, systems theory and ecological theory are ones which have been 'borrowed' by social work as they are generic in terms of their greater understanding of sociological and psychological conceptions of human nature. However, facets of these theories can be used and developed in order to inform the type of interventions proposed with those who require social work support. So, attachment theory is frequently referred to and used in understanding developmental stages of children and adults and often referred to within the 'triangle' of assessment (for example see Department of Health, Department for Education and Employment, Home Office, 2000).

Moreover, the contention here is that the way in which some of these theories are applied relies on a clearer understanding and knowledge framework of the cultural context, social history, service-user and carer narratives, as well as the personal and professional values attributed to the social work profession. Following Fook (2002), personal and professional narratives might be used within the context of assessment and intervention, with these narratives underpinning a 'multidimensional approach' to social work, providing an opportunity for interested parties to explicitly relate multiple meanings and perspectives to the development of practice. This explication encompasses matters relating to gender, class, race, beliefs, religion and other cultural identities, and as these are applied to professional notions of anti-oppressive and anti-discriminatory practice.

It is from this multi-dimensional approach that the idea of 'praxis' can be better developed as a mechanism whereby students can engage in the interface between theory and practice. That is, by supporting the growing competence of the student practitioner, at the same time opening up critical debate of social work theories and practice rather than reducing it to a functionalist process. This approach also enables students to recognise the eclecticism of social work and how 'hybrid' theories of human nature can inform their professional judgement in relation to how they assess and intervene. It would also encourage the student social worker to consider the concept of 'creativity' within their work (to be explored further below) seeing this as a central feature in maintaining resilience and persistence within an increasingly recognised stressful occupation (Ramon and Morris, 2005, 43).

Creativity in Care Management

Competence-based practice relies on the student demonstrating 'traditional' expertise according to models of evidence based practice; whereas, creativity requires expansive and transformative learning which incorporates reflective and reflexive approaches (Karvinen-Niinikoski, 2005). Students are required to demonstrate the traditional model of expertise through the *National Occupational Standards for Social Work* by providing evidence from practice that they have competence in Key Skills. Therefore, it is a challenge for social work educators to enable creativity through the theory practice interface. Educators need to explore with their students how the integration of theory can assist in practicing skills and how creativity can contribute to the required 'traditional expertise'. In addition, practice assessors need to support students to make sense of this integration and to assist students in applying it to practice.

In its simplest form, creativity is defined by the Collins Concise Dictionary as '1. having the ability to create; 2) characterised by originality of thought; 3) designed to or tending to stimulate the imagination.' However, it is difficult to enhance creativity with students in respect to the unified assessment process for two overt reasons. First, they do not immediately see the relevance of creativity to their work, as at first glance it seems incongruent with the standards and performance targets they need to evidence. Arguably the nature of core competencies via the *National Occupational Standards for Social Work* risks restricting learning to only achieving and evidencing the standards stated. Second, in undertaking the task of assessment and care management the superficiality and specificity of form-filling can be perceived as a barrier to creativity. For example, completing an assessment form which is highly structured often requires specific information about the limitations of a service-user or carer rather than the strengths they bring to their situation, how they would like to achieve change, and the way in which they see this changing coming about. Nevertheless, the final contention here is that the notion of creativity in assessment and care management does have a concrete and valid role, if considered as a multi-dimensional and transformative process emerging from a dialogue between service-user and social worker.

More specifically, creativity in social work can be associated with reflective cycles where the practitioner 'steps back' from the doing, to thinking about what was done, why and what could/should be done within the context of their involvement. This supports reflexive practice and holistic assessment as it 'takes into account diversity (and) complexity' (Baldwin and Walker, 2005). In addition, this type of work can be aligned with transformational practice, whereby social changes are explored with 'others' in an effort to reduce inequalities and enhance social solidarity (Adams et al., 2005, 2). In short, transformational practice requires the use of reflexive and critical practice which supports the undertaking of assessment that considers the aspirations of the service-user, rather than identifying needs within the functionalist model. It also supports the notion of 'reflexiveness' referring to a cyclical process of reflecting-in-action, reflection after action, and changes in thinking.

Conclusion

This chapter has explored the application of theory in care management and the unified assessment process through evaluating the tensions that occur for social work practitioners and students. It has explored how the of lack of consensus over the definition of social work relates to the varied conceptual and theoretical understandings of social work, further noting that social work is much more than what social workers do. It also concerns how social workers critically reflect on their practice using these various understandings.

The chapter has also looked at the range of tensions within care management such as the lack of unity of social work theory and the way social workers are controlled by the organisational culture which accepts a single-dimensional competency based approach to practice. The danger in accepting this approach is that it erodes the practitioner's ability to use their knowledge, critical evaluative skills and creative thinking. This problem is compounded if the purpose of assessment becomes the evidence for social workers to demonstrate organisational outcomes rather than evidence being linked to service-user need.

Students require considerable support from the practice and educational environment to relate theory to practice, and vice versa, enabling them to explore the multidimensional nature of their role as social work practitioner and through utilising the concept of 'creativity' in respect to reflective and reflexive practice. This support can be enhanced by good supervision models that develop and enhance learning, and prevent theory from being seen merely as a classroom activity. Moreover, promoting a multidimensional understanding of social work that explicitly acknowledges the presence of a diverse range of perspectives and personal narratives from the service-user, and reflecting wider social, political and cultural contexts will assist the social worker in being creative in their work. That is, developing creativity and competence that allows social work students to both understand and utilise theories in order to support their social work role, and to practice beyond the boundaries of their roles as defined by their organisation.

References

Adams, R. in Adams, Dominelli and Payne (eds) (1998), *Social Work Themes, Issues and Critical Debates* (Basingstoke: Macmillan).

Audit Commission (1992), *The Community Revolution: Personal Social Services and Community Care* (London: HMSO).

Baldwin, N. and Walker, L. (1998), 'Assessment' in Adams and Dominelli et al. (eds).

Balloch, S., McLean, R. and Fisher, M.I. (1999), *Social Services: Working Under Pressure* (Bristol: The Policy Press).

Brandon, D. (1994), *The Yin and Yang of Care Planning* (Cambridge: Anglia Polytechnic University).

Chan, K.L. and Chan, C.L.W. (2000), 'Social Workers' Conceptions of the Relationship Between Theory and Practice in an Organisational Context', *International Social Work*, **47**(4), 543–557. [DOI: 10.1177/0020872804046260].

Department of Health (DoH), Department for Education and Employment, Home Office (2000), *Framework for the Assessment of Children in Need and Their Families* (London: HMSO).

Doel, M. (2006), *Using Groupwork* (London: Routledge).

Edwards, P. and Wajcman, J. (2005), *The Politics of Working Life* (Norfolk: Oxford University Press).

Ellis, K., Davies, A. and Rummery, K. (1999), 'Needs Assessment, Street-level Bureaucracy and the New Community Care', *Social Policy and Administration*, **22**(3), 262–275. [DOI: 10.1111/1467-9515.00150].

Fook, J. (2002), *Social Work: Critical Theory and Practice* (London: SAGE Publications).

Fox, N.J. (2003), 'Practice-Based Evidence: Towards Collaborative and Transgressive Research', *Sociology*, **37**(1), 81–102. [DOI: 10.1177/0038038503037001388].

Garthwaite, T. (2005), *Social Work in Wales: A Profession to Value* (London: ADSS).

Gorman, H. (1998), 'Frailty and Dignity in Old Age' in Adams and Dominelli et al. (eds).

Hanvey, C. and Philpot, T. (eds) (1994), *Practising Social Work* (London:

Routledge).

Harlow, E. (2004), 'Why Don't Women Want to be Social Workers Anymore? New Managerialism, Post-feminism and the Shortage of Social Workers in Social Services Departments in England and Wales', *European Journal of Social Work*, 7(2), 167–180. [DOI: 10.1080/1369145042000237436].

HMSO (1989), *Caring for People: Community Care in the Next Decade and Beyond* (London: HMSO).

Hornby, S. and Atkins, J. (2000), *Collaborative Care: Interprofessional, Interagency and Interpersonal*, 2nd edn (Oxford: Blackwell Science).

Horne, M. (1987), *Values in Social Work* (Aldershot: Ashgate Publishing).

IASSW and IFSW (2004) (2004), 'Global Standards for Social Work Education'. www.iassw.soton.ac.uk/en/GlobalQualifyingStandards/GlobalStandards/pdf, accessed 20/12/06.

Karvinen-Niinikoski, S. (2005), 'Research Orientation and Expertise in Social Work – Challenges for Social Work Education', *European Journal of Social Work*, 8(3), 259–271. [DOI: 10.1080/13691450500210756].

McLaughlin, H. (2007), *Understanding Social Work Research* (London: Sage).

Meinert, R.G., Pardeck, J.T. and Murphy, J.W. (eds) (1998), *Postmodernism, Religion and the Future of Social Work* (New York: Haworth).

Melton, F.R. (1994), 'Competences in Perspective', *Educational Research*, 36(3), 28–94.

National Assembly for Wales (2001), *Consultation Document: Assessment and Care Management for Adults: Developing the Single Assessment and Care Management System including Fair Access* (Cardiff: Welsh Assembly Government).

Nocon, A. (1996), 'Examining Outcomes in Community Care', *Research, Policy and Planning*, 14(1), 39–44.

O'Hagan, K. (ed.) (1996), *Competence in Social Work Practice* (London: Jessica Kingsley Publishers).

Parton, N. (1998), 'Advanced Liberalism, (Post)modernity and Social Work: Some Emerging Social Configurations' in Meinert and Pardock et al. (eds).

Preston-Shoot, M. and Agass, D. (1990), *Making Sense of Social Work: Psychodynamics, Systems & Practice* (Basingstoke: Macmillan).

Quinney, A. (2006), *Collaborative Social Work Practice* (Exeter: Learning Matters Ltd).

Ramon, S. and Morris, L. (2005), 'Responding to Perceived Stress in a Social Services Department: Applying and Participative Strategy', *Research Policy and Planning*, 23(1), 43–54.

Rogers, C. (1961), *Client-centred Therapy: Its Current Practice, Theory and Implications* (London: Constable).

Sarason, S.B. and Lorenz, E.M. (1998), *Crossing Boundaries: Collaboration, Coordination, and the Redefinition of Resources* (San Francisco: Jossey-Bass).

Smalley, R. (1967), *Theory for Social Work Practice* (New York: Columbia University Press).

SSIW/WAG (2001), Health and Social Care for Adults: Creating a Unified and Fair System for Assessing and Managing Care (Cardiff: (SSIW/NAW).

Thompson, N. (2005), *Understanding Social Work: Preparing for Practice*

(Basingstoke: Palgrave Macmillan).

WAG (2002), *The Core Essentials of Creating a Unified and Fair System for Assessing and Managing Care* (Cardiff: Welsh Assembly Government).

Webb, S.A. (2001), 'Some Considerations on the Validity of Evidence-based Practice in Social Work', *British Journal of Social Work*, **31**(1), 57–79. [DOI: 10.1093/bjsw%2F31.1.57].

Chapter 6

Theory, Practice and 'Teaching' Professional Ethics

Gideon Calder

[A]nything that we can call morality today merges into the question of the organisation of the world (Adorno, 2000, 176).

Introduction

This chapter explores a cluster of issues arising from the teaching of ethics on vocational programmes in higher education. Such teaching has mushroomed in recent years. More and more, professionally oriented degree programmes involve an ethical component at the centre of the curriculum, rather than at its periphery. Grappling with ethics is a requirement for trainee nurses, doctors, social workers, probation officers – indeed, across the range of caring and social professions, as well as beyond it. This is welcome, but brings challenges. It poses questions about the nature and scope of vocational education and about what education in ethics is (or should be) like. Broadly, the argument of this chapter is that doing justice to both of these requires a subtler calibration of educational priorities than cruder, more reductive and instrumentalist models of 'learning outcomes' are able to accommodate.

Another way of putting this is that 'teaching' ethics has its limits. Not because ethics is too complex to be taught, or is somehow too arcane for vocational purposes – far from it, as the recognition of its place at the core of such professions shows – but because it is a process which cannot be reduced to outcomes in some neatly delimited way. The implications of these issues transcend professional ethics as a discipline – though arguably, they are encountered there with a particular starkness. In turn they reflect important questions about the relationship between theory and practice which are particularly pressing in the delivery of vocational education.

Relating Theory and Practice

To say that theory and practice can, and should, be thought of as being mutually entwined is philosophically compelling, and opens up fertile educational ground. As with other contributions to this book, this chapter is informed by the stance that – to paraphrase Kant – theory without practice is empty, and practice without theory is blind. Or to corrupt Socrates: theoretically unexamined practice is not worth the term 'practice' at all.[1] Or still more boldly: practice, properly understood, is impossible without theory, broadly understood. Claims that somehow we can bypass 'theoretical' niceties and get straight down to 'practicalities' rest on the untenable notion that somehow we could 'do' practice without theoretical preconceptions (however well- or ill-formed, and whether subject to reflection or not), or that 'getting straight down to practicalities' might itself be somehow a theoretically 'neutral' kind of strategy. The call to prioritise practice will always have its ideological roots: one cannot escape these simply by asserting an intention to avoid the theoretical domain (see Calder, 2006, 22–27). To present some model of the 'given' as a natural or inevitable starting point – or to appeal to the 'common sense' wisdom of a practice – is always to reduce the plurality and complexity of the world to one, partial, simplified, reductive version of it.[2] And that, however modestly or 'pragmatically' presented, is not just a theoretical move, but one of a particularly extravagant variety (see Penna 2004 for historical examples of the abuses of theory along these lines).

Meanwhile, theory itself is a practice, impossible to carry out without reference to the world and our activity within it. Especially in vocational education (but also more generally), the notion that we can 'do' theory free from the constraints of the practical, broadly conceived, is, just as much as the reverse view, self-undermined as soon as it gets started. For theory is not just the stuff of painstaking abstraction. It does not exist in some kind of metaphysical outer space, severed from our engagement with the world, and with each other. Most of its 'work' is done in far more mundane ways, in the 'processing' of our experience, our negotiation of practicalities, and the acquisition of everyday knowledge. A passage from Andrew Collier helps elaborate this general point:

> We acquire everyday knowledge largely in the course of activities whose aim is not knowledge. Like Picasso, we don't seek, we find. But the experience acquired in such practically oriented interaction with the world around us is then sifted, criticised, ordered, explained, redescribed. I am not talking about any unusual or consciously "philosophical" self-examination. I am talking about virtually everything that we normally call "thinking". Without such thinking, experience teaches us very little (Collier, 1994, 39).

'Such thinking' is, broadly, the work that theory does: interrogating particular, concrete experiences and contexts via more generalised, transferable conceptual tools. If experience without thinking is by nature uninformed and uninformative, so equally would be the 'doing' of practice without theoretical entanglements (assumptions, generalisations from particular cases, identifications of correlations between different ones) somehow entering in on the act. Thus, again, the very idea of theory-free practice which actually means anything is, from this angle, simply a mistake. This would apply just as much to any notion of 'untheoretical' education.

---

1   Adapting, here, Kant's claim that 'thoughts without intuitions are empty; intuitions without concepts are blind' (Kant, 1963, A 51), and Socrates' that 'the unexamined life is not worth living' (Plato, 1954, 72).

2   A process for which the term 'reification' – less fashionable now than once it was – remains particularly apt (see Bewes, 2002, Chapter 1).

Viewed in this way, 'theory' – sifting, criticising, ordering, explaining, redescribing – is as inescapable in the academic context as thinking itself.

Yet even if doing theory is inevitable in any substantive educational scheme, doing theory well is not. Simply to assume that theory and practice always exist in neat, tight, symbiotic relation would be to assume that the world – and institutions – run more smoothly than they do. The 'organisation of the world', to use Adorno's phrase, does not necessarily reflect such fine-grained points of understanding. Sure enough, across many areas of education, and especially on vocational programmes, the illuminative reconciliation of theory and practice is present as a core aim. But considered aright it is precisely that: an aim, an achievement, rather than a given.

As an example, practising critically, with theory in mind, is a crucial element of 'reflective practice' – itself a key aim of vocational education in the social professions. Reflective practice is variously defined as: 'a set of abilities and skills, to indicate the taking of a critical stance, an orientation to problem solving or state of mind' (Moon, 1999, 63); and as 'an approach which promotes autonomous learning that aims to develop students' understanding and critical thinking skills' (HEA, 2006). But that orientation, and that autonomy of learning, is something which cannot simply be 'outcomed' early in a module and then set to rest, or dug up later for periodic tweaking. It is in need of constant upkeep. Reflection and reflexivity are not processes with an obvious end-point, or prospect of closure. For all their mutual entanglement, theory and practice are not such that they can neatly be slotted together without mess or remainder, as if this were one among other pedagogical 'jobs' to be 'done'. When the slotting is too neat or the fit too snug, we risk the same kind of artificial foreclosure and reduction of 'professional reality' that we find when theory imposes itself too hard and too hastily on the complexity of social relations.

Thus, while theory and practice exists in reciprocal relation, they are also distinct. Educative practice can wedge them too far apart from each other, for one strategic reason or another ('Let's deal with theory in this module, and practice in this one…'). But equally, it can also stick them uncritically together in idealistic ways, so that in effect, one is absorbed into the other. With professional ethics, this possibility looms largest when a given module is taught either by a 'practitioner' with a grudging tolerance for theory, or a 'theoretician' with no practical experience of the profession in question. Here, there is a strong likelihood of theory and practice being 'reconciled' by one side being more or less collapsed into the other, rather than them being held in fruitful dialectical relation. From whichever direction, this is clearly problematic. Speaking as a 'theory' person who has done a good deal of professional ethics teaching in areas I have never practiced in, I've been uncomfortably aware of carrying out exactly this kind of collapse for the sake of getting students plausibly from A to B, in the sense of achieving clear outcomes. The potential for this looms especially large when ethics is being taught as a core component on vocational degrees.

Thus, to my mind, teaching professional ethics provides as good an example of any of the kinds of issues and challenges that we are invited to negotiate by the overall themes of this book. In the section below I explore some of the general questions raised by the growing profile of ethics in vocational education. There seems little to object to in the notion that practitioners in the fields concerned should be expected to have a certain level of ethical literacy. Yet there are reasons to handle ethics with special care. Three, I suggest, are especially prominent: the contested nature of the field; the difficulty of talking about pedagogic 'outcomes' in ethical decision-making; and thirdly, the non-iterability of the ethically problematic scenario. None of these factors is unique to practical ethics, by any means. Still, their presence is felt especially strongly there.

As I suggest below, while most theoretical discussion of professional codes of ethics has tended to concentrate on the coherence and practicability of the principles involved, it has tended to overlook a certain paradox at the heart of the very idea of such a code of ethics. That paradox is roughly this: that if codes of ethics are adhered to strictly, this is likely to turn the process of ethical decision-making into a mechanical, uncritical, uncreative and so not particularly ethical exercise. The more directive a code, the less room for manoeuvre, that is, for the individual to display the virtues of a critically reflective practitioner. And yet the cultivation of the latter is typically at the heart of the stated aims of the profession in question. Mere obedience or conformity does not, as it were, an *ethical* decision-maker make. To make a related point: ethical reasoning is not (or is never simply) instrumental or strategic, and so assessable simply in terms of results. Neither is it equivalent to factual knowledge in terms of its relation to standards of right and wrong.

This brings us, again, to the scare-quotes around the term 'teaching' in my title. The notion that ethics can be 'taught' along conventional lines is complicated by the kind of thing that it is. 'Ethics training', to use a term sometimes favoured by Human Resources departments, is as a phrase even more strongly dissonant with itself. The reason for this echoes what we said above. Ethics is not just only about the learning of rules, but also (re-echoing Collier) their sifting, criticising, ordering, explanation, redescription – and their reflexive adaptation to the situation at hand. The rules themselves are contestable, and constantly in question. To be 'trained' in ethics is, if it means anything at all, to be trained not simply to accept and deploy the terms of one's training, but to establish a relationship of critical reflexivity with respect to them. Thus, if merely following a code is not ethical, and codes themselves are up for contestation, critique and creative interpretation, this makes the 'learning outcomes' of a professional ethics module definitively provisional. This is reinforced by the relation of vocational education to professional practice itself, which is, by nature, preliminary.

The next job of the chapter is to consider what this amounts to. If what we seek is to stake out space for contestation, creativity and critique in the landscape of professional ethics teaching, what would this entail? Thinking through this, a first priority is to consider how to do justice to the contested nature of ethical debate without collapsing into a dead-end culture in which, with everything declared to be undecidable, 'anything goes'. A second reflects what kinds of creativity apply in this context. And a third concerns the 'critical' relation between codes and individual practitioners at which one would want to aim. I argue that the concentration on codes of ethics runs the risk of distracting from the cultivation of such virtues at an individual level. This is not to denigrate the significance of such codes, or to deny the possibility of universal principles. Rather, it is to argue that to avoid these principles becoming reduced to depthless slogans, or examples of mere institutional 'box-ticking', the role of practice needs to be included in their construction, rather than being something to which 'all-purpose' principles are applied, as if an instruction manual. Interpreted in this latter sense, the code of ethics becomes an instrument for 'managerialism', rather than the genuine facilitator of 'bottom-up' ethical exploration and reflection which it otherwise has the potential to be. And it in this kind of 'under-labouring' towards critical practice, rather than as the simple dispensing of wisdom, that ethical theory[3] has most to offer. A fourth conclusion follows: that the notion of an 'outcome' needs to be re-thought in the context of professional ethics teaching, to accommodate the fact that the real challenges, and thus the fruition of the teaching, lie after the transition from academic to professional setting has been completed.

Situating Ethics in Vocational Programmes

More than ever before, institutions and professions are bothered about coming across as ethical. This need not be a purely cynical or defensive exercise, though clearly it sometimes is. Whatever the intentions behind it, the introduction of a core ethical component into vocational programmes has had implications for both for the programmes themselves, and for the practice of teaching ethics. The requirement that students emerge from a course as ethically literate 'reflective practitioners' – able to analyse their own and others' practice and find a vocabulary in which to explain, justify or criticise it – is easier to state than it is to enact. To teach students ethical theory is, academically, relatively routine. But how to ensure that students will be able to 'practice ethically' is a question which, in the validation of degrees, proves resistant to a simple answer. Being by its nature evaluative, accumulative and ongoing, ethical decision-making does not necessarily sit easily with the identification of learning outcomes. How can you demonstrate that you are an ethical practitioner? Three initial factors seem to complicate any answer to that question.

First: ethics itself is a contested field. On the one hand there are deep questions about the nature of ethics itself: what defines it, how ethical values differ from other kinds of values, what makes ethical judgements different from judgements of taste and other forms of evaluation, and so forth. Such questions tend to be passed over fairly quickly in professional ethics teaching, and understandably so. Metaethics (exploring the conceptual underpinnings of ethics, rather than issues about how we should be, or act) is philosophically contentious to the extent that delving seriously into it might mean the applied, professionally specific elements of the curriculum never get reached at all. Still, questions about what makes ethics the thing it is are important, and do linger and re-surface even when tackling issues that seem more prosaic.

On the other hand, there are competing approaches in normative ethics, always contrasting at one level or another, and often radically at odds with each other in terms both of how they would conceive an issue or problem, and in the ways they would resolve it. Tackling ethical theory at this level is unavoidable on a professional ethics course, because it's here that students will appreciate the different ways in which conclusions

---

3   For the sake of this discussion I will stick to the term 'ethical theory' throughout, when otherwise, at points, other terms might suit better – 'moral philosophy', for example. Important though they are, the detailed textures of the relationships between 'theory' and 'philosophy' and 'ethics' and 'morality' fall beyond our radar here.

to ethical dilemmas might be reached. Three, quite distinct traditions dominate modern ethical theory: Kantianism, Utilitarianism and Virtue Ethics. Professional ethics, wherever formalised and however construed, will bear traces of all three (though almost always obliquely; codes of ethics do not tend to credit their theoretical sources). Again, though, the three approaches are often flatly contradictory.

The contradictions centre not so much on the course of action each would recommend, but on the reasons for their recommending it. Say proponents of all three agree that in a given situation, professional A has a responsibility to attend to the needs of client B. Each will emphasise something different in backing up this stance. The Kantian will stress that in helping B, A is acting in accordance with a relevant moral rule. The Utilitarian will say that A is honouring the responsibility to maximise the well-being of those concerned. The Virtue Ethicist will say that in helping B, A is displaying appropriate characteristics: perhaps charity, or benevolence (see Hursthouse, 1999, 1). These reasons are conveyed succinctly here – but even so their divergence should be fairly clear. Seeking ethical answers, the three approaches look in markedly different places: in honouring a principle, in maximising beneficial consequences, and in embodying virtues of character.

Each angle has its strengths and weaknesses. Each, from the point of view of the others, is wrongheaded and misfocused in its 'take' on how to negotiate the complexities of our ethical relationships. Each has formidable proponents. And each has a point: both in what it emphasises, and in the complaints it makes about the others. In light of this, adherents of each perspective have sought to revise their own favoured model to accommodate challenges and insights raised by converts to the others. Yet each approach remains fundamentally distinct. The three of them sit alongside rich, vibrant alternative traditions arising from feminism, existentialism, post-structuralism, various religious sources, and ethical insights which emerge 'sideways' out of the theory attached to social movements. These too throw complexities into the mix – and codes of ethics also, sometimes bluntly, sometimes intricately, bear their imprint.

The upshot of all this is that in teaching ethics there is no 'received wisdom' in any easily packaged-up sense. This is not to say that anything goes when it comes to adopting one approach or another – but rather, that 'progress' in the field of ethical theory will not be as it is elsewhere. Other fields (though I say this as an outsider to them; doubtless those within them will dispute it) may have dominant paradigms or shared assumptions, such that these can be grasped by students and then applied to a series of different kinds of problem. Typically these paradigms will progress, so that previous models become outdated and superseded, and teachers can say things like: 'Once, everybody thought X. But now we know that X was based on crazy views about C. So these days, given what we know about C, most people think Y.' Of course, in any discipline, saying things like 'only crazy people hold that position now' risks crassly generalising. But when it comes to ethical approaches, saying that really wouldn't make any sense. One of the three dominant approaches (Virtue Ethics) dates back to ancient Greek philosophy, and the other two (Kantianism and Utilitarianism) are children of the Enlightenment. Each has been tweaked and finessed through time, and spawned different schools of interpretation – but the core insights of each are strikingly resilient. And again, they remain distinct. To say that as a field, ethics converges in a gradually unfolding consensus is true only in very particular, limited senses. Contestation is part of the nature of the beast. Thus, any notion of an 'ethical practitioner' or 'ethical decision-maker' is itself, in important ways, necessarily open to question.

Second: the achievement of an 'outcome' in ethical decision-making is not as it might be elsewhere. It is not just that there are no simple, uncontroversially 'right' or 'wrong' answers – or relatively few, at least (even 'torture is wrong' has recently been put in question by the Bush administration in the US). It is also that in this area there is an especially complex relationship between 'doing' (ethics) and 'being' (ethical), or between what is decided, and how it's decided. Say, for example, that a multinational car manufacturer – Chelsea Tractors Inc – sets out to develop a mass-market extravagantly gas-guzzling sports utility vehicle, in full knowledge that developing cars which guzzle more gas will have directly harmful effects in terms of contributing to climate change. This in turn will hit hardest on those across the globe who, having least resources, are the least likely to be able to afford a new-model Chelsea Tractor. Say that, purely inadvertently, in developing the technology required for this, the company discovers possibilities for a revolutionary new low-emission engine which in fact, if made a legal requirement, will help reduce the carbon emission threat posed by cars to the environment. Chelsea Tractors Inc duly sell this on. The car industry is transformed, and in time, the new low-emission engine becomes the norm.

Have Chelsea Tractors Inc thereby become an 'ethical' car manufacturer? Doubtless 'yes', if you ask their – now very lucky-feeling – public relations department. But clearly this signals an inadequate understanding of the process of ethical judgement. They have not, by any measure, engaged in ethical decision-making. They were not *being* ethical, even if their actions have had clear, concrete benefits. Yet if their decisions were assessed purely in terms of outcomes, they would look like paragons of environmentally conscious virtue. Hence while outcomes tell us something about ethical decision-making, they can't tell us the whole story. If we transfer this to the teaching context, challenges emerge. The quality of ethical decision-making lies not in whether the agent has happened to do something beneficial; such benefits may (for Utilitarians, for example) be a necessary condition for ethical action, but by virtually nobody's standards are they a sufficient one.

Teaching ethics is not about instructing students about correct solutions to problems. It is about facilitating students in thinking for themselves about good practice, and having the confidence to do this. Ethically literate students will decide differently, even when thinking with similar tools, and even when their decisions have the same outcome. Those who have never reflected on ethics at all may make the same decisions in quantifiable senses, but from an utterly different direction in a qualitative sense. Attention to the nuances of the decision-making process is, to a very great extent, exactly what professional ethics is for. Or should be, given the nature of the territory.

Third: no two ethically problematic situations are ever exactly the same. Life is not like that; it repeats itself, but always differently. This is important because so much of ethics teaching makes use of 'stock' dilemmas or scenarios in encouraging engagement with the 'real life' negotiation of decision-making. Looking at example situations may help focus students' minds on how to apply principles in practice, and how to critically analyse the issues at stake. But any future situation will be subtly different, even those that seem similar at first glance. While there will be rules and principles to apply, the way they apply will depend on the specifics of the situation, and the judgements of the individual applying them. Again, the vocational value of ethical 'education' (and again, given the outcomes-oriented educational tenor of the times, the term itself has a ring of inappropriateness about it for this very reason) is witnessed in the capacity for independent, critical, inventive thinking about how to respond to complex situations.

Add these three points together, and it becomes clear that teaching professional ethics cannot viably be a matter simply of teaching rules to be followed, or off-the-peg solutions to problems. The most ethically reflective answer may be non-conformist. Indeed, a certain, measured readiness not to conform is required by any model of ethical decision-making (consider 'whistleblowing' as an example). Making space for resourceful, independent thinking is thus, in many ways, crucial to the teaching of professional ethics. William Ruddick calls this 'discursive moral competence': the ability to address and discuss in appropriate moral terminology different kinds of cases with different kinds of agents involved in those cases (Ruddick, 1983, 21). But achieving this brings with it a particular set of challenges.

'Teaching' Professional Ethics: Challenges and Limits

Those challenges – along with the three points above – reflect the paradox mentioned in the introduction. Vocational education is geared towards acclimatising the student to the knowledge, skills and practicalities of the profession in question. Yet if this is understood on the model of rule-learning, it squeezes out the space for genuine ethical reflection. Ethical decision-making requires knowledge, certainly, and skills – but not in the same way that building a shed does, or flying a plane. If it becomes predictable and uniform, it is likely, by definition, to have stopped being ethical thinking. If it is understood merely in terms of obedience to codes of ethics, it has ceased to become the kind of 'skill' that it is. It is not (obviously) that ethics requires the valorisation of wanton disobedience, or wilful neglect of principle. Rather, it is that the learning of principles – indeed, the demonstration of an encyclopaedic knowledge of them – is by itself never sufficient to achieve what ethical judgement is.

D. D. Raphael offers a definition of moral judgement which captures the distinction between the rehearsal of rules, on the one hand, and ethical decision-making on the other. On the one hand we have what anthropologists and sociologists call mores: the following of 'customary habits of etiquette', or the learning and replication of whatever is the 'done thing' in a given social or professional context. With moral judgement, on the other hand, 'we are talking not of mores... but of what, when we reflect, we are prepared to stand by as right, irrespective of whether it is enjoined by custom or not' (Raphael, 1955, 14). Customary rules and conventions may contain the same words as reflective moral judgements, but without being invoked critically and reflexively they are just customs: tools for decision-making perhaps, but not for the ethical decision-making at which courses in professional ethics aim. This, again, is one reason why the idea of 'ethics training' is arguably profoundly in tension with itself – unless we understand training in a less instrumental way which itself allows more space for reflexive creativity than the conventional usage of the term suggests.

In practice, whether explicitly accounted for or not, this space opens up early in ethics teaching, even in the most well-defined and ethically precise vocational contexts. Rather than accepting moral jargon as conventions to be absorbed and enacted, tackling ethics is definitively interpretative. Teaching professional ethics will always involve the interpretation of relevant principles and priorities, usually enshrined in a code of ethics or similar set of guidelines. Such codes are littered with loaded, debatable terms which are no less important or substantial for this inherent contestability. Terms such as 'respect', 'autonomy', 'fairness', 'needs', or indeed oft-used adjectives such as 'appropriate' are not self-evident, and are often, for the sake of generality, left deliberately open when articulated as guiding values. They do not put themselves into practice. They are put into practice by individuals in testing situations where what is required to do them justice will not be transparent or formulaic. They are made concrete through reflection and action. Thus, if ethical practice is the goal, simply knowing a code of ethics is not enough. In any given situation, being able to justify one's actions in terms of such principles will require creative engagement both with the principles, and with the situation itself.

'Respect' provides a good example here. Here is a term invoked as frequently in professional ethics, where it is a staple item, as it is in political discourse (for example New Labour's so-called 'respect agenda').[4] As a value it is hard to object to. But looking at its use in codes of ethics, and its interpretation by practitioners across different fields, and within single professions, one finds a thicket of multiple conceptions of what 'respect' consists in, and amounts to. Its significance cannot simply be read off the page, and applied cleanly to practice in some uncontroversial way. In fact, taking respect seriously means recognising certain ambiguities in the concept itself. Thus, both the objects of respect and the forms it takes shift according to professional context. Taking the medical context as an example, potential objects of respect include: patients' dignity; patients' privacy; patient's views' patients' rights to be involved in decision-making; patient confidentiality; human rights; the patient's right to be self-governing; and patients themselves, as individuals (examples taken from Gibson, 2006, 77–78). The texture of respect as an orientation will shift in nuanced ways across each of each of these senses: each involves differing relations, priorities and reference points. The position of the patient himself, his condition, and his relation to the service provided will affect the nature of the respect to be afforded him (see Darwall, 1977) for an influential discussion of different senses in which respect might be enacted). Thus, mastering an off-the-peg definition of 'respect' and applying it across different practical contexts is precisely not a learning outcome at

---

4   On his re-election as Prime Minister in May 2005, Tony Blair stated as a 'particular priority' the desire to 'bring back a proper sense of respect in our schools, in our communities, in our towns and our villages' (Blair, 2005). Quite what a 'proper sense of respect' *is*, though, is not something with which his government has shown an obvious desire to get to philosophical grips.

which an adequately configured professional ethics course might aim. Rather, the student should emerge with a sense of the questions and lacunae characteristic of conventional usages of the term.

Again, this does not mean that 'anything goes' – or that ethical decision-making is a kind of spontaneous, unconstrained activity where people simply invent their own answers. Respect does not cease to be vital because it is a problematic notion. Indeed, it is partly *because* it is vital that is so urgently contested. Neither is it the case that values such as respect are somehow open to infinite interpretation, or that no one interpretation might be superior to another. Clearly there are parameters here, and limits to what counts as acting in the spirit of the value in question – and the educative process will be geared towards making those parameters clear, in the context of the profession in question. There are, in all cases, ways of making wrong decisions, both in the ethical sense and in other respects. But even so the place of individual interpretation and initiative – to think for oneself, and to 'own' one's decisions – is absolutely central to what it is to be an 'effective' ethical practitioner.

This poses genuine problems in the classroom, precisely because it relies on the student taking ownership of their own critical thinking in the relevant senses. This will never be adequately achieved through passive absorption of relevant ideas or theories. One problem here, arguably, is that the current education system as a whole is not, predominantly, geared towards the flourishing of this kind of critical thinking. Thus, viewed in the gloomiest light, it may be that the teaching of professional ethics at higher education level arrives too late on the scene to be able, by itself, to accomplish its task. Hence it can only operate within constraints which ill-befit the nature of the beast. This is not necessarily education's fault; it reflects, of course, wider economic and political trends and priorities. As Terry Eagleton has put it, 'Modern capitalist societies are so preoccupied with thinking in terms of means and ends, of which methods will efficiently achieve which goals, that their moral thinking becomes affected by this model as well' (Eagleton, 2004, 123). If education itself becomes increasingly consumerised and conceived predominantly in instrumental terms, so it becomes a less hospitable environment for the notion that students have a role in challenging what they are taught, rather than receiving a packaged-up service.

A further challenge reflects the relationship between theory and practice itself. This relationship is at the heart of vocational education. Again, though, it is more easily enacted in some fields than in others. With shed-building, the relationship between idea and practice is relatively straightforward. Principles will be learned, and put into practice through a confined, determinate process of construction. My knowledge of shed-building is limited – but my guess is that there are a series of discrete tasks involved, each with their own attendant pieces of practical wisdom, the learning of which will facilitate the process. With ethical decision-making in a professional context, this is not the case. Specific, isolated packages of 'practical knowledge' are not, in fact, what is conducive in such contexts. Just as it cannot be taught viably as dogma, ethical theory cannot be linked simply to discrete professional tasks in such a way that it serves as an 'instruction manual' for effective practice.

This puts the designer of a module in a tricky position, precisely because an academic course is not the same as, and cannot possibly replicate the experience of, the professional context in real life. In fact there are real limits to which the details and texture of the professional experience can be communicated in the classroom at all. There is an inevitable abstraction about the whole enterprise: not 'What will you do in this situation?' but rather 'What would you do in this hypothetical situation?' This means that if creative critical thinking is the aim, it must always be recognised that the precise forms of thinking required in 'real-life' practice may in fact be different from those which emerge in the classroom setting. To get around this problem, I myself make use of 'fly on the wall' video footage of relevant workplace scenarios in order to invite students to evaluate the decision-making of others, and to consider what they themselves would have done. This is an instructive exercise, because it opens up space for a range of different interpretations of the situation and responses to it – and highlights the point that different such interpretations can, in particular respects be valid. Watching the same piece of footage, students will offer widely varying verdicts on the quality of the ethical judgements made by the practitioners in question.

What's important here is not simply whether those practitioners have 'done the right thing', but how students reason in reaching a verdict. But while this does allow for something approximating to experience of real life decision-making challenges, it is only an approximation. Students are accountable for their responses not to clients or their professional peers, but to a university lecturer. Their responses do not affect people's livelihoods. When they are in that situation, they may, very likely, think differently – and in fact, that seems entirely natural. Thus, again, marrying theory and practice is not, in fact, as straightforward a matter as the wording of module aims and objectives (my own included) often tends to make it sound. This is because, in obvious ways, the classroom lends itself to abstraction (to the theory side) but not, authentically, to the messier, more visceral stuff of real-life professional happenstance. Vocational education is designed to teach people about the specifics of the professional life they are due to enter into. But in fact, the extent to which such details can actually be conveyed in the classroom is limited. Michael Loughlin has voiced the concern that in fact, there is no real substitute for 'hands-on' training in terms of the immediate, contextual knowledge it has the scope to provide. For Loughlin, this points to deeper concerns about the way the theory/practice relation operates in vocational programmes. For in the absence of such direct experience, a version of 'what doing this job is like' will be constructed in the classroom. This – to return to the themes of the introduction – effectively reduces practice to a particular, partial exemplar of the theoretical 'take' on the issues involved. He expands the point:

> The problem with much of what now passes for vocational education is that it confuses the roles of theory and practice... In order to show that its theoretical components are 'relevant' to practice, theories are taught which attempt to communicate not general thinking skills but bits of alleged 'practical knowledge' which are claimed to be necessary (and sometimes, even, sufficient) to practice well. The result is that certain conceptualisations of practice are effectively taught as dogma, being presented as the definitive view of what the practice is 'really' all about (Loughlin, 2002, 237).

One might add to this that in such a process, theory is impoverished just as much as practice is. For Loughlin the result is a way of marrying theory and practice which is 'abstract in all the wrong ways' (ibid.): it winches theory away from the immediate experience of professional contexts, and drains theory of much of its critical purchase. At worst, the student may presume that on completing the course they have all the advance knowledge they require of what issues and concerns are 'relevant', such that they risk discounting all features of the professional world which do not fit within the particular rubric they have been 'trained' in (ibid., 238; see Dracopoulou (2005) for a response to Loughlin's case).

Another, supplementary concern follows – again applicable to vocational education in general, but again particularly acute in the context of professional ethics. By definition, broaching ethics offers not a self-contained process, but the start of a rather bigger story, which transcends the formal educative process itself. Engagement with ethics is not a ladder to be climbed up and then kicked away once the student has reached the goal of employment in their chosen field. It is ongoing. Vocational education is often taken as a kind of epitome of 'means-end', outcomes-oriented, instrumental educational culture, in which the roundedness and subtler textures of a 'liberal education' are sacrificed on the altar of employability. Maybe this picture fits, to some extent, and captures something of the climate of the times. But whether accurate or not, it is clearly way wide of the mark in terms of the deeper purposes of vocational education. By definition, its outcomes are provisional, awaiting confirmation and consolidation in the workplace. It is once they are there that students will begin the process of becoming 'skilled' ethical decision-makers (whichever way in which we interpret that phrase). And it is precisely once they are there that students no longer have access to the classroom context in which ethics itself can be considered and negotiated.[5]

Thus, again, there is a tendency for vocational education to offer selective, 'advance' theory, to which the realities of workplace priorities may or may not match-up. By the time the latter are reached, there is no longer recourse to the classroom. This will tend to reinforce the impression that the educative experience itself is a necessary means to an end, but in fact rather irrelevant to the real-life business of doing the job in view. Anybody teaching professional ethics will be reminded of this by a fairly typical experience (at least I hope it's typical for others too – it certainly happens to me a lot). It goes something like this. A year or two after they have completed your module in Probation Ethics, and gone off into their chosen field, you bump into two of your ex-students in a bar. After they've said 'Hey, it's the ethics lecturer guy' and all parties have managed to remember each others' names, and they've said some polite things about quite liking your module, one of them says something you're expecting, but nonetheless still induces a little sinking, squeezing sensation in the stomach each time: 'We never use any of that stuff, you know.'

'Using that Stuff': Some Conclusions

The teaching of professional ethics provides good examples of how easy it is for the theory/practice relation to be mishandled. Sometimes, in validating courses and in

---

5   I am grateful to Mimi Thebo for a discussion of this point which reinforced its significance in terms of the issues I'm raising here.

the classroom, it's easier that way for all concerned. Facing up to the theory/practice question can raise thorny, taxing issues, and these, as we have seen, may highlight limits in the very function of the professional ethics course. But the clearest example of why it is worth it – perhaps imperative – to face up to it is given in the ex-student's comment above. What we want is precisely 'stuff' on professional ethics courses which people can 'use' – not just in the sense that it has instrumental value, but in the sense that it remains alive, and keeps informing professionals' thinking, long after the course's 'learning outcomes' have been achieved. Enhancing such 'use value' in our courses would be the surest sign that we are getting closer to honouring the nuances of the theory/practice relation.

To achieve this, I think, we need primarily to pay attention to what is particular about ethics as a field. First: the necessity of contestation. There is no denying this. It is there at the start of ethical inquiry, and at the end of it, and everywhere in the middle. It is, as it were, an inevitable part of the furniture. The trick is to get comfortable with it. It is crucial to remind students that this does not point towards shapeless relativism, or introduce a kind of 'dead-end' in which further critical discussion is pointless, but rather the reverse. It necessitates critical engagement. Such engagement forms a crucial part of equipping people, as Loughlin puts it, with 'the general thinking skills necessary to distance themselves from the conceptualisations which affect how they view their practices, and to comment critically upon them' (2002, 237). This is part and parcel of any substantive definition of reflective practice. Contestation may clutter things up and pose problems, but to talk instead in terms of false consensus is to deny the very nature of the terrain.

Second: the space for creativity. What kinds of creativity are we talking about here? Not 'originality' as such, or spontaneous invention – for reasons already mentioned, ethical decision-making should not be conceived as equivalent to creative processes in a freeform sense. Meaningful, substantial languages of evaluation and critique of practice can only be constructed through deep engagement with practice itself. They are not created *ex nihilo*. They can be more or less accurate at capturing the nature of a situation, and in applying general principles and values to the problems it presents. But still, skilled decision-making is necessarily creative in the sense that it involves the capacity to synthesise the different priorities at stake and produce a particular, one-off decision which reflects those priorities. Again, this is where the deployment of codes of ethics comes up against a certain limit: they cannot interpret themselves, or somehow be rolled out automatically to resolve the subtleties of a particular dilemma.

Third: the relation between rules and agents. Codes of ethics themselves should play only a subsidiary role in educational dealings with professional ethics. Whereas there is a tendency for modules to begin and end by 'unpacking' the core principles within, there is a case for saying that this process should also arrive relatively late on the scene. The implications of codes is realised only when a contextual understanding of the profession at stake has been achieved – to the extent that this is manageable in the classroom setting. Ethical reflection needs to work from the bottom up. It needs to start with the individual, and with personal reflection on their own values and the basis for them. Building from this towards a critical, practical understanding of what values such as 'respect' actually mean in concrete contexts is something which is achievable only through a personal, creative process rather than simply through the learning of pre-established rules. This too is crucial to the fostering of a self-critical understanding in the individual of the extent to which their decision-making should be determined by their professional role, and on the other hand the importance, in due measure, of remaining reflexively critical of it (see Oakley and Cocking, 2001, Chapter 6 for helpful reflections on this theme).

Of course, these are only brief, sketchy outlines of an answer to the question: 'If the arguments offered here are at all convincing, then what do we do about it when it comes to designing and delivering classes in professional ethics?' They are something to be built on in future work. Also to be explored further is the extent to which the issues I have highlighted here in connection with one specific field – professional ethics – have echoes elsewhere in university teaching. My own sense, worth restating, is that they do – and that the echoes may be surprisingly strong. Much of education rests on answering similar riddles involved in finding a balance between delivering a structured, directional curriculum and achieving what, in almost any field, counts as a truly successful outcome: a self-critical, self-reliant student equipped to operate independently of such input. While disciplines are distinct, they are at the same time enmeshed in overlapping, mutually informing ways in 'the organisation of the world'. To supplement the epigraph to this chapter: while morality is tied up with the organisation of the world, it is still possible, through critical engagement with it, to reach a place from which that world can be better understood, and constructively addressed. This is an end to which professional ethics might indeed be understood as having the potential to serve as a means.

References

Adorno, T. W. (2000), *Problems of Moral Philosophy*, trans. Livingstone, R. (Cambridge: Polity Press).

Andre, J. (1991), 'Beyond Moral Reasoning: A Wider View of the Professional Ethics Course', *Teaching Philosophy*, **14**(4), 359–373.

Bewes, T. (2002), *Reification* (London: Verso).

Blair, T. (2005), 'Speech on Returning to 10 Downing Street', 10 Downing Street Website, http://www.pm.gov.uk/output/Page7459.asp, accessed 19/10/06.

Calder, G. (2007), 'Creativity and Conformity in Professional Ethics', *paper delivered at the conference Creativity or Conformity, UWIC*, January 2007. Draft available at <http://www.creativityconference.org/abstracts.php>.

Calder, G. (2006), *Rorty's Politics of Redescription* (Cardiff: University of Wales Press).

Collier, A. (1994), *Critical Realism* (London: Verso).

Darwall, S. (1977), 'Two Kinds of Respect', *Ethics*, **88**(1), 36–49. [DOI: 10.1086/292054]

Dracopoulou, S. (2005), 'Applied Ethics, Health Service Management and Critical Thinking', *Res Publica: A Journal of Legal and Social Philosophy*, **11**(3), 301–310.

Eagleton, T. (2004), *After Theory* (London: Penguin).

Gibson, S. (2006), 'Respect as Esteem: The Case of Counselling', *Res Publica: A Journal of Legal and Social Philosophy*, **12**(1), 77–95.

HEA (2006), 'Higher Education Academy: UK Centre for Legal Education, 'What is reflective practice?', http://www.ukcle.ac.uk/resources/reflection/what.html, accessed on 23/10/06.

Hursthouse, R. (1999), *On Virtue Ethics* (Oxford: Oxford University Press).

Kant, I. (1963, orig. 1781), *Critique of Pure Reason*, trans. Kemp Smith, N. (Houndmills: Macmillan).

Loughlin, M. (2002), *Ethics, Management and Mythology* (Abingdon: Radcliffe Medical Press).

Meagher, G. and Parton, N. (2004), 'Modernising Social Work and the Ethics of Care', Social Work and Society **2**(1), 10–27.

Moon, J.A. (1999), *Learning Journals: A Handbook for Academics, Students and Professional Development* (London: Routledge).

Oakley, J. and Cocking, D. (2001), *Virtue Ethics and Professional Roles* (Cambridge: Cambridge University Press).

Penna, S. (2004), 'On the Perils of Applying Theory to Practice', *Critical Social Work*, **4**(1), 1–13.

Plato (1954), 'The Apology' in *The Last Days of Socrates*, trans. Tredennick, H. (Harmondsworth: Penguin, 1954; orig.c. 399 BC).

Raphael, D.D. (1955), *Moral Judgement* (London: George Allen & Unwin).

Ruddick, W. (1983), 'What Should We Teach and Test?', *Hastings Center Report*, **3**(1), 20–22.

Schön, D. (1991), *The Reflective Practitioner: How Professionals Think in Action* (London: Arena).

Chapter 7

Bradford's Programme for a Peaceful City: An Experiment in Social Theory and Political Practice

Alan Carling

Introduction

This volume is concerned with the social contexts of interaction, and related issues of theory and practice, explanation and justification. Many of the contributions here are focused on the face-to-face relationships of individuals, as practitioners with service-users, offenders, clients and so forth. This chapter aims to explore the same range of issues, but with respect to a different set of problems, concerning the relationship of different social groups within the specific historical and geographical context provided by the city of Bradford in West Yorkshire, UK over the past few years. It thus focuses on the collective dimensions of experience, and deals with some issues that are directly political.

Bradford shot to international fame, or rather notoriety, during the evening of 7 July 2001, when sustained rioting took place in the Manningham area of the District.[1] The disturbances occurred on the date that had been set for the final day of the (month-long) Bradford Festival, whose events were cancelled because of police fears about an intervention from the far-right National Front (NF). Police had prohibited a march through Bradford planned by the NF, and the disturbances arose from an anti-fascist rally that was permitted to take place in the city centre. The disturbances lasted from around 17.00 until they died out in the early hours of the following morning. These events left 326 police officers injured, a number of buildings burnt to the ground, and hundreds of local citizens traumatised. Twenty-three people narrowly escaped death when fire was set deliberately to the Manningham Ward Labour Club, where they were drinking. The riots were the most serious civil disturbances on the British mainland for 20 years, and gave rise to a painstaking Criminal Justice effort – *Operation Wheel* – that has led to the convictions of 190 individuals for a variety of public order offences. Custodial sentences have totalled some 513 years, with a mean sentence of 3.7 years for adults and 1.7 years for juveniles. Those convicted

---

1   The Bradford District is the name for the whole Metropolitan area governed by the Bradford District Council. It includes several distinct urban centres, such as Keighley and Ilkley, in addition to the city of Bradford itself. I am most grateful to Philip Lewis, Marie Macey, Peter Nias and Ian Vine for their comments on an earlier draft of this chapter.

were nearly all male;[2] a clear majority of the offenders were previously known to the police (62 per cent), and almost 60 per cent of the non-student offenders were unemployed. The youngest person convicted for Riot was 14 years old, and the oldest was 46, with a median age of 20 years for all defendants. An analysis of names made directly from police records suggests that about 90 per cent of those convicted were of South Asian family origin and Muslim faith background. Nearly all of the defendants – 92 per cent – were Bradford residents.

The historical background to the 2001 riots includes the disturbances in Manningham in 1995, which involved up to 300 people on the streets, episodes of fascist provocation and popular response in the 1970s and early 1980s, and the public burning of Salman Rushdie's *Satanic Verses* in 1989, which attracted international publicity to Bradford. The most serious public order charge of riot had not however been used by the prosecuting authorities prior to 2001 (Carling et al., 2004).

Shortly after the events of 7 July 2001, a previously-planned report was published which reflected the concerns of a group of Bradford academics and practitioners, chaired by the then-Head of the Commission for Racial Equality, Sir Herman Ouseley, about the character and trends of social relationships within the District. Among many other factors, *The Ouseley Report* (2001) highlighted the tendency of groups from different ethnic-faith backgrounds to live 'parallel lives' within Bradford. Although the appearance of the *Report* at almost the exact moment of the riots was coincidental, it was difficult to resist the temptation to link the two as theory and practice, whereby the hypothesis of 'parallel lives' seemed to offer some explanation at least of the fact of the disturbances, and the form taken by them. At all events, the occurrence of the riots and the near-simultaneous appearance of *The Ouseley Report* concentrated the minds of all those living in Bradford who were anxious to understand what was happening to, and within, their locality... and all this was taking place just a few weeks before 9/11.

This conjunction of events provided the impetus for the initial growth of the Programme for a Peaceful City (PPC). The PPC had been established by Jenny Pearce, Professor of Latin American Politics in the Department of Peace Studies at the University of Bradford, and by her colleague Professor Donna Pankhurst, who had both served as members of the Ouseley Commission. The Programme aimed to develop a network of concerned local academics, citizens and practitioners, who would reflect together on the situation in the District, and think about strategies of fruitful intervention. I served as Chair of the PPC in its formative period, from July 2002 until June 2004, and I am most grateful for the opportunity provided by this chapter to reflect on this attempt to bring theory and practice together in a specific context of action. I will also draw on my experiences as a local radio producer and broadcaster with Bradford Community Broadcasting (BCB 106.6 fm),

---

2   Two women were convicted for offences in connection with the disturbances. One received 4.5 years imprisonment for Riot; the other was fined £200 for later Obstructing the Police (Carling, 2004, 19).

and as an Independent candidate in the local elections of 2004, which have provided unexpected research vehicles of slightly different kinds.[3]

The Remit of the 'Programme for a Peaceful City'

There is no doubt that the PPC was conceived of from the beginning as different from a conventional academic initiative. It is slightly more difficult to identify what the differences are, and there may be a variety of views about this in any case among members of the PPC. At a minimum, the distinguishing features of the PPC include the facts that:

1. Many of those involved have not been academics from either Bradford University or its neighbouring Bradford College, but have been located professionally within the school system, the local authority, faith organisations, the health service, community activism and community development, the police service, regional government, media organisations and a number of other agencies and fields, mainly within the Bradford District;
2. All those taking part have done so partly in a civilian capacity – as concerned citizens or residents – in addition to any professional engagement or affiliation;
3. The PPC's brief was never purely academic, but included a direct orientation to practice, with a specific aim of linking the University of Bradford in a new way with its immediate local environment.

The last aim arose from a feeling shared by a number of those who had worked in the University over the years that the University was *in Bradford* but not (or not sufficiently) *of Bradford*. I am sure that Bradford University is not alone in this perceived disconnection from its local community, but the lack of connection assumed a particular historical form in our case. The evolution of Bradford as an institution had taken it from a Mechanics' Institute to a College of Advanced Technology, and thence to the achievement of full University status in 1966. In the process, the University had in a sense emancipated itself from (the perceived confines of?) its local environment, and in particular from local authority control. The 'universe' in 'university' suggests moreover an unrestricted scope of intellectual ambition, not to mention a limitless generality of knowledge-claims. In the social sciences, Bradford had by the 1990s made this ambition good through a pronounced emphasis on international relations and European studies, modern languages, and issues of economic development, conflict and conflict resolution around the world. It is worth noting that this outward-looking, international orientation corresponds with local circumstances. As Priestley (1977, [1934], 152) observed many years ago, the

---

3   I have worked at BCB in conjunction with David Fitch on two series of programmes entitled *The Bradford Experience*, broadcast in 2005 and 2006 respectively. I stood as a 'Better Bradford' candidate in 2004, on a platform emphasizing the need for an open and constructive dialogue between different sections of the population. I am most grateful to the 342 residents of Heaton Ward who entrusted me with my votes.

secret of Bradford as a locality is its global connectivity, derived historically from its international supremacy in certain branches of wool textiles: 'Take down some of those greasy or dusty samples and you bring the ends of the earth together.' To be local in Bradford is to be global.

The most pointed contrast here is with Bradford's urban sibling-rival Leeds, which is a regional capital that has not been dependent in the same way on the extended reach of its industrial and commercial base.[4] The shock of the riots in Bradford in 2001 was nevertheless felt particularly by those academics who had dealt mainly in abstract or theoretical issues, or conflicts far from home. Here by contrast was a conflict on our doorsteps (literally so in the case of those who lived in central Bradford), which revealed a set of social problems that had been developing under our noses, whilst our professional attention had often been focused elsewhere.[5] And if the University as an institution needed reminding that its fate was tied to the image and reputation of its native city, confirmation was duly supplied by the 25 per cent fall in undergraduate applications in the year after 2001. Reaching out to the local community was not only a matter of civic duty for University staff; it began to look like a question of professional survival.

The issues then arose of what contribution a University-based initiative could make to the situation in Bradford, and how such an intervention should be organised. I will not pretend that these issues were formulated with adequate precision at the outset of the PPC, still less that the relevant answers were immediately forthcoming. What follows is my reconstruction after the event of some of the answers towards which the PPC has felt its way over the last five years. I will address the 'how' question – the kind of intervention involved – before the 'what' question – the learning about Bradford that has taken place as a result of the intervention.

The 'Aims and Principles' of the PPC

It is by no means unique to the PPC that it came to adopt an explicit set of ethical principles. Most academic and professional activities, not to mention many business enterprises, are conducted these days under formal codes of practice of various kinds, and other chapters of this book bear ample witness to the ethical concerns of thoughtful practitioners in many professional fields. *The Statement of Aims and Principles of the PPC* (2005) has nevertheless figured prominently in its self-definition, and is addressed to some specific ethical concerns, as well as advancing general principles.

The main preoccupation was to create a balance between two impulses that pull in different directions. On the one hand, there was (and is) a felt need 'to confront

---

4   Leeds has not therefore been subject to the same degree to the changing fortunes of particular international markets for its products. This is one factor, but only one, behind the greater economic success of Leeds than Bradford in recent years.

5   I should emphasise that I am speaking here for myself, and for anyone else to whom the description applies. There were a number of Bradford-based academics, including Sheila Allen, Marie Macey, Philip Lewis, Yunas Samad and Ian Vine, who had been professionally concerned with the situation of the District over a much longer period.

difficult issues' (PPC, 2005). This reflects a widespread perception in Bradford that the fear of initiating local public debate about issues of racism, religion and ethnicity could play into the hands of the far right. The emphasis is therefore to be placed on 'dialogue and learning' as a way into the challenges facing the District. On the other hand, the raising of 'difficult issues' is bound to carry risks of unproductive misunderstandings, unnecessary discord, or even social conflict – this is, after all, part of what makes the issues 'difficult' in the first place. This risk gives rise to a countervailing concern that the required dialogue should be constructive, in the sense of contributing to the long-run health of the social relationships in the District, rather than simply reproducing their pathologies. The twin requirements are therefore to open-out the dialogue rather than to close it down, and yet to channel the necessary dialogue in ways that will ultimately prove beneficial in promoting social and political goals of community cohesion and so forth.

The PPC's ethical stance undoubtedly overlaps here with the ethical concerns of other academic and professional initiatives – there is nothing particularly novel, for example, in the references to confidentiality in the research process and 'sensitivity to social differences'. But the PPC *Aims and Principles* go beyond these standard requirements by speaking also of the 'tensions within the District', the need to 'build[] bridges between theory and practice and between academics and practitioners', to 'support... initiatives for change' and make available the results of research to research subjects. The last point reflected a concern from the early days of the PPC that Black and Minority Ethnic (BME) groups in Bradford – especially those of Muslim faith and Pakistani heritage – were over-researched, and indeed subject to exploitation in the research process. But this particular concern dovetailed with the general view that the PPC should shift the ground-rules of academic engagement wherever possible in favour of a collaborative and inclusive approach, which would reach out beyond the academy itself.

What this stance might entail in practice was the subject of lively debate in the early years of the PPC. The question was raised whether the PPC should be an organisation or a network, and, relatedly, whether it should see itself primarily as a campaigning or as a facilitative body. Should the PPC take positions on potentially controversial issues as well as providing a forum for dialogue concerning them? Underlying these concerns is a question about the appropriate role for the University as an institution in an initiative like the PPC, and indeed the place for academic knowledge or expertise amongst a welter of different perspectives on questions of community cohesion.

The initial debates on these issues were resolved firmly in favour of the network conception, and against the view that the PPC should exist primarily as a campaigning body in relation to the local community. One of the great advantages possessed by the University as a venue for debate was the combined perception of its high status and relative neutrality. It also transpired that the University – indeed the PPC – was almost the only place in Bradford where sustained critical engagement was occurring around the social and cultural problems of the District. The PPC has acted as a meeting point where practitioners from a variety of different fields and backgrounds can compare experiences and exchange ideas. But it has also turned out, more unexpectedly, that the PPC has sometimes provided a venue to meet colleagues from the same field or organisation in order to participate in discussions that were not happening elsewhere. I recall, for example, a conversation that took place with a senior Police Officer in Bradford's central Police Station, in the course of which he said words to the effect that 'the trouble with people round here [in the Police Station] is that they are obsessed with law and order'. I could well understand this view, but then performed a mental double take: 'that's fine', I thought to myself, 'but don't we pay the police to be obsessed with law and order'.

The point is that employees of the local authority or the police service, say, might welcome the opportunity to come to the University to discuss issues with colleagues in their own professions – about the underlying forces or trends of social relationships in the District, for example – that were difficult (or inappropriate) to raise within their own professional milieux. In some of its activities, most notably an on-going speaker series arranged by Philip Lewis under the title 'God and Caesar', the PPC has also managed to attract mixed audiences – that is, audiences including reasonable numbers of both Muslims and non-Muslims – to discuss issues of diversity and faith. The PPC has also helped to stimulate other 'networks of concern' (Lewis, 2007). These may not sound like spectacular achievements, but the situation in Bradford is such that they should not be underestimated, and the University has clearly played a useful role in this respect via its support for the PPC.

The expertise contributed by the PPC to these activities has consisted mainly in the techniques of process, especially the maintenance of the ground rules of what came to be called 'safe spaces' – the term of art for arenas designed to promote constructive forms of dialogue. Again, the basic 'safe space' principles are not in themselves especially novel, consisting in a version of the Chatham House rules (PPC, 2006). Nevertheless, the PPC has taken these seriously, and most meetings of the PPC have begun with a recitation from the Chair of the creed containing the principles of respect, openness and confidentiality, but not necessarily politeness.

The aim, then, was to create the conditions for an inclusive and constructive dialogue between a variety of different individuals and groups, with a light touch, and the necessary minimum of bureaucratic intervention from the University. The only question of principle to arise was how inclusive this dialogue should be: should it extend to everyone within the District? The debate on this issue concluded that the PPC should not engage with representatives of racist or fascist organisations, but that the field should otherwise be left open. The *Aims and Principles* were then called into play once more to create a membership criterion for the PPC, with members asked to endorse the *Aims and Principles* explicitly. It was envisaged that this rule could be used to determine the limits of membership, should the need ever arise. It seemed reasonable to confine the dialogue in principle to those who were willing to enter into the spirit of dialogue, as defined by the *Aims and Principles* (and amplified by the 'safe space' rules). Although there have been one or two challenging moments on this score, there has been no need in the end to invoke this principle in order to limit the PPC's membership in its history to date.

The last section of the *Aims and Principles* outlines the structure of the PPC as it had crystallised by 2003. The regular membership had grown significantly, and it was inevitable that members were not equally interested in all the activities of the Programme. In addition to a regular series of meetings open to all members and to newcomers, it was decided to organise the work of the PPC around three 'hubs', concerned respectively with research, safe spaces and training.

Although the meetings of these hubs remained open, it was anticipated that a degree of specialisation would take place, and that each hub would constitute a nucleus of reflection in its given field. Thus, the safe spaces hub would not only organise meetings under safe space rules, but would ask the meta-questions of its own practice, such as:

1. What exactly makes a space 'safe'?
2. When is safe space dialogue most effective?
3. Can it be used in the same way with all groups?
4. Are social goals like 'cohesion' best aimed at directly, or as a by-product of other activities?
5. Are there circumstances in which 'single identity' work is preferable to 'mixed identity' work? (Kelly and Philpott, 2003).

In what follows, I will however concentrate on the differences that are made to the research agenda by organising research activity in part via an entity like the PPC, rather than under more usual academic arrangements. The differences will be illustrated through one specific case study before tackling the issue of what has been learned about Bradford generally through the activities of the PPC over the last five years.[6]

Fair Justice for All?

It was mentioned at the outset that a large number of local people, mainly young men of Muslim faith background and Pakistani heritage, were arrested and charged with public order offences in connection with the 2001 riots. Very soon after the first sentences were passed, a vigorous public debate began about the justice of the sentences handed down. At one end of a spectrum of views about the issue, the young men were seen as the perpetrators of a 'sustained and vicious mass assault' against the public and the police (*Yorkshire Post*, 11 December 2004), and those amongst them who came to be serving long custodial sentences were held to have received no less than they deserved. At the other end of the spectrum of views, the young men who were imprisoned were thought to have been subject to harsh and unfair treatment at the hands of a racist Criminal Justice System, notwithstanding the evidence of guilt presented against them in Court (Allen, 2003).

Although it would be wrong to assume that the views on this issue were polarised along simple ethnic or religious lines, it became clear that the division of opinion on the justice of the sentencing had the potential at least to feed into other divisions and conflicts in the District, and thus exacerbate tension. This conclusion was reached as part of a preliminary analysis published soon after the riots, which built on the early discussions within the PPC (Bühler et al., 2002). The sentencing issue was

---

6   The PPC has recently modified its internal arrangements once again (Summer, 2006), to emphasise thematic priorities. I will not comment further on this change, since it is too early to know what effect it may have on the development of the Programme.

thus perceived to be important as a research topic not only for its intrinsic interest but also because of a judgment reached about its possible impact on the evolving community relationships within Bradford. The research agenda, in other words, was situation-driven, rather than topic-driven, or indeed theory-driven, as would be the case more usually with academic research. It was on this basis that funding was secured from the Joseph Rowntree Charitable Trust for a specific enquiry into the sentencing issue.

The question then arose of what form a specifically academic (and University-based) contribution to the debate about sentencing might take: what kinds of expertise would be involved? The first point was to present the question of justice *as* a question, rather than a foregone conclusion – which was the way the issue tended to be treated by those on either side of the public controversy, including some contributors with academic connections (Allen, 2003). The second point was to present the relevant facts, in so far as these could be ascertained. This was achieved by gaining access to the police database for *Operation Wheel*, whose information was cross-checked against publicly-available sources, especially from the local press. The third point was to recognise that the question of justice is inherently comparative. If the sentences were held to be too harsh (or too lenient), the issue was: harsh or lenient in relation to what?

Here the relevant comparators include:

1. the provisions of the law;
2. sentences passed in the same jurisdiction for similar offences at other times or places;
3. sentences passed in the same jurisdiction against defendants with a different sociological profile;
4. sentences available to the authorities for similar offences in different but comparable jurisdictions.

Because there are a number of different avenues of comparison, the question of justice may not be unequivocal, since a given sentence may be high in relation to some comparators and low in relation to others. And even where a comparative difference exists, this is not conclusive either way in terms of the justice issue. It was interesting, for example, that the Bradford sentences were higher than those given typically in Northern Ireland, where the law differs and sentences for public disorder are often lower than in the rest of the UK. But this led to a debate in Northern Ireland about whether the law was too lenient (or applied too leniently) in the *Province*, not that the Bradford defendants had been treated unduly harshly (Carling et al., 2004, 33–34).

Given this range of possible comparisons, and the corresponding – typically academic – propensity to complicate the issue, it is perhaps not surprising that the Report did not come to a definite conclusion on the fairness question, but rather provided a frame of reference within which the reader was invited to make up his or her own mind (Carling et al., 2004, 7). The academic contribution – and the implied expertise – was thus partly *critical* (in treating the issue as problematic in the first place), partly *empirical* (in collating the facts about the operation of the Criminal

Justice System in this case), and partly *analytical* (in drawing attention to a range of considerations relevant to the evaluation of the justice issue).

At the same time, the report highlighted a number of issues and concerns. These included the central importance of the video evidence to the outcome of the public order prosecutions, the length of the maximum sentence for Riot under the 1986 UK Act (which is high by international comparison at 10 years) and the corresponding importance of the decision to prosecute the Bradford defendants for Riot, as opposed to lesser offences such as Violent Disorder or Affray. In particular, it looked as if the operative criterion for prosecutions for Riot was set higher in practice than stipulated by law – that is, the authorities in the UK would prosecute for Riot only for assemblies involving considerably larger numbers than the 12 participants required for a riot to exist according to statute.[7] A brief discussion was included at the end of the Report about the principles of Restorative Justice, and whether these might have some role to play in the approach to public order problems, alongside the conventional sanctions of either custody or community service.[8]

As mentioned above, the PPC played a crucial part in identifying the sentencing issue as a research topic. It was also important in the dissemination process. The question here is the responsibility of academics – or perhaps of intellectuals more generally – in releasing the findings of research in situations of potential tension or conflict. A preliminary draft of the Report was therefore presented at a PPC seminar, exposing it to the criticism of local practitioners, in order to assess its likely reception in the District and to guard against misunderstandings or misrepresentations. This turned out to be a very useful exercise, and the final version of the report was significantly modified as a result. The completed Report was then launched formally at another PPC event with a broad, invited audience.

The launch of *Fair Justice for All?* was covered in two local newspapers. The report in the Bradford *Telegraph and Argus* (11 December 2004) appeared under the headline 'Offenders Must Meet With Their Victims'. The news item alluded to the restorative justice issue, but as part of a balanced report which covered most of the main findings.[9]

On the other hand, the Leeds-based *Yorkshire Post* (11 December 2004) led with the statement 'Jail Not Best Remedy, Says Riots Report', and concentrated almost exclusively in its news story on (the misreading of) the report's argument concerning restorative justice expressed by the headline. This coverage was backed by a quote critical of the (alleged) conclusion of the Report obtained from the Bradford West MP Marsha Singh.

---

7   The Manningham disturbances of 1995 are a case in point: there were many more than 12 people involved, but no charges of Riot were brought, only (a small number of) charges for Violent Disorder. It has been suggested in discussions that this history generated an unfortunate sense of immunity from prosecution for public order offences within the local community prior to 2001.

8   Restorative Justice 'represents a new direction that emphasises rehabilitation and healing as a method of dealing with offenders.' (Carling, 2004, 47.)

9   I am grateful to Peter Nias for supplying me with copies of these newspaper reports. *The Telegraph and Argus* had also contacted a member of the research team, which helped to ensure balanced coverage.

Having grasped the wrong end of the stick so firmly in its news pages, it is perhaps unsurprising that the *Yorkshire Post* proved unable to let go in its editorial column:

> maybe the authors of the report claiming the Bradford rioters should not have been locked up did not witness the events of that sultry July night in 2001,

said the lead editorial,

> if not, they can perhaps be excused for failing to realise the true nature of what occurred... to say, as Bradford University's Programme for a Peaceful City does, that those found guilty of taking part should have received 'creative options' – i.e.) non-custodial sentences – 'to meet the needs of the community, the victim and the offender' is to talk arrant nonsense.

Perhaps the moral of this story is that, however hard one tries, it is impossible to prevent the misrepresentation of research findings by those with agendas of their own.[10] But I take it that this ever-present hazard should not prevent researchers taking care over the presentation of their findings, or indeed discourage them from undertaking research into contentious social issues in the first place.[11]

Learning about Bradford

It was mentioned above that the PPC deliberately adopted a 'network' conception of its structure, and set its face against a campaigning role within the District. This was interpreted to imply that the PPC as an organisation would abstain from public statements about controversial issues.[12] I have no doubt at all that the no-campaigning

---

10   Nowhere does the Report say either that a) restorative justice should replace conventional justice for public order offences, or that b) restorative justice entails an abandonment of custodial sentencing. *Both* statements would have to have been made in order to warrant the *Yorkshire Post*'s criticism of the Report. In fact, the treatment of restorative justice in the Report emphasises its adaptability to local conditions, its tripartite concern with the victim and the community as well as the offender, and its rehabilitative potential. The Report's conclusion on restorative justice reads: 'given that disturbances have often been a vehicle for voicing social discontent, restorative justice methods provide some promising tools in restoring a sense of justice for both victims and offenders. It seems particularly appropriate that where riots tear the social fabric, the sanctions against disorder should incorporate some awareness of how the fabric might be re-sewn together.' (Carling, 2004, 47.)

11   It is also disappointing that the West Yorkshire Criminal Justice Review Board has not taken up the opportunity to consider the findings of the Report, which was referred to it by the former Chief Constable of West Yorkshire, the late Colin Cramphorn.

12   Note that the *Yorkshire Post* attributes the (alleged) views about custodial sentencing wrongly to the PPC in its editorial, rather than to the authors of the Report. This is despite an explicit disclaimer printed prominently on the title page of the Report. Again, it is always necessary to take precautions against misrepresentation, but this does not guarantee that they will always have the desired effect!

stance was the correct one to adopt in the early years of the PPC.[13] The issue I wish to raise in the latter half of the chapter is whether this agnostic stance needs to be modified in the light of the learning that has taken place during the subsequent period.

Recall that the PPC has brought together a wide range of practitioners over a number of years, all focused to various extents (and from various perspectives) on one pair of questions:

1. What is happening to community relationships within the Bradford District?
2. What if anything can be done to improve them?

Although it would be misleading to claim that a consensus has been reached over the answers to these questions, there has been a significant convergence of opinion around some elements at least of those answers. Again, different members of the PPC might well describe this convergence in different terms. For what it is worth, my reading of the convergence (which I will call 'the convergent view') is as follows:

1. Separation along ethnic-religious lines is a marked feature of social life in Bradford, which is evident in patterns of residence, education, recreation and a variety of other fields.[14]
2. The levels of residential separation increased during the 1990s in some respects, whilst decreasing in others.[15]
3. The incidence of educational separation at school level is high, and (if anything) higher than the incidence of residential separation in the areas immediately surrounding the schools in question (Miller, 2004, 2; Burgess, Wilson and Lupton, 2005, 1050).
4. There is much anecdotal evidence, and some evidence of a more systematic kind, that the observed social separations are caused in part by deliberate choices to separate made by individuals and/or families, amongst a range of other factors that influence the observed levels of separation.
5. Social separation may not be a harmful phenomenon in its own right, but it creates the possibility of more harmful forms of social polarisation – that is – social, cultural and/or political antagonism between members of the local population with different ethnic-religious backgrounds.
6. There is some evidence that such social polarisation is occurring in Bradford, together with many examples of individuals and organisations who are working against any polarising tendencies, to prevent polarisation and to enhance community cohesion and mutual understanding.

---

13   Some members of the PPC argued however that it would have been possible for the PPC to take a higher public profile on controversial issues without infringing the 'no campaigning' principle. This may well be the case.

14   I have used the term 'separation' here for the tendency of individuals from different ethnic-religious backgrounds to live in different areas, go to different schools, follow different leisure pursuits, and so forth. This expression is preferred as a more neutral alternative to the term 'segregation' that occurs more frequently in the literature.

15   The Dissimilarity Index for ED-level residential separation was 0.75 in 1991 and 0.74 in 2001; the S.A. Isolation Indices were 0.53 and 0.62 respectively (Simpson, 2004).

7. It is not clear whether these ameliorative efforts (directed against the polarising tendencies) are a) operating on a sufficient scale, b) sufficiently well coordinated and c) conducted against a background of sufficient public understanding and consent, to be as effective as might be necessary to ensure a non-polarised future for the Bradford District.

This is not the place to rehearse all the argument and findings that have led to these conclusions.[16] I cannot resist a few theoretical comments, however, before turning to a practical example that for me encapsulates the issues currently facing Bradford.

First, it is quite interesting in itself to observe, against a background of postmodern scepticism, that such a convergence of opinion has indeed come about through the discussions within the PPC and related contexts. This is a blow in favour of a rather old-fashioned view of the research process as a cumulative accretion of knowledge achieved through collective deliberation.

Second, the process has in one sense vindicated the findings of the *Ouseley Report*, despite the fact that this was never a main concern of the PPC. Recall that the hypothesis of 'parallel lives' put forward by Ouseley was just that – a hypothesis. It is true that this hypothesis was grounded in the submissions made to the Ouseley Commission by a number of figures with long experience of dealing with community relations in Bradford.[17] It also reflected some prior publications by others (see especially Allen and Barratt, 1996). But Ouseley's work did not rest on new academic studies, or specially-commissioned research. It might be said therefore that the 'parallel lives' hypothesis 'came through from the grassroots' into the academic arena via the Ouseley process. But the hypothesis – both the facts and the significance of social separation – has now been subject to a more systematic appraisal in discussions connected with the PPC, which have tended to confirm the hypothesis.

The question then arises of whether the novel form of research initiative pursued through the PPC was necessary to this outcome. Could the same conclusions have been reached by a more conventional academic route? Although it would be difficult in the nature of the case to reach a definitive answer to this question, there are at least two comparisons that are instructive, and tend to highlight the merits of the PPC approach compared with more conventional ones.

As a first example, the Joseph Rowntree Foundation commissioned a team, based at Leeds Metropolitan University, to conduct a review of the academic literature on the situation in Bradford. The resulting document (Darlow et al., 2005) makes a very useful contribution, especially in areas such as business activity and health care, but it presents an exposition of a variety of different work rather than a critical assessment of the main issues facing the District. The authors themselves acknowledge that their review has been less successful in some of the more contentious areas, which, at the

---

16   For more discussion, see Carling (2008). I should emphasise that whilst most of the elements of the convergent view have arisen directly from discussions within the PPC, the concluding point was influenced more by the interviews conducted for the *Bradford Experience* series broadcast on BCB in 2005. There were more than seventy interviews in total, with a range of local (and a few national) figures, all concerned in various capacities with community cohesion issues.

17   See especially the submissions published as Appendices to the *Report*.

risk of oversimplification, consist of all the topics that are never to be mentioned in polite company, namely sex, politics and religion. But sex (or at any rate gender), politics and religion are at the heart of the issues facing the District. So this study represents an opportunity missed, possibly because most of the researchers involved stood outside the situation, and were reluctant to venture too far into controversial areas requiring local knowledge. The PPC has by contrast gathered together insiders to share insights and experiences, under an explicit remit to address 'difficult issues'. This has given the members of the PPC an advantage, and a confidence perhaps, not possessed by other researchers pursuing a similar academic agenda.

Second, if the convergent view outlined above had merely confirmed existing academic opinion, then it would be difficult to claim distinctive merits for the PPC. But this is not the case. The convergent view differs substantially from what might be regarded as the received academic-cum-official view of the situation in Bradford. The most influential exponent of this view is Ludi Simpson, who has tended to downplay the incidence and significance of the factors emphasised above, describing various aspects of social segregation, for example, as 'myth[s]' in relation to Bradford (Simpson, 2004, 668, 677). A fuller treatment of the issues raised by this difference of views is available elsewhere (Carling, 2008). Some of the issues are technical, and concerned to establish for example whether Census data from 1991 and 2001 bear the interpretation placed upon them by Simpson in his published work. Others are more general, and raise the question of whether a culture of denial has affected the academic treatment of the situation in Bradford. No one could possibly describe Simpson as an outsider to the Bradford scene, given his distinguished contribution to the intellectual life of the District over many years.[18] But it is an interesting question whether the debate about the received view would have taken the same course if it had been confined to *academics and researchers* within Bradford. The strength of the PPC approach from this perspective lies in the fact that non-academic practitioners with a wealth of local knowledge were involved directly in the academic debates, bringing with them the capacity to anchor the debates in local experience.

If the input of practitioners can thus be a good thing for research, what about the other side of the coin: how can research contribute to the work of practitioners? The practical issues at stake were crystallised for me recently by the following bricks and mortar example.

A Tale of Two Centres

The government's *SureStart* programme, which has brought much-needed public investment to many disadvantaged neighbourhoods throughout the UK, set out recently with the intention of building a new community centre to serve an extended area of Keighley, within the Bradford Metropolitan District. But the relevant parts of Keighley are built on a hill-side, so it proved impossible to find a site that was large enough and flat enough to accommodate the new centre in the middle of the area it

---

18   Simpson worked for the local authority in Bradford as a demographer for many years, and established the pioneering Bradford Community Statistics Project, before moving to a post at Manchester University.

was intended to serve. Two new Community Centres have therefore been built, a few hundred yards apart, located in the distinctive neighbourhoods of Guardhouse and Highfield at the two respective ends of the area under discussion. Because of the perceived characters of these neighbourhoods, and the perceived characteristics of the Centres' customary users, the Centres came to be perceived locally as 'White' and 'Asian' respectively. As a result of this, the staff at the Centres set up a number of different schemes designed to link the facilities offered by them both, and to encourage contacts between their users (BXp7, 2005).[19]

This example is instructive because it illustrates the kind of issues created by the informal processes of ethnic separation, regardless of the best intentions of the public authorities, and despite the official pronouncements about the achievements of multiculturalism. The authorities were undoubtedly right to build two separate facilities when they could not find a central site for one, since locating a new facility in either one of Highfield or Guardhouse but not the other may well have contributed to political tensions, and thus polarisation, between the two neighbourhoods. Fascist propaganda is certainly alive to such issues of 'equal treatment' (Cromie, 2005).

But the options available in this case also illustrate the policy options available generally to those concerned by separation. These are either: a) to create a single integrated facility, so that separation does not arise as an issue in the first place or b) to accept that separation is liable to happen (or has happened), and then introduce special measures designed to counteract some of its effects, essentially by bridge-building between members of the population with different cultural backgrounds.[20] In the case of educational separation, for example, the perceived inviolability of the principle of parental choice has ruled out option a), which has led to the pursuit of option b), in the form of the *Linking Schools* project, which is designed to familiarise pupils with those of different backgrounds who attend different schools.

An important recent study (Raw, 2006, 51–4) has also shown that the *Linking Schools* project works, in the sense that attitudes have changed positively as a result of pupils' contacts, and that the inter-cultural relationships established via the project have tended to endure beyond the end of the project. This holds out some possibility of lasting benefit for community relations.

Considered more generally, the work communicated through the PPC has created a frame of knowledgeable reference for the situation in Bradford. We know roughly what the main problems are in the field of community relations (as expressed in the convergent view); we have a reasonable idea of what we do not yet know but need to know (that is, we possess a sketch map of our comparative ignorance); we know

---

19   I have often heard it said that 'Keighley is different from Bradford' and that one should proceed with caution from one place to the other. All I can say is that, in this instance, Keighley seemed to be a microcosm of the local authority District that includes both places.

20   The issues here are not entirely straightforward, since it may not always be the case that the best way to reduce polarisation is to create an 'integrated' solution immediately. The attempt to create an artificially integrated solution may backfire under certain circumstances, leading to increased resentment and therefore polarisation (Robinson, 2005, 1424). This possibility is reflected in the view that, in the context of a highly polarised society like Northern Ireland, it may be necessary to start with 'single identity' work as a prelude to 'cross-identity' work. See Kelly and Philpot (2003).

in broad terms what needs to be done to address the problems, and we even know something about which particular initiatives work well in addressing the problems (see the discussion of the *Linking Schools* project immediately above).

It was mentioned at the beginning of the chapter that a concern existed in the early days of the PPC that the population of South Asian origin was over-researched. It is quite possible, of course, that some individuals *felt* over-researched, given the upsurge of academic interest following the riots. And it is certainly true that there has been more research conducted into the population of Muslim Pakistani background than among other ethnic and religious groups (Darlow et al., 2005, 10). But this does not mean that Bradford is over-researched; far from it.[21] As the summary above implies, we know something about some of the significant areas of concern, but surprisingly little about others.[22] For example, we know something about the facts of social separation, but surprisingly little about the reasons for it.

It would be wrong to say that Bradford is in a pre-conflict situation, since that would imply wrongly that violent social conflict is inevitable. But the underlying ingredients of conflict exist, and it is not obvious that the tendencies towards social polarisation have abated in the five years since the riots, despite the best efforts of numerous agencies and individuals. Indeed, some of the evidence – above all, the strong showing of far-right candidates in elections held between 2004 and 2006 – points in the opposite direction.[23] It follows that an entity like the PPC is needed as much as ever, and yet we are in the fortunate position of being able to rely on the prior learning already achieved via the PPC.

In particular, I would argue that any responsible agenda for academic research about Bradford needs to be informed by the convergent view of the problems of the District, aiming in part to overcome the significant areas of ignorance revealed there. Topics of immediate interest include:

1. the microfoundations of social separation;
2. the relationship of separation to polarisation;
3. the dynamics of polarisation.

---

21   Nor does this make Bradford an easy place to research. For a candid and in places entertaining view of some of the problems involved, see Sanghera and Thapar-Björkert (2007).

22   See also Darlow (2006, 10): 'Based on the evidence we have gathered it is clear that while a great deal of material has been identified, *significant gaps remain in knowledge and understanding about Bradford District*' (original emphasis).

23   The British National Party (BNP) elected 4 councilors in the Bradford local elections of 2004, with over 12,000 votes recorded for a party widely regarded as racist and fascist. The mean share of the vote in the nine wards with BNP candidates (out of 30 in Bradford as a whole) was 26.5 per cent. The BNP polled 13,688 votes in total in three Bradford constituencies in the 2005 General Election, with between 7 per cent and 9 per cent share of the vote in each case. The BNP increased their number of candidates to 16 in the local elections of 2006. They lost three seats gained in 2004, and gained just one other seat, but the overall number of votes cast rose to 18,212, 13 per cent of the total in the election (Schofield, 2006).

The emphasis throughout should be on *all* the ethnic and/or religious groupings in the District, and especially the evolving relationships between them.[24] It is arguable that the exclusive attention to one section of Bradford's population in any study tends to reproduce the phenomenon of separation at the level of research methodology, thus compounding in a small way the general problems of the District.[25]

In addition to rounding out our knowledge in existing areas of concern, it has become possible for the PPC to go one step further, and open up the debate about the future that is suggested by the convergent view. The debate could focus more explicitly on the values that might underwrite a common future, on the policies that might be required to reach it, and the institutions that might help to secure it.

The values in question include equality, as adapted appropriately to a multicultural context (Barry, 2001; Kelly, 2002), and toleration, which is the subject of revived philosophical interest (McKinnon, 2006). The policies involved include the exploration of choice mechanisms that are less likely to lead to separated and/or polarised social outcomes, either through market processes or official allocation systems, such as parental choice of school. The institutions would be those that are more likely to facilitate productive exchanges between members of the population with different backgrounds as a matter of course in everyday life – an attempt to ensure, in other words, that all social spaces in the District are safe for every citizen.

A New Departure for the PPC?

Suppose that the PPC were to move forward with such an agenda. Would that turn it into a campaigning organisation, at odds with its location in a university? This is undoubtedly a serious question requiring careful consideration. A reputation for neutrality is a source of strength for both the University and the PPC. It is hard to win, and easy to jeopardise. It is also true that a movement in the contemplated direction would raise issues of policy that are both controversial and fraught within the Bradford District.

It is a commonly-held view, for example, that one of Bradford's main problems is the poor quality of its political leadership over the past decade and more – both within the three main political parties and at the higher levels of management within the Council (Vine, 2006). It was put forward as part of the convergent view above that actions to tackle the possibility of social polarisation have been a) insufficient in scale, b) insufficiently coordinated and c) insufficiently discussed and communicated with the public at large to match the requirements of the problem at hand. This finding might or might not imply a criticism of the political leadership in the District, depending upon the explanation given for the state of affairs described. It might be, for example, that it is not the individual leaders or managers who are to blame,

---

24   Darlow (2006, 10) makes the same recommendation, which is a helpful outcome of the JRF review process.

25   Here again we can see where the PPC approach has made a difference to the received research agenda. The latter has tended to see BME populations as relatively-disempowered minorities within a broader social context that is taken as given (and taken as racist), rather than as active and substantial participants in creating a joint future that remains significantly open.

but the impossible situation in which they have been placed by circumstances and events. I am not taking a view on this issue, because the investigation required to resolve it has not been undertaken, so far as I am aware. The point is however that merely raising the issue, which *does* follow from the convergent view, is liable to prove controversial with the District's powers-that-be.

In any event, if the PPC were to move from saying 'we are here to host discussions on policy issues' to saying 'these are the broad directions in which we think policy should move', this would inevitably bring the PPC into a political arena within the locality.

Despite these potential reservations, I think that there are three sets of considerations that speak strongly in favour of such an initiative.

First, it is true that the PPC would be adopting a policy stance, but the content of this stance needs to be borne in mind. The aim that follows on naturally from the convergent view is *to work to prevent and to reduce the mutual polarisation of the different ethnic-religious populations within the District*. Although this aim has not been articulated very explicitly in local public debate (which is part of the problem with politics in Bradford), I take it that this objective would command clear majority support (perhaps overwhelming support), across all sections of the population, among all the reputable parties, and at all political levels – both popular and official. The only people to oppose this aim would be those who have a vested interest in the 'Clash of Civilisations', who are, roughly speaking, the fascists on the one side and the jihadi Islamists on the other. This level of (presumed) consensus, and its peace-building intentions, would seem sufficient to dispel any suggestion that the PPC had become unduly political, if it were to adopt an anti-polarising stance as part of its self-definition.

Second, the contemplated move is fully in line with the *Aims and Principles* of the PPC, whose stated aims are (among others) 'to demonstrate the value of collective learning through reflection on practice' and 'to build a consistent and coherent understanding of issues facing the District'. Part of the PPC's 'Strategic Vision' is 'to influence University, local and national policy agendas' and a further aim is 'to offer support where possible to initiatives for change in the area under study [arising from research]' (PPC, 2005). Reviewing the situation reached within the PPC to date in the light of these aims, we have indeed undergone a collective learning experience that seems to have arrived at 'a consistent and coherent understanding', which has fed through over time into 'initiatives for change in the area under study' that could well 'influence... policy agendas'. The PPC set out moreover 'to develop a practical and intellectual agenda for addressing issues of diversity, equality and cohesion within the Bradford District'. It is difficult to imagine a credible agenda for such issues that is not based on the anti-polarising premise. To continue along this path seems simply to be taking seriously the mission statement of the PPC.

Thirdly, the convergent view is not just any old view, but a view that is, as said above, based on 'collective learning', which has been governed, so far as is possible, by the general rules of academic discourse. As long as this orientation is maintained for the future, so that all positions are regarded as corrigible, debate is open, and the evidence respected, what problems of principle would arise? This simply seems to be taking seriously a commitment to the practical ideals of social science. Who could argue that such a commitment was inconsistent with the essential purposes of a University institution?

References

Allen, C. (2003), *Fair Justice: The Bradford Disturbances, the Sentencing and the Impact* (London: Forum Against Islamaphobia and Racism).

Allen, S. and Barratt, J. (1996), *The Bradford Commission Report* (London: HMSO).

Barry, B. (2001), *Culture and Equality: An Egalitarian Critique of Multiculturalism* (Cambridge: Polity).

Bradford Community Statistics Project (2006), http://www.communitystats.org.uk.

Bühler, U. et al. (2002), *Bradford: One Year On. Breaking the Silences* (Bradford: Programme for a Peaceful City).

Burgess, S., Wilson, D. and Lupton, R. (2005), Parallel Lives? Ethnic Segregation in Schools and Neighbourhoods', *Urban Studies*, **42**(7), 1027–1056.

BXp7 (2005), 'Keighley Part 1: Local Issues and Concerns', *The Bradford Experience*, Programme 7, first broadcast on BCB radio (106.6fm), 3 April 2005, produced by Alan Carling and David Fitch, and presented by Alan Carling.

Carling, A. (2008), 'The Curious Case of the Mis-claimed Myth Claims: Ethnic Segregation, Polarization and the Future of Bradford', *Urban Studies*, **45**(7), forthcoming.

Carling, A. et al. (2004), *Fair Justice for All? The Response of the Criminal Justice System to the Bradford Disturbances of July 2001* (Bradford: The Programme for a Peaceful City in association with the Joseph Rowntree Charitable Trust).

Cromie, P. (2005), *Election Leaflet for the Bradford West Constituency* (Welshpool: BNP).

Darlow, A. et al. (2005), *Researching Bradford: A Review of Social Research on Bradford District* (York: Joseph Rowntree Foundation).

Kelly, P. (2002), *Multiculturalism Reconsidered* (Cambridge: Polity).

Kelly, R. and Philpott, S. (2003), *Community Cohesion – Moving Bradford Forward: Lessons From Northern Ireland* (Leeds: Government Office for Yorkshire and The Humber).

Lewis, P. (2007), 'Faith in the City – Religious and Secular Traditions Collaborating to Limit the Appeal and Impact of Radical Islam: Bradford, a Case Study', *International Relations*.

McKinnon, C. (2006), *Toleration: A Critical Introduction* (London: Routledge).

Miller, J. (2004), *Community Cohesion* (Bradford: RAISE Project Case Studies). www.insted.co.uk/raise.

Ouseley, H. (2001), *Community Pride not Prejudice: Making Diversity Work in Bradford [The Ouseley Report]* (Bradford: Bradford Vision).

PPC (2005), *Statement of Aims and Principles* (Bradford: PPC).

— (2006), *Ground Rules for PPC Discussions* (Bradford: PPC).

Priestley, J.B. (1977 [1934]), *English Journey* (Harmondsworth: Penguin Books).

Raw, A. (2006), *Schools Linking Project 2005–06: Full Final Evaluation Report* (Bradford: Education Bradford).

Robinson, D. (2005), The Search for Community Cohesion: Key Themes and Dominant Concepts of the Public Policy Agenda, *Urban Studies*, **42**(8), 1411–1427. [DOI: 10.1080/00420980500150755]

Sanghera, G.S. and Thapar-Björkert, S. (2007), 'Methodological Dilemmas: Gatekeepers and Positionality in Bradford, West Yorkshire, UK', *Ethnic and Racial Studies*.

Schofield, S. (2006), *Bradford's Local Election 2006 – the Resistible Rise of Anti-Democratic Politics?* (Bradford: PPC).

Simpson, L. (2004), 'Statistics of Racial Segregation: Measures, Evidence and Policy', *Urban Studies*, **41**(3), 661–681. [DOI: 10.1080/0042098042000178735]

Vine, I. (2006), *Shared Future v Blinkered Vision? – Addressing Bradford's Unsolved Dilemmas* (Bradford: T-CUP [Toller Citizens' Unity Project]).

Chapter 8

Eurocentricism, the Philosophy of Liberation and the Social Model of Disability: The Practice of a Social Movement within a Latin American Context

Nadia Heredia

Introduction

To speak about disability always seems to open up new horizons for discussion. Disability exists as a human reality, but has not necessarily been understood as an important topic for consideration, unlike many other human differences. This Chapter will argue that from an ethical and philosophical perspective, the notion of social responsibility profoundly connects difference and disability, which requires that history is reinterpreted by new theories and philosophies of liberation. That is, theories and philosophies which open up new horizons so as to hear the new voices of the excluded.

A 'Normal' History

Philosophical modernity arose in the eighteenth or 'Enlightened' century, where reason was assumed as a guide and foundation to human thought and action, marking a break or turning-point in history. Paradoxically, this break also signified the beginning of 'Universal History' which although was told 'for all', was unilateral, derived from a particular social process and a unique cultural, political and economic movement initiated in Europe.

From this moment legitimated voice, speech and reason were made one, describing 'The Other' categorically and judging whether persons should be seen as acceptable parts of 'The Whole'. Hegel's *Philosophy of History* perhaps best represents this European 'voice' or conception of the world, in which everything and everyone was viewed and examined. *Categories* of 'superior' and 'inferior' were used as a simple way to understand reality, where superior always referred to European culture, and inferior referring to other 'ways of life' – that is *not* cultures – 'discovered' in Latin America, Asia or Africa. Human beings became part of this categorised reality and so by doing 'naturalised' the process of seeing 'The Other' as part of an inferior social reality, and as inferior to nature.[1]

In this context, an European constructed 'Universal History' created a history of 'normality' and the image of the ideal human being as man, and only man; as white and opposite to all different colours of people discovered, as the New World was colonised; as scientifically knowledgeable and opposite to all ancient knowledge embodied in native or other cultures, such as China; establishing particular norms such as heterosexual, in sexuality, and healthy as in non-disability. This construction process left many people excluded from the right to be part of the 'normal' whole and so from have any rights to participate in social spheres. In addition, it was a process that was supposedly underpinned by science and theories of the egoism of man developed in the liberalism of Adam Smith and Thomas Hobbes. Consequently, regarding 'The Other' in part became a permanent attitude of suspicion and the norm for any human relationship, whilst 'The Other' was also seen as dangerous, and in the extreme, the enemy.

However, with capitalism strengthening, characterising 'the normal' was widened, including all those people capable of work. This led to a new conception of the valuable, or useful, where people previously excluded were more included in a long chain of exploitation that let them inside 'the us' of the world of work. Nevertheless, although women, black people, and 'natives' were included relatively easily, disabled people and those diagnosed with mental illness were not. For these latter groups, segregated institutional structures were put in place that reinforced the distinction between workers and non-workers, as well as more generally what is the 'desired way of life' or 'ideal' human being. Specifically, institutions such as schools, hospitals and prisons, under the guise of care and rehabilitation made the 'abnormal' 'normal' and the 'ill' 'healthy'. For example, Foucault's historical view of these institutional processes, identifies how 'the subject' becomes an object of study by the social sciences within this period, where policy-makers begin to establish 'normality' as a desirable end of political and social life (for example Foucault, 1975). Moreover, being different was considered a sufficient condition to being socially punished, where the control and monitoring of the body and its behaviour was the motor that operated social life.

The Latin American Context

As well as the above political and economic conceptions of human value, specific cultures and their particularities were part of the construction of the 'ideal person'. For example, in the Latin American academy, Eurocentric conceptions of 'the normal' were never questioned. That is, until a new movement of Latin American philosophers started to raise the possibility of establishing a distinct Latin American tradition of thought (see, for example, Kush, 1968; Bondy, 1969; Martí, 1990).

---

1   For other discussions concerning Latin American and geopolitical bordering of philosophy see, for example, Lander (1993); Dussel (2000); Mignolo (2001).

This intellectual movement began a long journey of discovery to uncover the meaning of being Latin American. This meaning or meanings had to give new and re-owned answers. That is, socio-political answers about the place that Latin America occupies in history; ontological and metaphysical answers about Latin American identity that were different from what had been taught or imposed; and ethical answers concerning the values that were necessary and relevant to revalorise oppressed Latin American culture. Adopting certain types of philosophy from the early twentieth century, difference and 'otherness' were now seen as valuable in re-creating new identities. This adoption relocated and reprioritised Latin American consciousness, as distinct from European conceptions of the world, showing that inside Latin America there were multiple ways 'to be' reflected through centuries of cultural development.

In short, Latin America was disembarking from the train of 'progress' and was deconstructing its dependency on Europe, now seen as an urgent and necessary socio-political, economical and intellectual task. An increasing awareness of the connection between poverty and liberation motivated this movement to denaturalise conceptions of 'progress', 'underdevelopment' and 'social delay'. However, there is a dialectic operating within this move toward independence. On the one hand, independence meant Latin America needed to unify its speech, and so ignore Hispanic social, economical and political impositions and oppressions. But on the other hand, within Latin American countries, independence also had to be thought of as a way to promote a critical discussion about how colonial political regimes can be transformed. That is, via democratic systems with the participation of all excluded classes being centrally involved in creating a historically unique state project (for example, see Castro, 1985). The option was clear. The liberation of Latin America from oppression was more than a fashionable slogan and the social and political mobilisation experienced in the twentieth century is its proof.

Moreover, the presence of the Catholic Church as a founding partner of the New World had become permanent in all or most social and political processes throughout Latin America. Following the dialectic described above, the Catholic Church both reacted against and added to the exclusionary social and political dichotomy between 'unnaturalness' and 'normality'. In conservative Catholic quarters, naturalness and normality became associated with 'the divine', with 'unnaturalness' and 'abnormality' being associated with 'sin' and 'ungodliness'. Whereas, the 'Theology of Liberation' (see Gutiérrez, 1990) born in Latin America in the early 1970s, became a controversial Catholic movement, affirming for its followers that the Church had to be part of the revolutionary process to end the oppression of the poor.[2]

More generally, philosophy and theory is seen as having a central role in this liberation, as the axis of this new thinking appeared as a concrete option re-thinking social and historical categories learnt from Eurocentrism. The theological and political movement alongside so-called 'Dependence Theory' denounces structural dependence and dominance, even within the intellectual domain. The principal bases of this Philosophy of Liberation is to explore the possibility of creating a way of

---

2   For a comprehensive analysis of the theory of Theology of Liberation, see, Dussel (1976); and Petrella (2004).

thinking and living that is a real alternative, with the intention of liberating all 'the Other' oppressed and excluded, so producing in effect a new geopolitical map.

The above theme of the oppressed 'Other' is represented through these theories and philosophies as the problematic of 'the poor' who are unable to live life to its full potential within various spheres. The woman in a machismo and patriarchal system, the native cultures oppressed by occidental cultures, and others excluded by social, political and historical violence, prevent members of these groups from developing various aspects of their lives. To put it more abstractly, the theory of liberation promises a 'something' or 'somebody' that is beyond 'being' and 'non-being' and points to an existence that is more real, whilst also allusive. That is, 'beyond sense', given the presence of oppression and exploitation. As Dussel maintains:

> The philosophy of liberation seeks to re-think the whole of philosophy (from logic or ontology, to the aesthetic or the political) from the Other one, the oppressed one, the poor person: *no-being*, the barbarian, the *nothing* of 'sense'. There is 'somebody' *beyond* the 'being': it is real although doesn't still make sense (Dussel, 1983, 55).

To *make* sense of this exteriority or otherness we need to examine prior philosophical work. Following Dussel, one of the representative founders of the Philosophy of Liberation, the exteriority of the excluded appears in Latin American thought via Emmanuel Levinas who emphasises and explores face-to-face encounters with 'The Other', and present and past pain noticed and experienced in these encounters (see Dussel, 1985). To exist in exteriority is to exist outside of what the whole as Totality establishes always in an oppressive way. So, the hard work of liberation theory and the Philosophy of Liberation is to show the urgent necessity of 'seeing' 'The Other' and feeling the historical and social responsibility of hearing its claims of justice. In this context, beginning to see Otherness as excluded implies that we must also see these ways of life and existence as being suppressed by every homogenising system, whilst also allowing the Other *to be itself*. Therefore, to be conscious of oppression via a liberating theory or philosophy is the first step in the long journey that finishes in the concrete praxis of liberation.

To summarise so far, although the South American academy is still often acritically Eurocentric, the contribution of Liberation Philosophy, and other critical theories, give tools to re-think and deconstruct social, cultural or educational practices that homogenises races, knowledge, traditions and languages, and have as their objective the attainment of a European ideal. Also, this philosophy as a theory is highly valuable, because from its inception it does not avoid talking about socio-political power asymmetry and structural poverty from a Latin American perspective and reality. What is permitted is a relocation of thought in a new geopolitical context, from a place that recognises historical oppression and points to real possibilities for liberation.

Working within this new Latin American context, discussions about difference also permits us to talk of realities that are represented by a wide variety of social movements that, from different places of exclusion, claim a right to be heard. However, despite the emergence of social movements from indigenous people, women, workers of recuperated factories and university students, amongst many others, Latin America does not yet have a coherent and established social movement of disabled people. Within these different emergent speeches the voices of disabled people still do not appear as 'one voice', participating in the public sphere. Therefore, the challenge for the above theories and philosophies of liberation is to add disability to the differences in social, academic and political speech.

Disability in Latin America

As highlighted above, although social movements are presently emerging in Latin America, it still does not have a disability movement akin to Europe as begun in the 1960s and 1970s. During this period, the European (and North American) disability movement started to articulate the claim that discussions of disability issues must centrally include the voices of disabled people. One consequence of this historical development has been to challenge dominant academic models or theories of disability from a closed medical, psychological or scientific paradigm, to a social paradigm of disability. In addition, it is important to acknowledge that the Second World War is also part of this development, obliging Europe not only to change abruptly the architectonical physiognomy of its principal cities, but also change other public policies toward disabled servicemen. It was also forced to accept disability as a social reality brought about by war, albeit within the context of a social imagery that closely identified disability with personal, individual tragedy.

The social and academic appearance and development of disability theory and practice in Latin America has been substantially different. The historical, cultural and political process of colonisation and evangelisation experienced in Latin America has generated a particular perception of disability in the public consciousness. For example, the enormous influence of the Catholic Church in all matters relating to Latin America, affected the social perception of disability, and the popular culture that conceives disability as divine punishment. One social outcome of this was that disabled people were literally hidden by their families, as a result of the social stigma attached to families that had a disabled member – a stigma based on the belief that the family and the disabled person were receiving divine punishment for unknown sins. This way of thinking has been well-established throughout Latin America and effectively accuses disabled people and their families of having produced something wrong or unclean, and so increasing an irrational feeling of guilt that is vividly expressed through social concealment.

In contrast, another distorted view from Christian charity has described or defined disabled people alongside all 'defenceless people' – namely, that the Christian community has the duty, but not necessarily a *social* responsibility – to help. This conception of charity, mixed with strong feelings of pity – and so making the action more ethical or religiously 'correct' – also produces substantial negative outcomes for disabled people, as well as for others that are 'helped' or 'cared for'. The main problem being that charitable action conceived in this way puts all those who are pitied in a place of inaction defined as passive objects of this help. The theoretical premise underpinning charitable action is that 'The Other' has to be helped, because it cannot do anything for itself. In this context, the only way to think of disability – that is something that must be lived with but conceived as an illness of the body and the soul – was to look for some kind of salvation. The institutions that could realise this were the Church through a miracle that recovers the body and soul to health and peace, or the hospital, through various medical and rehabilitation practices. The miracle that the power of faith could not make, the hospital tried to substitute for, leading to very intrusive intervention that often occupied most of the disabled person's life.

From the above, the medical model of disability can be thought of in the first instance as complementing religious practices, in the hard work of eliminating disability. However, with the progressive secularisation of thought and institutional life and practice in all parts of society, the medical discourses about disability, sustained by the scientific model, started to acquire more authority over and above religious paradigms of sin and divine punishment. Parallel to this process, it is important to note the increasingly significant impact of medical institutions on the lives of disabled people in Latin America, which helped to move lives from a home-based or family-closed sphere to social and public arenas. In the latter context, disabled people could at least begin to participate in social life through the hospital institution and via the only non-religious place that can deal with and try to end the 'social problem' of disability. These institutional developments in Latin America have marked the start of what might be called the socialisation of disability. Therefore, paradoxically the Latin American experience of the medical model of disability is responsible too for its social exposure. Whereas, the permanent connection established between disability and health reinforced by the medical model (and as postulated by the European social model of disability) has made it difficult in a Latin American context to conceptualise disability as a social phenomenon.

Nevertheless, the institutional reference to the medical model of disability in Latin America as the only secularised context for discussing disability, leads to a number of challenges – both theoretical and practical. First, there is the challenge of deconstructing medical speech about disability and offering alternative more radicalised and liberating discourses and theories. Second, there is the task of showing that the reproduction of discourse as 'social common sense' through this medical paradigm generates more exclusion for disabled people who are seen as principally ill, with all the limitations that an illness can bring to a person. Given this, it is necessary to specify in Latin American theory and practice that these medical conceptions are not unique or universal, nor are they the most appropriate to apply in public policies relating to disability.

The Medical Model and the Role of the State

In the twentieth century the social role assigned to disabled people in Latin America was that of someone who is ill and has to be cured. In the public sphere, the natural – and naturalised – connection between disability and illness or disability and medical treatments, has produced a long chain of social consequences. These consequences are reflected not only in legislation formulated during this time, but also in state policies and the general conceptions within collective cultural domains that have defined disability issues.

All public policies generated by the state relating to disability have been guided by rehabilitation practices seen as a basic necessity for disabled people. For example, the importance of establishing a medical pathology in relation to individual disabled people is prioritised over the rights they might have to certain social services. So, the presence of a social demand for educating disabled children has often been answered by Latin American states through the development of therapeutic centres, rather than a fully integrated education policy. In addition, underpinned by the medical model, there is a collective social or 'common sense' promoting the thought that illness is inextricably linked with being disabled – or the illness *of* disability. That is, leading to a permanent state of suffering and pain which in turn legitimates the view that disabled people cannot think for themselves. Therefore, as someone assumed to be depressed or with serious health problems, disability is seen as a condition that necessarily reduces individual autonomy to its lowest levels. This assumption in turn reflects the above religious and medicalised theories of disability – but is still maintained in some areas of social consciousness – namely, that disabled people need special care given their child-like status and despite their physical maturity. In the process, these conceptions adopted by the state also reproduce an 'assistencialist role' that emphasises the passivity, or incapability, of disabled subjects to change their unfavorable situation as a result of the impediments they have.

Moreover, another serious consequence of the medical model of disability is that the responsibility of state and society is transferred and/or understood to be within the individual sphere. In this way, 'the problem of disability' is individualised or belongs to a minority group within society. Here, the division between 'them' and 'us' and between 'The Normal' and 'The Other' is maintained as a basis for state practices. The responsibility of the state demands positive actions for the welfare of all in society but from the medical model perspective a major state obligation is to help those people in 'special' situations, including the ill and disabled. Special parts of society require special attention, so in these cases the state responds, but by doing so installs a further division between what is beneficial for all and what is beneficial for that special part, the latter being defined as in an 'abnormal' and 'less than ideal' condition. The structural problem of responding to the needs of all is changed by this practice of responding to an individual problem, or at best a problem of 'a minority'. So, when education is provided for all, only a 'special' education is provided for disabled people. This special provision does not reflect the establishment of a more inclusive society but, informed by the medical model of disability, emphasises the medical deficits of individual subjects.

It is important at this point to highlight that, for at least the past three decades, the main problem with Latin American disability policy is that disabled people have been targeted as a minority group with 'special needs'. The state has a specific role of making 'special' policies for disabled people based on the medical model which then permeates all the 'solutions' to 'the disability problem', despite the overall social and political context for disabled people being far more complex. It is in this arena that language and words have a crucial role to play in the creation of a social and 'common sense' about disability. The reiterated perception of disabled people being a 'social problem' to be 'solved' and the continual reference of political speech-making that reassures the public that the 'specialness' of being disabled means extra resources are being targeted toward this group, generates a feeling that people are being helped, and not that people are making use of a social right. As a result, commensurate with the state's role above, disabled people occupy the position of perpetual debtor to the state or to particular politicians with goodwill. That is, displacing the notion that there is a social responsibility of the state to all its citizens that then would require positive actions to be implemented for disabled people as an included part of the whole. Given this exclusionary process, it is understandable that disabled people in Latin America (unlike their European counterparts) have not mobilised around a 'consciousness of rights' and so leading to positive and concrete actions and practices as mechanisms for claiming these rights. The resulting inaction and historical passivity of disabled people in Latin America has furthermore naturalised the practice of politicians that they should think *for* disabled people and not *with* them.

Following from the above, the most urgent political action that needs to be taken in Latin America is to abandon the belief that the state, through its disability policies should answer an individual or 'special' problem, and so should reject the medical model underpinning these policies. On a wider social level an educative process has to be initiated that deconstructs the 'old view' conceiving disabled people as being in a state of perpetual childhood. Or, at best that disabled people are only capable of experiencing a low degree of autonomy because they need to be assisted in some special way. Briefly put, these misconceptions fail to recognise that all persons in any society need to be 'assisted' in order to exercise autonomy, albeit disabled people sometimes require different forms of assistance to maintain theirs.

In addition, we must begin to promote a new social vision for disabled people, presenting autonomy and the value of 'The Other' as something that should be respected, where difference does not mean inferiority, and disability does not mean eternal childhood. Promoting this vision is a necessity, not only for disabled people, but also for the whole of society in order that we might be enriched by this difference. Whilst structural changes are not a sufficient condition for radical reform, these changes are necessary to start this transformation, and it is in this context that theory matters crucially to the way in which practice develops. For Latin America, with its long history of oppressive theoretical conceptions of disability and disabled people, the social model appears as a radical political alternative or paradigm for seeing the world, and thereby provides a basis for structural transformation. Once policies are changed then this provides a further foundation for transforming entrenched social conceptions. In this moment of praxis, which combines theory and practice in new ways, we can move the axis of discussion from the disabled person presented as 'the problem' to open up new horizons of debate about social responsibility and so include those who have been previously excluded.

The Social Model in Latin America

If we understand that disabled people are one part of a greater whole, the distinction between 'them' and 'us' is unnecessary. But this distinction has been made historically, not only in Latin America but all over the world, and not only in relation to disabled people, but many other groups too. Consequently, it has led to a reinforcement of the divide between what is defined as 'normal' and 'ideal' and what is defined as 'abnormal' and 'lesser than'. As explored above, difference and similarity is established by the Totality of the Moment (that is the status quo), Us like each other, but separate to the different Other, them, with the 'them' including women, black people, disabled people, native cultures and many other 'minorities'. It is this, what might be called a fallacy of the minorities, which has repeatedly justified the historical oblivion and omission of rights being afforded to 'Others' who are different.

However, social, economic and political realities demonstrate that 'minorities' often only exist by virtue of unequal power relations that reinforce their oppression. For example, women are not a minority, but gender oppression throughout the world reinforces minority status. Similarly, in Latin America, native cultures are not a minority as recent studies have consistently shown that the majority of the population has indigenous ancestors.[3] Nevertheless, rights for these cultures are still not respected, again reinforcing minority status. Consequently, the characterisation and categorisation of minorities is often not only false but ideological, because this naturalises the oppression of certain groups by reproducing a fatalist vision that it is always going to be this way.

This fatalism produces a double-effect. First, it puts the oppressed in a place of inaction and passivity that appears unchangeable. The future is therefore presented as an abyss – that is not unknown and full of possibility but as an eternal return of the same. Second, the structurally oppressive 'Totality of the Moment', also appears as perpetual and unalterable. In this way, fatalism discredits the power of transforming action and prevents change. For these reasons, the social model of disability can be seen in Latin America as not merely an academic theoretical alternative, for its fundamental contribution is to destructure the passive historical roles assigned to disabled people who are oppressed, and so providing a political option in concrete practice. Therefore, to start thinking about the themes of disability in a social way demands a change in the axis of discussion and practice. This also obliges us to speak critically about those 'common sense' assumptions that are not argued for but merely assumed. In other words, engaging in theoretical discussion *as* a critique initiates a serious debate about the role of the state, and the existence or otherwise of public policies promoting the active participation of disabled people and guaranteeing social practices of inclusion.

If we understand the political as the public sphere, where social themes are discussed, transforming understandings of disability in political discussion means that disability must become a public and not an individual 'problem'. Or, it is merely a 'problem' only affecting disabled people. Moreover, in this public or social debate, it is necessary to abandon the belief in the authority of knowledge as provided by medical or psychological discourse derived from scientific theory and experiment, and to open doors and minds to the knowledge of subjective experience. To hear the voices of those involved in public discussion, therefore requires a transformation of the public sphere, which respects the place of difference as related to the different interpretations of these experiences. This respect also implies that we should all be open enough to understand that when these voices say that things made *for* them are simply wrong because they don't respond to their needs, then these interpretations

---

3   For example, a study by the Service of Genetic Fingerprints of the University of Buenos Aires, showed that 56 per cent of Argentinians have indigenous ancestors.

of subjective experience should be listened to and taken seriously. Consequently, the complex process of opening-up public discussion about disability with disabled people, being principal participants in the design and planning of what their needs are, requires a change in the way disabled people's experiences are perceived by themselves and others. This change would represent a first-step in transforming political decision-making from its entrenched historical practices leading to further changes in the manner by which public policies are developed and implemented. The powerful idea contained within this aspect of the social model of disability as applied to a Latin American context, is the fundamental challenge it makes to past medical and psychological theories of disability promoted within both academia and socio-political contexts. The challenge is to centrally incorporate a subjectivist cultural view of personal experience when evaluating the successes or failures of policy as measured against the long-term social inclusion of disabled people.

Another important point to be clear about is what conception of difference is being used and valued as related to these competing theories of disability. If we understand disability as a human difference revealing more the inexhaustible spectrum of differences that human reality and experience shows and uncovers, then every time society is made increasingly accessible for all it also becomes, in principle, a socially realisable project that facilitates this wider revealing of difference. However, when making 'special provision' only for disabled people, as has been the case in public policy for decades in Latin America, it undermines the possibility of respecting difference across the whole of society, and so does nothing for disabled people who seek to be included. If it cannot be understood that society not only is, but also must be re-made in order to manage better an open place for reform and change, then the focus will always be on the problematic 'individual subject' who must change so as to fit into society.[4] In matters relating to disability, this has been translated into the old practice of rehabilitating the subject, to cure them or become 'more normal' as defined in a particular historical context. Following from this, to abandon what was described above as an assistencialist medical view of disability, also demands that we are conscious of the state's responsibility for promoting an active social role for disabled people. That is, derived from a different conception of what capability means as distinct from disability, with the former being redefined in the revaluing of difference. In this scenario, the social model of disability appears as a radical break between old and new ways of understanding disability by linking the celebration of difference with capability, and so offering a concrete but radical social and political alternative to the medical model.

The idea of conceiving disabled people as part of a whole, emphasizing that the whole has to be modified and not the individual, encourages the belief that the social model is the best and only way forward. However, whilst this theory of disability offers a new more profound paradigm for investigating issues concerning difference and disability/capability, there may be limits to its use – both practical and philosophical. One of these limitations concerns how the emphasis on difference

---

4　　For other applications of social and critical models of disability in Latin America in public policy spheres such as education, see, for example, Skliar and Duschatzky (2001); Aramayo (2004); de Oliveira (2004); Skliar (2002).

as linked to capability rather than disability, might result in the explicit denial that disability exists at all, or at best that the experience of disability is implicitly thought of as secondary to a disabled person's lived experience. From this perspective, even for those disabled people who have opted for the social model, there are deeper philosophical and ethical issues and questions concerning what difference might mean that in turn underlies further possibilities for discussion, as we will see.

'The Other', Social Structures and the Power of Social Images

Examining the treatment and theoretical explanations of 'The Other' is essential in all ethical and political discussions orientated to political practice and concrete social action. More specifically, in disability debates the definition of 'The Other' as disabled in the context of promoting the social model, has initiated a long discussion about the ethical and political inferences of emphasizing certain aspects of this theory of disability over others. Following from this, it is also important to highlight that social and cultural perceptions about 'The Other' necessarily produce concrete effects when guaranteeing particular welfare outcomes in the population via the implementation of specific policy. Consequently, in Latin America it is essential when initiating structural changes to policies that affect disabled people, that, alongside, a transformation of oppressive cultural and social theories of disabled people occurs, so these changes can be real and long lasting.

However, all theory has its limits, particularly when we are trying to use it as a tool for guiding and explaining social and human action, given that subjective human experience (as explored above) is highly complex and diverse. Therefore, the social model of disability has limitations when representing aspects of the complex reality of being disabled. If the final objective is to create an ethical and political base in which society can generate better conditions of life, then depositing all the trust in the power of changing social structure via state reform based on a particular theory of society and disability, can weaken that social and political project. In this context, to assume that the presence of disabled people in the public sphere has to be initiated only or first by the state or by other social and political institutions is not politically or ethically sustainable. That is, given we want to revalorise a new active role and a new conception of 'The Other'.

One strong criticism of the above structural conception of change is that reform in social structures does not guarantee a deep and real change of mind in the social understanding of disability and the impetus for the so-called social inclusion of disabled people. Consequently, revisions to the normative goals of disability legislation based on a broadly social model of disability, although might try to provide comprehensive policies for inclusion, may generate more complications for service-users. For example, social processes of inclusion can become highly bureaucratic in their procedures and paradoxically make benefits inaccessible, so undermining any commitment to guaranteeing more accessibility as a simple question of establishing equal rights for disabled people.

Nevertheless, this problem should not belie the connection between the analysis offered by the social theory of disability in general – and of the state in particular – and the identification of the systematic reproduction of excluding practices and social segregation. As explored above, the main outcome of such practices is the inactivity or the passivity of those affected, and that they have to permanently face this state of affairs understood by the social theory of disability to be unfair or unjust. The full participation of disabled people in different aspects of social life involves, therefore, a 'conscience of responsibility' within all spheres of society.

It is the case that the constant reception of social messages and information reproducing medical or other oppressive images of disabled people delay genuine attitudes of transformation. The mass-media, and the use of language generally, play a determinant role in the categorisation and social perception of disabled people. For example, providing disabled people with basic resources for mobility, such as a wheelchair, is often portrayed in a dramatic way encouraging the belief that making the life of 'the disabled' better can be reduced to social and charitable assistance. This type of representation has the effect of hiding the reality that, although having a wheelchair may be basic to social participation for some disabled people, providing this kind of resource should be a mundane and everyday matter of establishing a disabled person's equal rights to access. These media images of disabled people accentuate a social conception of diminution or restriction, not only in relation to physical mobility, but other social functions that disabled people might legitimately perform, such as being a worker or a student. Furthermore, restrictions concerning what a disabled person might want to be or do relate not only to structural features of a person's life concerning work, study or participation in other public activities. These also concern personal spheres where being disabled is portrayed as incompatible with wider aspects of human experience, such as sex, love or even happiness.

One paradagimatic example of this representation which now will be briefly explored is the movie *Butterfly Effect*. This film raises deep philosophical questions about the 'fracturedness' of time, the power of choice and agency, the importance of every second in the decisions that build the life of a person, and the still intriguing theories of quantum mechanics, and yet has as its main character a disabled person who is portrayed as unique in his suffering and loneliness because he is not able to choose 'the woman of his life' as a direct consequence of being disabled. In this 'disabled life' the only viable option presented for the character is death by suicide. However, this choice is not realised, not because he chooses life – in the last second – but because the dependence created by the disability means that the act of suicide cannot be performed. Following this ending, another more general point regarding the film, is how conceptions of the future cannot be connected with present-life and disability in any meaningful way. If the future is not represented as feasible or meaningful for the disabled person, the present also becomes irrelevant or meaningless. In other words, the power of individual action loses its sense because there are no purpose-based goals ahead. This lack of sense and purpose pushes the main character to choose death, where the importance of individual agency in the present and the creation of a life in the future are portrayed as essentially unobtainable for disabled people.

Although there are lots of representations of disabled people that are not as extreme as this, it is clear that the individual tragic representation of disability found in the medical model is writ large in this film. Consequently, the overall message finds resonance with the audience because of the medical model's prevalence, which presents the life of a disabled person as dysfunctional and tragic. A good life with a disability is not therefore an eligible option. However, this outcome is not the result of institutional oppression as such, which might be remedied by social benefits being re-distributed through various structural transformations. Rather, it is a consequence of deeper underlying societal conceptions and misperceptions of disabled people that are then reflected through film and other media. In short, disability is defined as incompleteness, which poignantly reminds us of the urgent task ahead. As stated above, we must create an alternative critical view of diversity and difference. That is, fundamentally undermining the false security of the dictum stated by Skliar that: '… "diversity" is not us: they are the other ones' (Skliar, 2002, 22).

Some (Final?) Thoughts from a Particular Place

In Latin America we are living in a particular moment, which not only has implications for political aims and objectives but also for wider social mobilisation. These activities in turn have led to various pertinent revisions in questions concerning who we are and who we want to be, with debates about the ways ahead only just starting. The theoretical critique of Eurocentrism and a re-examination of Latin American roots as derived from 'native cultures' provide a solid base to build a new and open system of social and ethical relations. It is this notion of systemic openness, both in theory and in practice that is essential to being open in relation to the new and the excluded 'Other'. Moreover, openness also implies a respect to all the new 'Others' that, when are fully included, challenge the security of the homogenous whole. That is, they challenge the security of a closed system that operates as an oppressive 'Totality' and by so doing allow oppressed voices in this system to be heard that previously had been silenced. To quote Dussel:

> To know how to listen to the voice-of-the-other one, is to know how to prepare for their interpellation, the trembling of my security, my installation, my world, as a risky and disturbing clamour for justice (Dussel, 1973, 58).

Therefore, to learn and teach a culture of listening is a political and ethical challenge in a context where 'the correct way to be' has been institutionalised and reproduced historically through powerful legal and educational systems. The alternative objective is that people, as a matter of political and ethical conscience, should recognise 'The Other' as someone who deserves respect for the mere fact of being human, with equal dignity being afforded to individual identities and characters. To revalorise the encounter with the "Other" in this way means that one is open to hearing the new. It also implies being open to different futures, because the new necessarily demands that the future does not have to be just one path. This is the deeper sense in which ways of liberation can be talked about (Dussel, 2000, 32). What must be prepared for is that the future can always be different, because encounters with exteriority (with otherness), is disruptive and unpredictable, where 'The Other' demands to be heard. Again, to quote Dussel:

The ethical conscience or meta-physics is then the *encounter* of the *voice-of-the-Other* one that interpellates and demands justice from its dis-tinct exteriority, encountering this voice which knows how to *hear-the-Other* (Dussel, 1973, 59).

In Latin America, during the last few decades, an enormous variety of new Others have literally occupied the streets demanding to be heard and seen. It is a crucial moment when disabled people have to decide what role they want to play in this new social scenario. To have a conscience requires a theoretical appreciation of historical oppression and to know from what place we are conceiving disability and difference, these qualities being essential when drafting effective strategy for action and practice. More specifically, it is important to move medical discourse from the place of privileged and authorised knowledge and abandon the medical and assistencilist perspective that presently surrounds dominant medical social and political misconceptions of disabled people. To start to hear the voices of disabled people is therefore not only a matter of ethical conscience but also a matter of historical justice, if these matters can ever be thought of separately.

Moreover, it is important to see that changing our attitudes to difference is necessary for changing the axis of discussion regarding disability. In a context where the different subject is presented as someone who has to be recognised *as* different, always talking about 'the subject' is not necessarily helpful or liberating. The proposal is not therefore to continue talking, rather to refuse to continue reproducing oppressive ways of thinking about 'The Other', and so initiate a responsible debate about difference. If we start to talk about difference as a multi-dimensional concept and value as it relates to the positive promotion of human diversity, we can see that there is no simple opposite to 'different subjects' that is reflected in the false concept of 'normality' and its associated value of 'conformity'. To provide this critical understanding of difference and diversity requires us to 'educate the look ... a look that can also be rebellious' (Skliar, 2002, 54). The experience of disability and the encounter with it can consequently be healthily disruptive of "the whole". To quote Skliar again:

> To follow surprised, disjointed, for not continuing to believe that 'our body', 'our space', 'our culture', 'our language', 'our selfness', means 'the whole time', 'the whole space', 'the whole culture', 'the whole language', 'the whole humanity' (Skliar, 2002, 17).

What is deeply problematic and oppressive is if one body, space, culture, and so on assumes it is the whole, and so doing commits violence to the continuity of those who are different and do not belong to this whole. This understanding is reminiscent of Levinas' definition of violence who states: '... violence doesn't consist so much in hurting and annihilating as in interrupting the continuity of people' (Levinas, 2002, 47).

Therefore, we can affirm that reproducing theoretical structures and concepts that define 'The Other' as different and 'lesser than' and so a target for special treatment, inevitably excludes those who are defined *as* different from universal provision. This process of exclusion in its most extreme form also undermines the possibility of experiencing human personhood. In short, those who are defined as different and abnormal are reduced to definitions *about* themselves and so are unable to recognise the subjective experience and interpretation *of* ourselves. Consequently, solitude is experienced by the 'outsider', but who nevertheless has solace in the knowledge that others experience something similar, and that the promise of liberation for all is found in this experience and paradoxically brings hope through insecurity. In the words of one famous Latin American writer: '(our) solitude is happy with that elegant hope.'[5]

Finally, the 'new look' proposed is from an insecure place that is not fully known or understood but in recognising these epistemological limitations allow people to be seen and not looked at. The attentive reader will realise that 'our' new look is not advocating a closed-theory of whatever kind, but rather a more modest contribution that needs permanent revision and re-thinking, through its ongoing encounter with practice and the interpretation of this practice via critical reflection. In other words, we are advocating a provisional and open-theory that is a place to begin good practice, nothing more and nothing less. Consequently, there are a lot of questions, just a few and sometimes improbable answers, but as theory and practice reflects this process, we then don't go through life believing all is *just* like it was said.

References

Apoluceno de Oliveira, I. (2004), *Saberes, Imaginários e Representações na Educação Especial. A Problemática Etica da "Diferença" e da Exclusão Social* (Petrópolis: Editora Vozes).

Aramayo, M. (2004), *La Discapacidad. Hacia un Modelo Social Venezolano* (Venezuela: Zamora).

Bondy, S.A. (1969), *¿Existe una Filosofía en América Latina?* (México: Siglo XXI).

Borges, J.L. (2004), *Ficciones* (Buenos Aires: EMECE).

Borón, A. and de Vita, A. (Comp.) (2002) *Teoría y Filosofía política La Recuperación de los Clásicos en el Debate Latinoamericano* (Buenos Aires: CLACSO).

Castro, G. (1985), *Política y Cultura en Nuestra América, 1880–1930* (Panamá: Centro de Estudios Latinoamericanos Justo Arosemena').

Dussel, E. (1973), *Para una ética de la Libración Latinoamericana* (Buenos Aires: Siglo XXI).

— (1976), *History and the Theology of Liberation. A Latin American Perspective* (New York: Orbis Books).

— (1983), *Praxis Latinoamericana y Filosofía de la Liberación* (Bogotá: Nueva América).

— (1985), *Philosophy of Liberation* (New York: Orbis Books).

— (2000), *Ética de la Liberación en la Edad de la Globalización y la Exclusión* (México: Trotta).

Foucault, M. (1975), *Discipline and Punish* (New York: Pantheon).

Gutiérrez, G. (1990), *Teología de la Liberación: Perspectivas* (Salamanca: Sígueme).

---

5   Borges, J. L. (2004), *Ficciones* (Buenos Aires: EMECE).

Kush, R. (1968), *América Profunda* (Buenos Aires: Bonum).

Lander, E. (comp.) (1993), *La colonialidad del saber: eurocentrismo y ciencias sociales. Perspectivas latinoamericanas* (Buenos Aires: CLACSO).

Larrosa, J. and Skliar, C. (eds) (2001), *Habitantes de Babel. Política y Poética de la Diferencia* (Barcelona: Alertes).

Levinas, E. (2002), *Totalidad e infinito*, 6th edn (Salamanca: Sígueme).

Martí, J. (1990), *Philosophical Discourse of Modernity* (Cambridge: Polity Press).

Mignolo, W. (Comp.) (2001) *Capitalismo y geopolítica del conocimiento. El eurocentrismo y la filosofía de la liberación en el debate intelectual contemporáneo* (Buenos Aires: Signo).

Padawer, M., *La Construcción Discursiva de la Discapacidad: un* Análisis De Dos Discursos In. http://www.avizora.com/publicaciones/ciencias_sociales/ciencias_sociales_17.htm 13 March 2006.

Petrella, I. (2004), *The Future of Liberation Theology An Argument and Manifesto* (UK: Ashgate Publishing).

Skliar, C. (2002), *Y si el Otro No Estuviera Ahí? Notas para una Pedagogía (improbable) de la Diferencia* (Buenos Aires: Miño y Dávila).

Skliar, C. and Duschatzky, S. (2001), 'Los nombres de los Otros. Narrando a los otros en la cultura y en la educación' in Larrosa, J. and Skliar, C. (eds).

Chapter 9

Beyond Practice and Beyond Theory?

David Morgans

Introduction

This chapter examines some of the limitations of using any theory as an explanatory mechanism for understanding the social world human beings occupy. These limits do not just relate to problems in application for the reasons discussed throughout the book, but also relate to issues in philosophy and epistemology concerning the nature of philosophical pursuit and the problems of defining and/or describing any foundational explanations of human behaviour and relations.

On one level at least, human beings, in their social relations with others, assume a common understanding as to the nature of their world. This is not to say that at particular times and in particular situations, for different people, the world around them can and may be apprehended or comprehended differently – for example physically, socially, psychologically, politically, ethically, personally. This may be dependent on a number of factors, some of which I will mention later, but still such misunderstanding will, without analysis, commonly be treated as mistaken or inappropriate functioning. In analysis it is assumed that human relations demand as a necessity, an essential degree of systematic understanding and this is a role for theory. But there also exists a province where fundamental disagreement about the nature of reality and social reality is more common and even expected that is in the realm of theory.

Competitive Theory and Its Relation To Practice

Explaining and providing understanding of the world; the nature of physical and social phenomena is the responsibility of theory, but such phenomena is difficult and its analysis complex, and if one views this activity simply, thus one finds a competitive relationship between theories; a competition for the mantle of 'correct theory' – that is that which is the best in having its content correspond or represent its object. In this way competing theories lead to an incommensurate relationship with one another, this incommensurability is often a product of each theory upholding contrasting explanations of the same phenomena. It is no wonder that the non-theorist generally sees 'theoretical discourse' at best as confusing and at worst having no application to the 'real' world. It is no surprise then to find a typical initial question asked by trainee practitioners on applied social studies courses: 'why do we have to study social theory?' This is not an easy question to answer given the complexity of the subject in question and given, admittedly, that a lot of theory and the way it is presented, seems difficult and even impenetrable. This attitude is also all too frequently communicated to practice. To combat this we could suggest a beginning of an answer to this question by stating that both applied social studies and social theory are concerned with human behaviour and hence social interaction and social relations.

If our definition is fair, the way that theory relates to policy and practice is then obvious. Theory can provide the knowledge that policy and practice can apply in its practice to assist to bring about its specific aims and goals here stated. But while theory is taught to practitioners through their training, most practitioners in their practice, I think it fair to say, do not give much weight to thinking theoretically about their practice. Indeed, they seem generally to find 'prescriptions derived from practice-experience of considerably greater immediate use' (Sheppard, 1995, 265). That is not to say that practitioners do not think in a systematic manner about their practice. Yet, the social problems, whether they be social, psychological, ethical, political or personal, that make up, what I shall call from here on, the 'social problematic', are often thought by them to deserve a more empathetic and emotive kind of attention, in that it concentrates a number of different types of responses to a certain types of social behaviour. They indeed call for description, prescription, definition and action, yet these responses are often seen to be more 'subjective' and less 'objective' (we will explore the problems in making such a distinction a little later on) than those which take place within the phenomenon of a theoretical definition. In short, the prescriptions of theory have, for many practitioners, often appeared distant, esoteric and hardly relevant for the complex and pressured world of practice (ibid.). Past studies have concluded in relation to practice that: 'with [a] body of practice wisdom as a basis for their activities, the need to use abstract theories and generalizations from research were minimal' (Carew, 1979, 354). We can even conclude that '[i]n some quarters there has been what Hardiker and Barker (1981, 2) call an 'anti-intellectual stance' in which the role of theory is avoided.' (Howe, 1992, 8–9). This element brings out the fact that not only is there a question mark around this relationship between the theories of science and social science and the views of societies' actors, but it is also true that such actors (as in the case of our practitioners above) also develop meaningful theories of their own, that compare and contrast with the theories of science and social science. In later discussion I will be concerned in detail with these issues, and I will also want to look closely at the problem of meaning in the process of theorising, especially at the discourse of social science theories. First, however, let us look at the process of (social) theorising in a wider context.

The Sense of Theory

During social interaction, when people encounter physical objects or other human beings, certain things happen. One way of describing such encounters is to say that the processes are a way of 'trying to make sense of the encounter'. The actors' experiences we take to be simple ideas, such as 'what is going on' and 'why things are as they are and do what they do', may be a simple survival technique in any and every given situation. For human beings, feeling uncertain about the way the material or social world is liable to behave is often disconcerting. From a scientific and a social scientific perspective, we are taught that ideas are produced historically and chronologically in one by such interaction with the material and social world; they have regularity and form and are constructed, in one way or another (for example philosophically, psychologically, sociologically, and so on) out of a chaotic range of sensory stimuli. This socialising activity in itself seems to assume that the universe (or at least something in it or outside it) is neither random nor chaotic but rational; that there is reason in being. Consequently, we more often than not, tend to act on the assumption that to every event there is rhyme and reason, and of such order we can have knowledge. A question that arises from this type of description, and one that will tax us later on, is to do with the relation between the individual and his world, and whether we do not merely recognise these patterns, they being caused by an external reality, or whether we seek to actively create them.

If I am right this description demonstrates that human situations are necessitated by reference to some preconceived notion of the possible order of things. But what gives us this preconceived notion and what is it? The simple act of description requires in itself some mechanism by which to organise sensual perception. Yet what is the nature of this mechanism?

A specific feature of modernity was that knowledge might be gained from a scientific analysis of society, of just the kind that is entailed in social scientific activity. What then does such a science of society entail? As we are aware, the natural sciences seek to describe and explain natural phenomena. But does it, in its activity, simply describe or prescribe? Well one may be drawn to consider that mere description of a natural phenomenon does not only add to one's knowledge but can enhance it. That is, that knowledge can be applied and thus bring about change without the description that led to such knowledge logically entailing that change. So we can say that there are occurrences within the sphere of scientific activity which have a cause and effect relationship with social life and which do not feature in the description of the activity itself. Moreover, this feature is not insignificant. Developments within this activity have had considerable implications on the way we think about ourselves and the way we apprehend the social reality we experience. What is important for us is how such knowledge is normatively perceived. It is fair to say, I think, that the claim science has generally made concerning the knowledge it produces is that it involves the notion of certainty. That is, that such knowledge stands in direct contradiction, to statements of belief or opinion and certainly, those claims that are based on pure faith. The question that concerns us is what kind of knowledge does theoretical activity produce? The growth of confidence in the discoveries of natural sciences and the way they progressed through the growth of a body of empirical knowledge has been well documented since the renaissance. The developing methodology (that is the way or method that the sciences utilise to achieve their goals) of the natural science, also gained credence with their every success. Thus, thinkers of modernity expressed immense confidence in the findings and methodologies of the natural sciences, so much so that they began to hold the notion that a science of society could be upheld. As theories are developed in science to test and discover and describe the nature of natural phenomena, so the same system could be applied to social phenomena. In short, they believed that social theories could be formulated to explain how society works, or at least certain aspects of how society works. This is the influence the natural science model has had on social theory as a whole. However, this confidence was not total, as other theorists have argued that there was and is a major logical difference between the sciences concerned with material objects and those concerned with human beings. Unlike most natural objects human beings have ideas about their world. They have subjective views about their own, and others' situation. It is the individual's understanding of what is going on which is every bit as important to the social theorist as the external characteristics and behaviours that others may observe. As one other theory of human behaviour has it, social sciences and the natural sciences have different subject matter.

This paradigm maintains that there is a fact-value distinction. It provides an analysis of the relationship between description and prescription maintaining that values are not logically entailed by the facts. Human beings are conscious and in this they are different from matter. Persons have feelings, emotions, intentions, imagination, ideas, beliefs, and so on, and as such it is impossible for science with its empiricist foundation to establish an explanation for such phenomena. Matter does not have meaning and purpose it only reacts to external stimuli, where as human beings act. Social actions have meanings and thus any understanding of society must be grounded in the explanation of individual social action and social interaction. Of course, once one gives up the idea that thoughts, feelings, intentions are not just of physiological ontology, one must invest some other explanation to the cause of human action and thus invest the 'meaning' of such phenomena with some other logic. But this can be problematic. Certainly, this paradigm accepts that the acts of consciousness, so to speak, are the result of individual choice and decision. But how is it then to explain the regularity and pattering of social relations, the existence of social groups along with their methodical values and belief systems and even more so the co-existence of different social groups and cultures with different values and belief systems? All may have invested different meanings to the same behaviour and the same social actions. This theory places a lot of faith for answers to this question, for a description of society and for a science of society in the concepts of understanding and intuition, but this is where it too has its problematic.

Despite this divergence of theoretical thinking, the search is then on for a theory that is more successful in solving those problems that the practitioners and operators in the field recognise as 'acute' (Kuhn, 1970, 23). Certainly social science theories, whether based on the natural science model or not, describe a complex network of relationships, but with such descriptions that are often 'ideal' models which may or may not conform to social reality. As such, the 'structures' of society are seen as analytical constructs, an interpretation of the social relationships as a pattern, and the test of social change is whether the pattern is altered. As long as the theory one is using describes this pattern, that is as long as the society can be compared with the model in its basic essentials, it will allow the theorist to claim that society can be reasonably described in those terms. The problem is at any one time there will be more than one model, more than one theory. Each model and each theory can interpret the structure and the pattern of social relationships, differently. Each model and each theory will make claims to systematic description (for example, logical, scientific) and thus epistemological content. From such a basis it will claim the ability to infer rational means and ends. Only too often, however, do such models, having determined that there are elements of society that demonstrate correspondence with their 'ideal', pass over other aspects of social relationships which do not fit the particular perspective. It is thus often construed as a blinkered way of looking at the world, but one that has been underpinned with an appeal to either some kind of scientificity or other systematised rationality. Therefore, it will take more than a mere appeal to these kinds of cognitive activity to separate the epistemological claims of particular theories in the social sciences from subjective or value affiliation.

Also important to this enquiry is the role of theory and research in the social dimension. The question we must ask is whether it is possible to oppose the injunction that claims that to test theories against 'the facts' is impossible in the social sciences? The problems for the theory that have been described can imply that there is no-theory-neutral language in which to generate 'facts' or 'data' such that these can be used to adjudicate between competing theories. Any set of observations, or statistics, have to be organised and based upon concepts held either explicitly or, more typically, implicitly but yet not necessarily consciously by the theorist(s). These concepts in turn, will depend upon some view of the world, or some theory derived from science, a moral position, a political position, a religion, or merely a 'commonsense' view of the world which itself depends upon a point of view, a set of interests, held by some group or groups in a social formation. Facts, one can assert from this viewpoint, do not speak for themselves. They only speak to those who share the same view of the world as that of those who generated them. One has to acknowledge the consequence this must have for any practice based on theory.

While not discussing any particular theory in detail this 'theory problematic' does throw up major difficulties for sociologists, social scientists, social philosophers and indeed practitioners. It may affect the latter more than many, for it raises the question of the ontology of values. Whatever practice we adopt it will influence social relations, social action, social interaction and of course practice. And practice based on a 'theoretical world view' will invest our role as social actors with a particular interest, the interests of the world view to which the practice belongs. This 'constructionist' view claims that depending on which view we accept will affect the way we view social reality.

This 'constructionist' claim amounts to one of two things, either it is a metaphysical claim that something is real but of our own creation. Or it is an epistemic claim that a valid explanation for why we have some particular idea about either physical or social phenomena has to do with the role that that idea plays in our social lives. If we make a claim in the former sense, we end up saying, that something like to reject the force of gravity would contravene no law of nature: but as it is a law of nature it thus leads us into a logical contradiction. 'Real' is something we dreamed up then, an idea constructed in the latter sense which we could reject without fear of contradiction.

The latter sense makes sense in relation to our discussion of the relationship between theory and practice. If we have an idea or a concept, not because there is sufficient or even necessary evidence in its support, but because we subscribe to some contingent underlying social principle that it underpins. But it also means that if we do not happen to share the idea or concept in question we ought to be free to reject its underpinning underlying social principle. There are many examples of important work in the name of this social theorising for example under the heading of social rights, inequality, social exclusion, respect for person, and so on, which have important ramifications for practice and practitioners. Let us illustrate the above discussion by applying its thinking to a specific example from practice.

An awareness of these points has led to a widespread general scepticism about many 'fixed' categories in health and welfare. For example, the concept of mental illness has for a long time become subject to scepticism which has been voiced by many sociologists, psychologists and philosophers. One has argued, for example, that our belief in schizophrenia is socially constructed (Boyle, 1990). The claim is that there is no adequate reason to believe that the symptoms commonly lumped under this label are manifestations of a single underlying disease and, hence, that the search for its aetiology by neurochemistry is doomed. Her argument is not, of course, new, anti-psychiatry theorists were taking an anti-realist and anti-objectivist stance against the 'medical model' of mental illness decades before Boyle; for example, see the work of R. D. Laing (1967) and David Cooper (1967, 1971).

Such theories that point to the social construction of 'ideas' in the second sense we have mentioned have been valuable and illuminating and led to much critical and important work concerning social prevailing attitudes – and such an activity is nothing less than an essential precondition for a critical approach to the practical problems that come under what I have called the 'social problematic'. However, despite their escaping labels of metaphysical confusion and logical contradiction, and providing a 'political' rationale for many practitioners in work with their service-users, they still do not provide the kind of indubitable correctness that the theories of modernity were expecting. Indeed, that they do not, still opens them up to the criticism of being 'value-laden' and 'subjective' or even an incorporation of these two in the label of politically motivated. Moreover, if we take our example, as there appears to be increasing evidence that the symptoms associated with schizophrenia are predictable significantly before their onset and that the condition is highly heritable, and these facts point in the opposite direction (Boghossian, 2001).

The Problematics of Social Theorising

Rather than, despite and indeed because, of its critical function, all such theorising, that is, social science or social theorising, is characterised by the idea that the acquisition of knowledge combined with a critical dialectic dimension, necessitates improvement, and this implies progress in the human condition. Nevertheless, we still know that this creates a dual problematic; firstly, this system has not produced merely one social theory but a collection of social theories, which are as varied as they are contradictory. Thus, we do not have a lone paradigm of social reality but a series of incommensurate paradigms, which do not admit readily to an independent arbiter even if we could conceive of one. Secondly, there is notion that the production of knowledge, scientific or otherwise, is not as detached from other types of social relations as some would like to make out. We cannot always separate the progressive of science from the ideas of social life and therefore, our welfare, education, scientific, legal and political systems will reflect to some extent the interests of those who have an interest in how ideas are put to work in society.

According to the discussion above on both the history and the condition of social theorising, we have been introduced to two ways in which the divisive head of contradiction is raised. Firstly, there can be a plethora of incommensurate theories of the world (either conceived physically or socially). We have seen that one way of interpreting this, then, it to adopt the philosophical claim that there is a world that exists independently of human minds. This means that we do not have to make that uncertain metaphysical claim that we created the world or that the world is 'mind-dependent'. But in and of itself this world is structureless: it is not broken up into things, kinds of things, or facts. We impose structure on the world by thinking of it in a certain way, by having one set of beliefs about it rather than another.[1]

What I am attempting to emphasise here is the claim that there are two different ways to understand the claim that we impose structure on the world. On the one view we literally make it the case that there are certain kinds of things in the world – mountains – by thinking of the world in terms of the concept 'mountain', by believing there to be mountains. Nevertheless, such theories will be commensurate in their idea that there is a reality that corresponds to the 'things' that are discovered, whether or not there is disagreement on how the concepts of these 'things' are interpreted or constructed. These theoretical perspectives imply that while the 'physical world' exists and may (a) be mind-independent, and (b) have some sort of causal role in the structure of the social, it may also be something that is beyond the human subject's apprehension. We have noted the problems with holding both these aspects of this view in relation, in that neither perspective admits readily to an independent arbiter even if we could conceive of one.

The second view is that the structure remains entirely on our side of the divide: the claim that there are mountains is just a way of talking about what is true according to our conceptual scheme or language game. It is not even to try to make a claim about how things are in some mind-independent reality. In other words, the creative role that human subjects play in the construction of their social world, and, indeed, in the production of 'themselves', may be total. Indeed, some such theories will stress the impossibility of an independent arbiter and the impossibility, even logical absurdity, of attempting to conceive of one. This second view could be seen as evolving from a loss of faith in the former, that is, a loss of faith in scientific paradigms and their role in the ordering of our world. Is there, then, any way of resolving this division, that will allow theory to play an authentic role in practice and restoring the faith in theory to practitioners?

This way of establishing knowledge about the social world is, or can be called its cognitive dimension (Craib, 1992), and we find 'cognitive fault lines' in social theory which help to make sense of the process of this seeming fragmentation that arises out of a character can deem its critical dialectic. The division we have touched on in the above examples is, it could be argued, and is argued by many, a consequence of what could be called the 'post-modern' evolution of the social. Social theorising as

---

1   These views bare not just a passing resemblance to the problematic 'transcendental idealism' of Immanuel Kant.

well as an attempt to understand the world is part of the world. This is problematic in two ways (Craib, 1992).

Firstly, the activity of reflecting the actuality of social has become both increasingly important and problematic over the last decade. Contemporary Western society with its perpetual, technological and consequent social change has led to social life and the inner life of individuals becoming increasingly fragmented. Societies, institutions and organisations for which we work are becoming increasingly complex and perhaps experienced as more beyond our control than ever before. Social theory, thus reflects some of this, both in its own fragmentation and in other ways. This portrays how the optimism of modernity, with its reliance on the scientific paradigm and technological developments, has given way to the pessimism and even nihilism of 'post-modernity'. While there is confusion over how to define this term, it arises perhaps more from the difficulty in determining the standpoint of this era, or age; what it is about, in terms of theory and the place of the 'subject' within it. Post-modernism, in its broad usage, is a 'family resemblance' term; a nomenclature for pluralism of movements in art, literature, and so on, which rejects the pretensions of high modernist culture. In philosophical terms, post-modernism is essentially a critique of the values and truth-claims of modernity.

In this world view, we see its roots in the social theories that reject 'scienticism', thus societies do not 'determine' agents, but they survive and change only through acting individuals. We see the introduction of 'transformative' model of human action, where social phenomena provide the raw material, on which human subjects act, and forms of life come out at the other end. In this process, 'the deed, the activity is primary, and does not receive its rationale or its justification from any theory we may have of it.' (Monk, 1990, 306). A crucial property of human action, as far as this type of thinking goes on, is that it is intentional; it aims at achieving something. To make the same point in a rather different way: human subjects not only monitor their action (that is know what they are doing) but monitor the monitoring – they can reflect on what they know they are doing, assess it, make judgements and choices. In this respect they are crucially different from societies, which are structures of social relationships. An important point here is that there is no simple relationship between a subject's action and intention and its effect on society or a particular social relationship. The social world then is made up of two distinct and different types of being: social structures and subjects. Thus, we may see that epistemological questions depend upon ontological questions. Evidently, this has certain implications for theory.

This theoretic perspective raises the second problematic that is given in this way of thinking. It is the realisation that far from producing 'objectivity' the method of theorising clearly cannot escape 'subjectivity'. That is, as each language of each society has its meaningfulness and legitimacy guaranteed by its practices, by its 'social life'. Therefore, it cannot be undermined by any other theory of reality, hence, it cannot be refuted by any other cognitive world view, no matter how more discursively legitimate that view claims to be. Moreover, while there can be different subjects, their origins rooted in their language and their culture, their internal order, whether it be unfair or unjust, cannot change. For example, in a certain view of this kind there is a rejection that there is a standpoint of Western science which can and should be used as a critique of other 'forms of life', for example religious or cultural practices (for example see Winch, 1979).

This is also the stance of 'the perspective' that can be called 'non-theory', where 'sociological' understanding of a form of social activity, in order to count as understanding, must be couched in terms of only those concepts involved in the activity itself. This is not merely a criticism of scientificism within the social sciences or social theorising, this is an absolute rejection of a kind of 'objectifying' within theorising. Thus, there can be no 'real' subject, for all subjects are defined within the parameters of the 'forms of life' and are subordinate to the relations within. How then do we establish preferences between practices? Practices cannot be evaluated from a set of correct principles or absolute values, they cannot even be established through any kind of social consensus. In this perspective there can be no such thing as neutral objectifying, all knowledge emanates from discourse and all discourses are power-laden.

An example of this approach can be taken from Foucault, a protagonist of the view I have outlined. In his work, with discourse comes the possibility of knowledge: the social, political or epistemological object is the possibility of the subject of a particular discourse. Discourse is located in the theory of power for Foucault. He stresses the intimate connection between the production of knowledge and the exercise of power. The 'groups' that dictate the 'subject' of discourse demarcate the sphere of experiential reality. In other words, reality and its subjects have no purpose or identity per se; they are the products of the relations of power; these forces themselves are collective units or quanta of power, their nature varying depending on the position they occupy within the changing hierarchies of domination and subordination. Our cognitive structures are but so many of configurations of force. Consciousness is merely an effect of particular relations of force. Hence, Foucault has this to say:

> The power-knowledge relations are to be analysed, therefore, not on the basis of a subject of knowledge who is not free in relation to the power system, but, on the contrary, the subject who knows, the object to be known, and the modalities of knowledge must be regarded as so many effects of these fundamental implications of power-knowledge and their historical transformation (Foucault, 1977, 27–28)).

Power is then a relation or rather a multiplicity of relations that pervade social reality in the 'apparatus of production [for example], families, small groups, institutions' (ibid.). It is not a negative in the sense of being merely repressive – but it is positive and productive in so far that it forces these relations into the social. Power is exercised through national and international strategies originated in the interaction of programmes and technologies which is not imposed on individuals as such, but rather it permeates every social relation through those psychological and cognitive limits we impose on ourselves; we are the victims of 'the cop in our own head; of our own exteriorization of the law' (ibid.).

A consequence of this type of analysis is that it can be no unique or unified 'universal view' which acts as an agency of social change. Discourse is the battlefield of the perpetual struggle between competing strategies for power. One can see here clearly the ramifications for practice, terms such as, 'need', 'client welfare', 'respect', 'acceptance', 'confidentiality', and 'conscious raising' do not reveal the 'real world, they merely assemble it' (Rojek et al., 1988, 137). Practice, therefore, is not care but discipline. Discipline 'makes' individuals; it is the specific technique of a power that regards individuals both as objects and as instruments of its exercise. Power, then, does not act upon pre-formed individuals, containing them through repression or deceiving them by means of ideology – it creates them. Self-emancipation is a plurality of struggles as irreducibly multiple as the relations of power themselves. Indeed, it is claimed, such relations of power 'can only exist in the function of a multiplicity of points of resistance: these play, in the relations of power, the role of adversary, of target, of support, of prize to be taken. These points of resistances are present everywhere in the network of power' (Foucault, 1976, 123–128).

I have only time and space here to cursorily point out the kind of criticism this position attracts and the argument I make is far from being extensive or exhaustive. Nevertheless, I believe it contains a crack in the structure of this perspective and if extended could bring about a collapse. Specifically this problem stems from the fact that the approach judges all 'world views' or 'forms of life' as if they are of equal value and that one cannot be seen to be more 'correct' than another. In other words, any concept of correctness becomes arbitrary; correctness preference of one for the other. Foucault (1976, 1977) and Deleuze (1983) go further than this and may be taken as maintaining that each theory creates its own reality. However, the present idea of totality as a succession or a competing milieu of incommensurable paradigms survives only until such theorists and their paradigms start to espouse an evaluative analysis. Then their theories, despite their expositions to the contrary, clearly start to define what looks very similar to a 'transcendental signifier' (in other words, an independent arbiter) which is meaningful and independent. Given the complexity of the paradigms approach it is difficult to assess whether this 'entity' exhibits 'needs', 'interests', and so on as simple concepts in its analysis of social reality. However, it does make much of the concept of 'struggle'. But struggle by whom, against what and towards what? Can any sense be made of this concept, without there being an answer to these questions? For instance, 'struggle' usually predicates an end to which it is a means – even if that end is conceived within the meaning of struggle itself. What looks very much like an end can be recognised within the writings of the post-structuralists Deleuze and Guattari in *Anti-Oedipus*. They claim that: 'the task of the revolutionary is to free the flux of desire from all codification, from all territorialization.'[2] They maintain that where the flux of desire is free from coding, organization and control, experience will more accurately reflect the nature of reality. This certainly looks like this type of 'perspectivism', that is, a theorising on the nature of reality. But, moreover, is it not proffering a 'flux of desire' which is a subject of 'experience'? What is this mystical even metaphysical entity? These two facts do not only open their theory to self-referential criticism but they allow their theory to be interpreted as having a subject close in conception to the 'self' or 'soul' of the old order empiricism. Couple this with the claim that such 'perspectivism'

---

2   To understand what this view would mean as a dictate for practice, we only have to substitute the term 'practitioner' for the term 'revolutionary' in this context.

has a Nietzschean influence that incorporates the belief that for Nietzsche man is able to will desire as a law unto himself, then it is no wonder that such theories are open to abuse. For example, they can be used to legitimate the decline of any egalitarian conception of society and to justify new right thinking in the arena of political discourse which is not apposite to their aims.

The Language Game of Social Theory and Practice

In finally turning to what I am calling the no-theory approach to understanding and explaining (in a way) social phenomena; I am still attempting to engage with an attempt of resolving the 'social theorising' division, that will allow theory to play an authentic role in practice and restoring the faith in theory to practitioners. And I am assuming, at least in this Chapter, that the postmodern approach has not done so.[3] This approach takes what has been called a 'therapeutic' turn; it portrays a more 'holistic' treatment of subjects: arguing that human action does not create society but either maintains or changes it in some way – this is the sense in which the two are not independent of each other. Societies do not 'determine' agents, but they survive and change only through acting individuals. A 'transformative' model of human action, where social phenomena provide the raw material, on which human subjects act, and forms of life come out at the other end. Both the approaches of, what I have termed, non-theory and no-theory, is that this emphasis is on particular rather than universal standards. The main criticism of such a stance is that it suggests a relative position. For these reasons some see the approach as open to the charge of both 'idealism' and extreme relativism, not only as described but in terms of the construction or production of the 'subject'. This is to say that in describing a form of life the sociologist is necessarily restricted to those explanations which are characteristic of the concepts of those being sociologically investigated. Anything more will still be reducible to such concepts when submitted to analysis. In short, the main feature of such methodology is its reliance on 'internal explanation.' But this reliance on a criterion of logic and rationality that is embedded in particular ways of life, within particular language games, some will argue, attests to a relativist position. Indeed, Winch, whom we can categorise as ascribing to this position, is thus attacked. Winch, also adopts a Wittgensteinan position. And it is true to say that Wittgenstein treated all world views fundamentally on par with each other. In his remarks on Frazer's *Golden Bough*, for example, Wittgenstein is careful to distinguish between the significance and rightness of world views:

> One could say 'every view has its charm', but that would be false. The correct thing to say is that every view is significant for the one who sees it as significant (but that does not mean, sees it other than it is). Indeed, in this sense, every view is equally significant (Wittgenstein, 1967).

---

3   I am sure there are others who would disagree with me here and my presentation and criticism of the postmodern approach as I have outlined it. See, for example, Rojek et al. (1988).

It can be conceived from this Wittgensteinian viewpoint that different societies can have different forms of life and thus have different ordinary languages. Again, as each language of each society has its meaningfulness and legitimacy guaranteed by its practices, by its 'social context', it cannot be undermined by any other theory of reality, hence, it cannot be refuted by any other cognitive world view, no matter how more discursively legitimate that view claims to be. For these reasons Edgley (1983)[4] sees the approach as open to the charge of both 'idealism' and extreme relativism: it is difficult to define concepts used in the Wittgensteinian approach, that is 'everyday usage'; 'language-game'; 'form of life', in such a way that they can mark theoretically, the distinction between the conceptual legitimacy of the non-metaphysical language and the conceptual confusion of a metaphysical use of language. In other words, the implication of this type of description seems to be that there is no language independent reality in relation to which concepts can be more or less adequate. It can only offer epistemological foundations which are open to sceptical relativism and cannot be considered as grounds for the possibility of cognitive objectivity.

Nevertheless, before we dismiss this perspective let us take a closer look at this view to see if it offers any way out of the problematic outlined and any hope for practice. Wittgenstein wants to argue that, instead of turning immediately to a study of how individuals come to know the objects and entities in the world around them, we should begin in a quite different way: by studying how, by interweaving our talk in with our other actions and activities, we first develop and sustain between us, different, particular ways of relating ourselves to each other – that is, that we should first study how we construct what Wittgenstein calls our different forms of life with their associated language-games. Only then may we turn to a study of how we 'reach out' from within those forms of life, so to speak, to make various kinds of contact – some direct and some indirect – with our surroundings through the various ways of making sense of such contacts that our forms of life provide. To explain this in Wittgenstein's words 'our talk gets its meaning from the rest of our proceedings' (1969, § 229).

Indeed, Wittgenstein's use of 'the term 'language-game' is meant to bring into prominence the fact that the speaking of language is part of an activity, or a form of life' (Wittgenstein, 1953, § 23) this is a claim that our practical usage of words draw their influence very little from our saying of the words, in themselves, so to speak, but from our use of them at significant moments, to make important differences, in the milieu of social life and social activity within which we are involved. Thus, again, it is our situated use of our words that is important, in social practice. For Wittgenstein the meaning of a word is in its use. Demonstrating that one understands a word is found in the use of a particular word in the correct grammatical context. Giving the meaning of a word will involve describing all the instances of that word's possible use. Furthermore, a word or concept does not have a correct use independent of the 'language game' as Wittgenstein calls it. In short, this term shows that language is part

---

4   Edgley's criticism one can see as a siding for a return to 'scienticism' albeit within a Marxist view. For more criticisms of this view from a more 'orthodox' scienticism see Gellner and Williams.

of and essential to the practice of social life; as he puts it, 'Here the term 'language-game' is meant to bring prominence to the fact that the speaking of a language is part of an activity or form of life' (Wittgenstein, 1953, §23). By emphasizing the use of words he moves away from empiricism's passive theories of language. Language is not simply read off from reality but is part of the reality creating process. It is not that language can express a community's system of beliefs about reality or can describe reality; it is that this is implicitly and necessarily present in the language that that community speaks. We see this point is reiterated by Winch who argues that 'Reality is not what gives language sense. What is real and what is unreal shows itself in the sense that language has' (Winch (1979, 9). Indeed, Wittgenstein's theory of language closely involved the possibility that, no one form of life or world view (epistemology) provides a complete and correct description of such a world, or ever can, they merely provide a paradigm for practice. The claim here is that our beliefs form a system of which we are cognisant and which are internally consistent, and against which each individual belief is compared and approved: 'When we first begin to believe, anything that we believe is not a single proposition, it is a whole system of propositions (Light dawns over the whole.)' (Wittgenstein, 1969 §141).

Thus, it seems the claim is, and this is very relevant to the application of practice, while disputes over truth and falsity; appropriate/non-appropriate, moral/immoral are possible and disputable, the concepts are grounded in a world picture that it is neither true nor false. To Wittgenstein the things we say the expressions we make are grounded in the forms of social life in which we participate. Thus, while language does not have meanings, which can be revealed by perspicuous representation of an underlying structure: a depth grammar that underpins the 'surface' grammar, we can derive an understanding of language by exposing the deep grammar of social practices: uncovering the 'depth' grammar of the term on the Wittgensteinian model is done by looking into the workings of language. This does not mean developing or discovering a theory of language. Rather, by describing and perspicuously representing language-games we come to see the part our language plays in human social interactions: that it is rooted in our forms of life. If this is so of linguistic expressions, given the way that language is seen by this approach, it must also be true that social actions too have their surface grammar and depth grammar. Thus, while we perform social actions and know that we do, such knowledge does not imply that we can give an account of the functions such actions perform. Again, such an account can only be given by uncovering the 'depth' grammar of these social actions.

If we can conceive this, would it be possible that the social scientists task could be construed as exposing mistakes concerning the forms of social action? The job of giving a correct prognosis would consist in uncovering the depth grammar of these forms. Or, in other words, it could be where the Wittgensteinian model provides a form of social inquiry which goes beyond the unreflective account people give of their lives and arrive at an authentic account of social life. This enables us to understand the role of language in our social institutions and how it is grounded in our forms of life. Thus, it is possible I want to maintain, that Wittgenstein distinction between depth (background 'grammatical' features of language) and surface (foreground use) may help us see the structures of oppression which keep socially challenged groups and individuals on the disadvantaged margins of society. To attempt this type of enquiry, of course we have to accept the cogency of a Wittgensteinian conception of language in which a matrix of rigid and largely unreflective assumptions and propositions operates in the background as we negotiate our linguistic interactions with others and deal with the affairs and situations of daily life. To help us here let me cite Wittgenstein's striking metaphor of the riverbed:

> It might be imagined that some propositions, of the form of empirical propositions, were hardened and functioned as channels for such empirical propositions as were hardened but fluid; and that this relation altered with time, in that the fluid propositions hardened, and the hard ones became fluid.

> The Mythology may change back into a state of flux, the river-bed of thoughts may shift. But I distinguish between the movements of the waters on the river bed and the shift of the bed itself: though there is a sharp division from one to the other....

> And the bank of the river consists partly of hard rock, subject to no alteration or only to an imperceptible one, partly of sand, which now is in one place now in another gets washed away or deposited (1953, §96–7).

Wittgenstein's idea here is that of a guiding framework with shifting boundaries. In this sense it constitutes the limits of the world for the group who share a world picture. But such limits or boundaries are in no way fixed and may fluctuate considerably. In other words, Wittgenstein is emphasizing that a groups' world view is a system of propositions, a set of concepts, a collection of language games relating to the 'forms of life' of that particular group, which are *taken-for-granted* as a condition for judgments, inquiry and experiments. In numerous examples Wittgenstein demonstrates how instances of the system, set or collection are acquired, thus revealing the limits to any theoretical enterprise, for each instance or form are built in to the condition of any such enterprise. And as such they are beyond the scope of any investigation. Referring to how these instances or forms are grounded, Wittgenstein maintains that at the basis of any world view is a way of acting: 'It is not a kind of seeing on our part; it is our acting that lies at the bottom of our language game' (Wittgenstein, 1969, §204). Then, it seems that doubts and certainties are grounded in the particular world view, thus:

> 'My life consists in my being content to accept many things'. Our certainty expresses itself in the way we act (Wittgenstein, 1969, §344).

Thus, here is the notion that everything that we think of, and talk of, as being the case about ourselves and our language – that we have 'minds', that we 'think in our heads', that 'words stand for things', that we can 'explain' occurrences 'in the world' in terms of 'theories', and so on – all these things can only make clear and intelligible sense from within the confines of specific language-games. This does not mean that language itself is unusable outside of a language game. Far from it, but it does mean that all such talk is, by its very nature, initially, of indeterminate meaning, open to determination only in the context of its use.

Given such a complex position, an understanding of the 'social problematic', is, in what occurs in the 'momentary gaps' between people as they respond to each other, while not forgetting the relation of such gaps to the surrounding circumstances in which they occur. It is in our 'momentary relational encounters' that everything of personal, social, psychological, ethical and political importance to us occurs. In this way we may be able to invoke a different way of positioning a social argument on a vantage point from which we can see the 'rough ground' of our ordinary language use and the river which runs through it. In other words, we can say from this that 'human problems' are fused into the very framework of the background and are made invisible by their commonplace nature. For example, crime, racism, sexism, homophobia, violence against women and children are all practices we are encouraged not to see, especially when doing so would reveal to us the relationship between oppression and privilege. On this Wittgensteinan view, theories and thus the social practice they support as such are both beside the point and after the fact. They are beside the point, in that they hide from us the actual forms of life from within which our talk makes sense (and whether they are, for instance, of an unequal, an equal, an official, an instrumental, a mechanical, or of a properly living and personal kind). And they are after the fact, in that they also divert our attention away from those moments in which the essential social struggles are (or would be) at work in their initial formation – struggles which are not pre-linguistic, by the way, but are prior to any particular forms of life.

Solving the Social Problematic?

The question here is, remembering the analogy of the river, how much, if at all, the background lies within our collective powers to effect. Slow change may not be good enough with respect to lessening and ending oppression that is generated by the 'social problematic'. The question for our current enterprise must be whether it can suggest a way where an agenda for effective practice can be grafted onto a Wittgensteinian analysis of language. If we allow the cogency of this Chapter's analysis as to the linguistic structures of the 'social problematic, for example oppression, domination, cruelty, repression, coercion liberty, and so on, the issue is what would count as grammar, how open to view our grammatical commitments really are and how amenable to deliberate adjustment; how hard the river bed? Can this analysis honed in the philosophical workshop be adequate to any excavation project that would bore us through to the linguistic substrates where our presuppositions lie buried?

One view would be that, like the foundations of a bridge, these are deep but with sufficient ulterior motivation ultimately accessible. Another would be, and perhaps this would be a neo-conservative Wittgensteinian position, such presuppositions are so deeply entrenched and so thoroughly insinuated in the cut and thrust of everyday life as to be almost completely invisible and impervious to any attempt to modify or adjust them for the sake of achieving some perceived better effect in the way of getting on in the world – the social problematic will always be with us. After all the claim is that shared linguistic practices and speech patterns of every-day social practice may conduce – imperceptibly, unintentionally – to what may legitimately be named the 'problems' of others. We must be willing to acknowledge our own shortcomings in the way of prejudicial speech which can easily be intuited, despite an assiduous effort (and social theories that aim at eradicating the social problematic are of course included here) to rise above it, for example the pleasure we take in a disparaging ethnic joke, the innate unease we feel in the neighbourhoods where 'we do not belong', the unreflective and sometimes disconcertingly unmet expectations we have of other people to their life-styles: all these are evidence of the tacit assumptions we carry around with us that for the most part never rise to the level of conscious, critical awareness but which structure our practices and influence the attitudes of those around us. We could here reverse a commonly rehearsed dictum of certain structural positions and claim that oppression is personal first and structural second.

I have to say that Wittgenstein himself was notoriously diffident about the prospects of using his 'method' for any such a 'political' undertaking. Such imperatives almost always involve making some sort of moral judgements; imperatives or/and moral prescriptions and Wittgenstein once described moral philosophy as a 'perfectly absolutely hopeless task'. But if we pursue the notion of 'language game' used above we make some progress. I do not have time here to describe all the vagaries of the 'language game' to the uninitiated save to say that from the above description we can judge that this notion is a rule-governed social practice involving the use of words, moreover, most language games are governed by two sets of rules one for the speaker and one for the hearer. If we were then to make a number of philosophical leaps of faith here – and whether they are philosophically legitimate leaps I have yet to test out – the first would be to assume that firstly, that all social 'practices' aimed at addressing issues in what I have termed the social problematic entail making some kind of value-judgement and these are *ipso facto* moral judgements; the second is to assume that the rules for the use of such values can be understood as rules of a family of language games and, finally, to argue that such rules in their primitive form are the rules for the use of certain very simple but universal imperatives, for example '*Help!*' and 'No!'. Accepting these moves we can claim that making value-judgements or applying morality is basically a set of rules for the use of these 'universal imperatives'. We will assume of these that under certain circumstances anyone may give to anyone else without any special social relationship (other than the speaker and the hearer) being required. Beings who do not have such universal imperatives among their use of language could be said not to have a morality. What I mean is if all their imperatives among their uses of language require a special relationship between speaker and hearer, then such things might be said to have an authority structure, a sense of tribal loyalty, friendship circles, family ties, and so on, but not morality. To be said to be able to lay claim to being good, fair, honest, and so on, a group of beings must posses at least some universal imperatives among their uses of the language. This is not to argue that these must be the same imperatives as our own, beings whose form of life is different from ours may use different imperatives, which operate by different rules. Among human beings, however, universal imperatives will have a use that is inclusive. The rules for the use of imperatives vary to some extent from one community of speakers to another but the basic paradigms tend to remain the same. Such uses of language could be said to be profound expressions of our humanity, including primitive reactions to our own suffering and distress as well as the suffering and distress of others without which the language game of 'universal imperatives' could not be taught or learned. The paradigmatic rules of such language games are the basic rules of humanity which are practiced, more or less imperfectly, by nearly all human beings.

Social Theory and Social Practice

I think it entirely plausible, then, if we can uncover or 'perspicuously represent' these 'universal imperatives' in the language game of social theory and its practices, that, in this way, we can come to be more aware of our own reflective prejudgements and we can make a more conscious attempt to eradicate the ones that are harmful and unjustifiable. It seems viable and at least potentially fruitful line of inquiry to pursue this perspicuous representation of linguistic practices to make our humanity visible and allow the eschewing of invidious practices that keep the 'social problematic' in place. However, despite this line of inquiry there is still the question of how far this type of linguistic analysis will take us is open to question, however, as some of the most entrenched forms of and gregarious instances of social problems may be beyond the reach of philosophical intervention.

What I am arguing, is that certain theoretical constructs including those we have considered in this chapter, that inform practice aimed at the social problematic may have (mostly) ignored the subject's embodied embeddedness in this routine flow of spontaneous, living, responsive activity. Not only have such theoretical discourse let it remain unnoticed in the background to everything that we do, but have also ignored its importance as a sustaining and resourceful setting that is always present in our attempts to make sense of, and in our lives. Especially, certain political philosophical thinking around social problems has, perhaps, failed to notice the occurrence within social life of those special but in fact everyday events, those departures from the routine, which enable us to gain access, not only to the 'inner worlds' of certain kinds of social groups forms of life – but also to the unique 'inner worlds' of the other individuals around us, including, sometimes, the bizarre worlds of those living in strange relations to their circumstances, utterly unfamiliar to the rest of us.

Conclusion

I will conclude by suggesting, then, that, following Wittgenstein, as far as our investigations into social theory and its practices are concerned, the task is not that of finding the single, Archimedean standpoint from which to construct a final, true theory for understanding the world of practice or the finding of the perspective that we can anoint with the title 'correct theory' for practice. Indeed, I want to suggest that it is not to do with finding any new theories at all. It is to do with creating new ways of acting, new practices within which to capture – to notice and characterise linguistically – the character of the living moments in which 'meaning making' occurs. Our ways of acting, or forms of life, are primary and do not, and cannot, receive their justification or rationale from any theories that we might have of them. They are themselves the source (the grounds) of all the justifications we might offer for specific actions, for the task of such justifications is to sustain our forms of life in existence. Indeed, as Wittgenstein puts it, a theoretical picture often 'stands in the way of us seeing the use of [a] word as it is' (1953, §305) – we need to be sensitive to the changing sensuous influences actually at work on us, moment-by-moment, in our ordinary, everyday social actions, interactions and transactions with each other. For, 'conversation flows on, the application and interpretation of words, and only in its course do words have their meaning' and 'what we [i.e., those who follow his methods] do is to bring words back from their metaphysical to their everyday use' (Wittgenstein, 1953, 116.) That is, we point out, not the explicit, conventional, cognitive, representational meanings of people's words, but meanings of a quite different kind: those implicit in people's unique, sensed, responsive reactions to their surroundings. Thus, my aim is to try to articulate the nature of the relational practices involved in investigating these fleeting, momentary, responsive meanings.

References

Boghossian, P.A. (2001), 'What Is Social Construction?', *Times Literary Supplement*. [PubMed 11786199,11557283,11174862].

Boyle, M. (1990), *Schizophrenia: A Scientific Delusion?* (London: Routledge), Kegan & Paul).

Capra, F. (1983), *The Tao of Physics* (London: Fontana).

Carew, R. (1979), 'The Place of Knowledge in Social Work Activity', *British Journal of Social Work*, **9**(3), 349–364;

— (1971), *The Death of the Family* (London: Penguin).

Cooper, D. ed. (1967), *Psychiatry and Anti-Psychiatry* (London: Paladin).

Craib, I. (1992), *Modern Social Theory* (London: Harvester Wheatsheaf).

Deleuze, G. and Guattari, F. (1990), *Anti-Oedipus* (London: The Athlone Press).

Edgley, R. (1983), 'Philosophy' in McLellan, D. (ed.);

— (1976), *Le Volonte de Savoir* (Paris: Gallimard).

Foucault, M. (1977), *Discipline and Punish* (Harmondsworth: Penguin).

Gellner, E. (1968), 'The New Idealism' in Lakatos, I. and Musgrave, A. (eds).

Goffman, E. (1968), *Asylums* (London: Harmondsworth).

Howe, D. (1987), *An Introduction to Social Work Theory* (Aldershot: Gower).

Kline, M. (1967), *Calculus, An Intuitive and Physical Approach* (New York: John Wiley and Sons).

Kuhn, T. (1970), *The Structure of the Scientific Revolution* (Chicago: Chicago University Press).

Laing, R.D. (1967), *The Politics of Experience and the Bird of Paradise* (Harmondsworth: Penguin).

Lakatos, I. and Musgrave, A. (eds) (1968), *Problems in the Philosophy of Science* (Amsterdam: North-Holland).

Latour, B. and Woolgar, S. (1979), *Laboratory Life: The Social Construction of Scientific Facts* (London: Sage).

McLellan, D. (ed.) (1983), *Marx: The First Hundred Years* (London: Fontana).

Monk, R. (1990), *Ludwig Wittgenstein: The Duty of Genius* (London: Vintage).

Rojek, C. et al. (1988), *Social Work and Received Ideas* (London: Routledge), Kegan & Paul).

Sceff, T. (1966), *Being Mentally Ill* (Chicago: Aldine).

Sheppard, M. (1995), 'Social Work, Social Science and Practical Wisdom', *British Journal of Social Work*, **25**(3), 265–294.

Vesey, G., ed. (1972), *Understanding Wittgenstein* (London: Royal Institute of Philosophy).

Williams, B. (1972), 'Wittgenstein and Idealism' in Vesey, G. (ed.).

Winch, P. (1979), *The Idea of a Social Science and its Relation to Philosophy* (London: Routledge), Kegan & Paul).

Wittgenstein, L. (1953), *Philosophical Investigations* (Oxford: Blackwell);

— (1967), 'Remarks on Frazer's *Golden Bough*' in Rhees, R. (ed.), *Synthese* 17, 233–253;

— (1969), *On Certainty* (Oxford: Blackwells);

— (1981), Zettel (2nd. edn), G.E.M. Anscombe and G.H.V. Wright (eds) (Oxford: Blackwell).

Index